HELLENIC
CIVILIZATION

HELLENIC CIVILIZATION

An Historical Survey

BY MAURICE CROISET

Administrator of the College of France

TRANSLATED BY PAUL B. THOMAS
WITH AN INTRODUCTION BY
EDWARD DELAVAN PERRY

New York ALFRED · A · KNOPF *Mcmxxv*

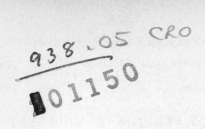

CONTENTS

INTRODUCTION

by

Edward Delavan Perry

An important indication both of the spread of interest in the civilization of Ancient Greece as a whole and of the gradual change in the points of view from which it is studied may be found in the publication, during recent years, of many works, whether as parts of more or less extensive series or as single issues, presenting one or more aspects of that marvelous achievement of human genius. The materials for our knowledge and comprehension of that period of the world's history are rapidly increasing. New evidence—archæological, inscriptional, linguistic, literary—is constantly being added, often modifying and sometimes completely overthrowing conceptions hitherto fondly held. Perhaps about no people of history have sweeping generalizations been so readily made and so slavishly adopted as about the Greeks of antiquity.

To make the more significant portions of such newly acquired information accessible to that part of the "reading public" which cares for these things, but has neither time nor inclination to enter upon the exacting yet necessary professional study in these fields, is to perform a most useful service. Certainly not less important is the presentation, in clear, precise, and agreeable form, of the most characteristic features of the Greek civilization, of the main lines of its development through the centuries that lie more or less open to our observation, and the

vii

interpretation to modern minds of ideas and customs in many respects so different from our own, yet forming so largely the basis on which our own civilization rests.

With every year it becomes more evident that the Greeks of historical times were a people (or rather a group of peoples) of extraordinary diversity of origin, religious belief and practice, and customs, never for long held together closely in any political union, constantly engaging in war with each other, living under many different forms of political organization which sometimes changed with great rapidity, restless, only too often fickle and treacherous, in some respects—particularly in religious ritual—deeply conservative, in others constantly eager for some new thing, commercially enterprising, highly emotional yet endowed with a sense of proportion which generally saved them from extravagance of taste though less often from extravagance of conduct; in short, a people whom it would be excessively difficult to describe adequately in any brief formulas. In dealing with such a subject the danger of failing to see the trees of which the wood is made up is not less that that of failing to see the wood for the trees. And not only were there striking differences of character, customs, political and social organization, among Greek communities at any given period, but almost any one community varied in such respects from one age to another; while of course the rate of change would itself show many variations. The evidence at our disposal for acquainting ourselves with this ancient Greek civilization is singularly uneven for different regions and periods. For example, the huge losses sustained by the mass of Greek literature in the process of transmission from one generation to another have left great gaps in the writings of some of the most famous and important among Greek historians, whose accounts at first hand we should so highly prize and so gladly utilize. It happens that for Athens we are vastly better informed than for any other Greek state, and vastly better today than thirty-five years ago, owing to the discovery, in 1891, of a manuscript of Aristotle's *Constitution of Athens*—the only one remaining of more than one hundred and fifty similar descriptions of Greek political organizations.

Very few scholars unite with the great learning by which the almost endless details are mastered that profound comprehension of the relation of parts to the whole which alone makes possible an accurate and adequate generalization. Still fewer add to these the power of concise, clear, and interesting description and exposition. The primacy of the French in these respects will hardly be seriously questioned even by the most patriotic scholars of other countries—just as there are many points in which the French language, with its highly developed and harmonious yet forcible prose style, its delicate and unfailing sense of proportion, its avoidance of involved constructions and exaggerations of every kind, is peculiarly well adapted to the exposition of Greek themes. This happy combination is to be seen, for example, in the famous work of Fustel de Coulanges, *La cité antique*, originally published in 1864, which after sixty years still remains a standard and invaluable help and guide. In this little book the paramount importance of a thorough study of ancient religion for the comprehension of the ancient state was—perhaps for the first time—strongly emphasized.

A similar insistence upon the necessity of understanding ancient religion if we would understand ancient civilization is a marked feature of the admirable little book, a model of condensed, clear, and accurate statement, which M. Maurice Croiset of the Collège de France has published in the *Collection Payot* under the title *La Civilisation hellénique*. Not less characteristic of the book is the adherence to the historical method of presentation, in which the gradual development of the more important features of Greek civilization is traced. While many valuable publications in the field of classical, particularly of Greek, investigation have given him a very high place among scholars, he is best known outside of France as the collaborator with M. Alfred Croiset —*par nobile fratrum*—in the monumental *Histoire de la littérature grecque*. Alfred Croiset is no longer living; but Maurice, in spite of his seventy-eight years, is still pursuing his life-work.

Mr. Thomas has done competently a most useful task in making the *aperçu* accessible, in an excellent translation, to readers of English to whom French is still a strange tongue.

PART I

ORIGINS AND BEGINNINGS

CHAPTER I

ORIGIN AND EARLY PROGRESS OF HELLENIC CIVILIZATION

Antecedents. Minoan and Mycenæan Civilizations.— Hellenic civilization, properly so called, begins for us about the eighth century B. C. But this apparent beginning was in reality only a continuation, or rather, a revival.

Archæological discoveries, especially in the last thirty years, have in fact shown us that a civilization truly worthy of the name had developed in the islands of the Ægean Sea, later in Crete, and finally in certain parts of the Greek mainland, during the second millenium B. C., and that it was particularly brilliant toward the middle of that period. The monuments of Crete—notably the palaces of Cnossus, Phæstus, and Hagia Triada—altho now reduced to ruins, bear irrefutable witness to it. Moreover, the character of the monuments seems to reveal an epoch of comparative peace, favorable to the advancement of the arts, to the increase of wealth, and to a quiet and well-organized life. The more or less legendary name of King Minos, represented as a peacemaker and law-giver inspired by the gods, may well remain associated with that succession of remote centuries, of which we know scarcely anything save what is attested by these monuments and their ornamentation.

Other no less imposing ruins, at Mycenæ, at Tiryns, at Orchomenus, and at other places, give evidence that

3

this civilization had penetrated to many points on the Greek mainland. They lead us to believe that for many centuries powerful chiefs and warriors lived there. These cities are in reality fortresses. They seem to preserve the memory of a sort of military feudalism. Protected by formidable ramparts, and located along the natural trade-routes, they had to be constructed so as at once to guard them and to exploit them. The riches which they contained were well defended, because it was felt, apparently, that they were in danger. Evidently redoubtable princes lived behind these massive walls; for them they were citadels, and for their subjects they were places of refuge in case of need. And yet in this state of hostile defiance among neighbors art was relished and cultivated. Today, beneath the crumbled palaces, the spade of the excavator discovers relics of brilliant decorations, fragments of columns, painted friezes, and sculptures. In imagination, guided by the remains unearthed, one may restore great banquet halls, royal apartments, and courts of regal splendor. Furthermore, imposing sepulchers bear witness to the pride of princes who sought, even in death, to assert their haughty superiority. This civilization may be called Mycenæan, since the ruins of Mycenæ today represent to us the highest development of culture in that period.

Period of Invasions and Migrations.—On the other hand, the epic poets tell us of a confederation of kings called Achæans; and the historians report that toward the end of the second millennium B. C. great movements of populations took place in Greece and completely overturned the previous civilization. They refer especially to a conquest of the Peloponnesus by Dorian tribes descending from the region of the Pindus. It is probable that there was in fact a long series of migrations extending over a period of several centuries—a period of incessant conflicts, of violent occupations leading to the forcible expulsion of ancient royal families and of a part of their subjects, and to the subjugation of others, sometimes even to the displacement of entire populations, which had to go forth in search of new settlements. This, we are told, was the time of the establishment of numerous Greek tribes in Asia Minor, along the eastern coast of the Ægean Sea. Gathering there in units, according to ties of kinship, they gradually formed from north to south along this Asiatic coast the groups called Æolians, Ionians, and Dorians, while on the Greek mainland were founded those states whose later glory now fills the pages of history. These several centuries of continuous conflict and disturbance might well be compared to a sort of Middle Age, in which the previous civilization declined, but from which, toward the eighth century B. C., the Greece of history emerged.

Further on, in speaking of epic poetry, we shall see what progress the Greeks of Asia, the Æolians and especially the Ionians, made at that time in advance of their brothers in Greece proper. For in leaving their native soil these vigorous exiles, who refused to submit to the law of their conquerors, carried precious traditions away with them. It was natural that civilization, temporarily endangered, revived first among them. Hence it was in their cities—at Ephesus, at Smyrna, at Miletus, at Colophon, in the islands of Chios and Lesbos—that the arts, poetry, a certain elegance of life, a sense of beauty, once more began to manifest themselves; and from there this brilliant culture gradually extended its beneficent influence to the Greek mainland. But the Greek cities of Asia were unfortunate enough to witness the rise of two dangerously powerful empires near at hand: first that of the Lydians, later that of the Persians. Thus it is not in this Asiatic Greece, fascinating as it is, that we can best study the formation of the Hellenic states; let us rather devote our attention to those which survived and endured—the celebrated states of Greece proper.

Formation of the Hellenic States.—The term "states," of which one is obliged to make use, is poorly suited, as a matter of fact, to those first attempts at political formation. Rather were they groups of clans or tribes, whose character was in most cases heterogeneous; but usually it came about that one group predominated over the others and thus gave its name to the region occupied. However, from the time indicated above, a definite tendency toward organization is to be observed in the majority of these communities.

At the time of the conquests and migrations just referred to, it is evident that the peoples who went forth in search of new settlements had to obey orders. But by no means were they mere roving hordes temporarily banded together; on the contrary, they represented a certain inherent system of orderly arrangement associated with them from time immemorial. They were composed of families, phratries, and tribes, each associated in a cult of its own and in the honor paid to a common ancestor, real or fictitious, whose name it bore; and from the moment when they settled down to live anywhere, these traditional groupings constituted the framework of their normal social life. Each family, in the large sense of the word, had its chief, or, as the head of a family was called in the phrase of that time, its king. It had also its own land and its own jurisdiction; and it supplied all, or very nearly all, its own needs. These family kings were more or less subordinate to superior kings, richer and more powerful, whose council they formed; and the superior kings, in turn, were able to recognize at least in certain cases, and especially in time of war, a supreme king. Here, then, we find the rough outline of an organization at once aristocratic and monarchic, altho we should not, of course, conceive such a society as subject to clearly defined hierarchical rules.

The geographic conformation of Greece, naturally divided into cantons, lent itself poorly to the political fusion of these incipient states; moreover, it was not even favorable to a close *rapprochement* of their own component elements. The fact is that none of the groups thus outlined was ever sufficiently powerful, for any considerable length of time, to dominate all the others, or even to attempt to do so. Consequently, they remained separate and independent. Many of them never achieved any real unification; only a few were successful in so doing, and it is among these few that we may best study the formation of the state in the proper sense of the term.

For the sake of simplicity, let us consider here only Sparta and Athens; and without entering into the details of their history—which the limits of this work do not permit—let us state the essential facts in a very few words.

Sparta, born of the Dorian conquest, had to organize its forces with a view to maintaining its domination over a conquered population. There, accordingly, the military spirit was from the very beginning, and always, associated with the oligarchical spirit. Not only did Sparta have to exclude from the government every element which did not belong to the conquering race, but it also felt the need of imposing upon itself a rigid discipline capable of maintaining the closest coherence

among its citizens. It wanted them all to be as much
alike as possible. Thus it was led to assume the character
of a sort of military camp, under the authority of its two
kings, its Council of Elders, and later its ephors, with a
rigorous code of laws resolutely hostile to every innovation and consequently to every form of individual liberty.
Everything was subordinated to the public interest. The
children were given a severe, almost cruel, training; the
life of the citizen was subject to rules and restrictions of
every kind. Accustomed to obedience from infancy, the
Spartan was to have no other desires than those of military honor and patriotism. In this way Sparta succeeded in developing among its people an extraordinary
moral force, and this, together with its remarkable
military efficiency, for a long time rendered it superior to
the majority of the other Greek states. Consequently,
it has left the world shining examples of those virtues
which it practised. On the other hand, in voluntarily
condemning itself to isolation and immobility, it lessened
its own share in the general development of Greek civilization.

The history of Athens is quite different. Whatever
were the origins of the Athenian people, every marked evidence of an ethnic diversity in them was early effaced.
The sense of racial unity made way for the sense of
human and social equality. The little patriarchal kingdoms were united in Athens, sooner than anywhere else,
in an association at once religious and political, the center
of which was the Acropolis, the principal seat of the cult
of Athena. Ruled at first by kings, the city was afterwards governed by hereditary (later, by elected) magistrates called archons, who were the leaders of a landed
aristocracy. But the growing importance of the small
landowners, favored by the nature of the country, the

laborious energy of the peasants, and the demands of a
rapidly increasing urban population, combined to develop
a democratic spirit in the masses.   There were conflicts,
civil wars, and adjustments.   At the beginning of the
sixth century B. C. the laws of Solon, in abolishing the
burdens of land servitude, marked an important step in
the progress of the people.   For a time they even established a certain social equilibrium.   They did not, however succeed in placing liberty on a solid foundation; it
remained for the tyranny of Pisistratus and his sons to
prepare the ground for that.   By promoting agriculture
and commerce, as also by encouraging intercourse with
foreign countries, this tyranny awakened in the people
a clearer consciousness of their power.   The result was
that in 510 B. C. they drove out the tyrants, and three
years later they laid the solid foundations of the democracy by the establishment of the constitution of Clisthenes
(507 B. C.).   In the first half of the fifth century this
movement achieved its final consummation when, after the
Persian Wars, the lower classes, inspired by victory and
by the memory of their sacrifices, swept aside everything
which still stood in the way of their ambitions.

We shall observe this institution in operation in the
following period.   What it is necessary to emphasize here
is the fact that Athens, from the end of the sixth century
B. C., had created a form of political organization founded
upon the equality of its citizens before the law.   Few
facts have been of greater importance than this in the
general history of civilization.

The City-state and the Citizens.—In almost every part
of Greece, broadly speaking, there was formed what was
called the "city" (*polis*), and what we call the "state."
Of what, precisely, did it consist?   This "city-state" was
a collectivity having a genuine moral unity and tending

to establish an effective solidarity. All its members were bound together, not only by common interests, but also by clearly defined legal relations—relations based on rights and duties inscribed in a constitution. Neither these rights nor these duties were everywhere the same; but everywhere the citizen was one to whom the city-state attributed certain positive rights that were born with him, and, on the other hand, one whom it looked upon as bound to the performance of certain precise obligations in the common interest. The most important of these rights and the foremost of these obligations was to participate personally in the government. In that respect there was an absolute distinction between the citizen and the foreigner, even in places where foreigners were favorably received, as at Athens; and the distinction was even more radical between the citizen and the slave, who had no rights at all. If man, as Aristotle was to say later on, can fully realize himself only in the highest of associations, which is the city-state, then the Greek citizen alone, as distinguished from the barbarian, was completely a man. To the title of citizen, therefore, was attached a special dignity, and he who bore that title was proudly conscious of the fact.

The Law.—From this conception of the city-state there naturally developed a corresponding conception of law. It was in the Greek city-state, indeed, that law was first conceived from the standpoint of the high moral significance which attaches to the word. Neither in theocracies, nor in despotic monarchies, nor among semi-civilized peoples, could there be law in the proper sense of the term. For theocracies knew only the commandments of God as expressed in the imperious dictates of a sacerdotal body, or of a superior man, recognized as an interpreter of the divine will; despotic monarchies had no

rules other than the orders of the sovereign; semi-
civilized peoples conformed to family customs and to the
wishes of their tribal elders and chiefs. In the Greek
city-state the law was essentially a product of the intellect, conceived with reference to the common interest.

The period with which we are concerned witnessed the
origin of the principal bodies of Greek law, some of them
historic, others semi-legendary—those of Lycurgus,
Charondas, Zaleucus, Draco, and Solon. These names,
and the traditions to which they are related, teach us a
unique fact: everywhere, at some time, the city-state felt
the need of laying down certain general rules governing
the relations of the citizens among themselves. Intended
to repress acts of violence, to determine due reparations,
and also to fix the obligations of every member of the
community, these laws were adapted to the conditions
and requirements of each individual state. Whether they
are authorized by divine sanction, or whether they lack
such sanction, in the last analysis they always rest upon
the at least tacit accord of the citizens; they represent a
common will, resulting from prevailing social conditions, of
which they are the consecration. Moreover, they are imposed less as a heritage of the past than as a guarantee of
the future peace and stability of the city-state. From
this conception sprang the feeling that, if the laws were in
any way to be modified, it was to be done with prudent
discretion—not for light and transient reasons, but only
in order to adapt them to the changes which time necessarily brings about in every form of human society.

Their real object was to establish the reign of justice—
a concept of the first importance, which in Greece becomes
more and more closely associated with that of law. For
the Greeks, having no decalog, could seek the formula
of justice only in their legislation. Essentially human,

this justice written in their laws is derived in the end
from the common agreement of those who are guided by
a sense of moral righteousness. It is true, no doubt, that
the gods also favor it, that they not only regard it with
sympathetic eyes but to a certain extent are even guard-
ians of it; but they are not called upon to formulate
it thru the mouths of their priests. It is determined of
itself by the conditions and requirements of the social
life; it is regulated and clarified by every-day experience.
Opposed incessantly by the passions, its very setbacks
serve to show that it can not be dispensed with and help
to emphasize the necessity of fortifying it. Defeated
every day, it is nevertheless victorious in the long, con-
tinous records of public life.

Slavery.—With regard to one essential matter, however, justice never succeeded in asserting itself. A cry-
ing injustice, slavery, was consecrated by custom from
the earliest times. Sanctioned by all the Greek laws
without exception, a universal institution everywhere else
in the ancient world, its origin dated back to the oldest
abuses of power, that is to say, to the earliest ages of
mankind. For the honor of their civilization, so humane
in other respects, it is to be regretted that the Greeks
did not manage to repudiate a custom so outrageous to
humanity.

First Expansion of Hellenic Civilization.—Everything
that has been said so far relates to the Greek peninsula,
to the Ægean islands, and to the Greek coast of Asia
Minor. But after the eighth century B. C. Greece did not
cease to expand beyond these limits.

As soon as it had regained its internal equilibrium after
the period of invasions and migrations, it had, for numerous reasons, to widen the sphere of its activities. The
first needs of its nascent industry compelled it to seek in

more or less distant places the materials it lacked—
copper, silver, and iron—and consequently to export
some of its own products in exchange. On the other
hand, the spirit of adventure animated a considerable
number of its inhabitants. At the same time its population was increasing, in many places, more rapidly than
the means of subsistence. Finally, civil conflicts, of such
frequent occurrence at that time, brought it about that
large groups of conquered peoples were sometimes obliged
to leave their native country. All this accounts for the
colonizing movement which began in the second half of
the eighth century B. C., the way for it having no doubt
already been prepared by earlier voyages and explora-
tions.

On the one side, toward the west, Corinth founds
Corcyra. Then Chalcidians, Corinthians, Megarians,
Achæans, and Locrians establish themselves in Sicily
and along the southern coast of Italy. One by one, cities
spring up there and in turn send forth colonies of their
own. On the other side, toward the east, Chalcis occupies the promontories of Thrace and there founds a
colony which receives from its mother-city the name of
Chalcidice. Miletus secures a foothold on the Hellespont
and along the Propontis thru the founding of Abydus,
Lampsacus, and Cyzicus; and from there it gains Pontus,
establishes a trading post at Sinope, and penetrates as
far as the Phasis. Megara founds Chalcedon, Perinthus,
and Byzantium, the mistress of the Bosporus. Athens,
finally, establishes itself in the sixth century B. C. in the
Chersonnesus of Thrace.

Nothing gives a better idea of the exuberant vitality
of Greece during this period than the intensity of this
colonizing movement. Moreover, in thus spreading out
she not only carried afar all the most vitalizing elements

of her civilization, but at the same time she steadily maintained her power at home; for these new cities remained in uninterrupted communication with the mother-cities which gave birth to them, piously conserving their spirit, their customs, and their traditional cults. Between them and the Greek mainland there was a steady commercial and intellectual intercourse.

Thus Hellenic civilization was propagated; and the type of humanity which it realized became known far and wide, even among peoples still barbarous. Let us now seek to discern its more intimate elements and to assign to each of them its proper value, beginning with religion.

CHAPTER II

THE RELIGION OF THE GREEKS

Importance of Religion in Hellenic Civilization.—
Everybody knows what constant and profound influence
religion exerted among the Greeks. We find it associated
with almost every phase of their public and private life.
Many important events of their history were either inspired or sanctioned by it; many of their artistic
creations were religious either in origin or in purpose.
Even the great movements of Hellenic thought were
closely bound up with the national religion, since nearly
all of these movements were either impelled by it or,
on the other hand, opposed and retarded by it.

(1) BELIEFS

Primitive Religions.—An analytical study of the historical religions of Greece, as well as the knowledge which
we have today acquired concerning still earlier religions,
enables us to recognize as the primitive basis of their beliefs the deification of the phenomena of nature or of the
unknown forces which were supposed to produce them.
Since the life of man was essentially bound up with these
phenomena, it was a question either of conjuring them
when they were feared, or of befriending them or even con-
straining them to appear if they were needed. Hence the
more or less magic rites designed to avert evils and to
multiply blessings. For a long time the popular imagi-

15

nation pictured these forces in vaguely defined forms, as so many spirits localized in the stars, in the phenomena of the air, in certain animals, in trees or plants, or even in inanimate objects such as water-courses, lakes, caverns, and rocks; and when they were pictured in any more concrete form, they were usually conceived as fantastic creatures, less human than monstrous.

Anthropomorphism.—But at the beginning of the his-torical period these barbarous conceptions had already become only scattered survivals. The form of religious belief which predomined in Greece from that time on, and which imposed itself upon all the more cultivated minds, was that called anthropomorphism. This con-sisted essentially in ascribing to the gods the essential characteristics of human beings.

Let us guard, however, against relying upon this definition to a greater extent than the facts allow. The anthropomorphism of the Greeks is known to us es-pecially thru their poetry, and thru the plastic arts, which are more or less dependent on it. But poetry, by its very nature, can not be regarded as an absolutely reliable interpreter of the conceptions of the great number. Like the plastic arts, altho to a less extent, it is obliged to lend to the figures with which it deals a reality much more fixed in its forms than the oftentimes vague conception of simple believers would be likely to ascribe to them. In the Homeric poems we see immortal gods endowed with incomparable beauty, strength, and swift-ness. Among them are differences of sex, age, charac-ter, and attributes; and each of them has a name and a set of traits peculiar to himself. Altogether they form a family, or rather, if one takes into account also the minor deities (a veritable people which figures only in the background), a city-state. This people has a supreme king and is divided into tribes occupying, respectively, the sky, the earth, the sea, and the subterranean world, each of these domains having its own distinct ruler. In this divine world, which one may suppose to have sprung from diverse origins, poetry endeavors to create a certain orderly system; and it succeeds, very largely, in the effort. Insofar as possible it arranges these gods in family lines, which it ingeniously joins together in more or less definite relationships. This is what we observe especially in the *Theogony* of Hesiod. A succession of generations unites the old gods with the new gods, who thereafter rule the world. In the center of the Olympus thus constituted stands forth the majestic figure of Zeus, sovereign of gods and men, and lord of the thunder, a weapon which renders him invincible and enables him to strike down all his enemies. A little below him are his two brothers, Poseidon, lord of the sea, and Hades, ruler of the dead, dreaded possessor of a dark subterranean empire. Close to Zeus sits Hera, his sister and his consort. The family group is completed by the children of Zeus: Hephæstus, the divine smith; Apollo and Artemis, both children of Leto; Persephone, daughter of Demeter; Ares, the grim warrior; and finally, the young and agile Hermes, messenger of the gods. This mythology is in itself a masterpiece of organization and of beauty; it reveals a characteristic gift of idealization not found, in the same degree, in any other nation. But its very perfection leads one to believe that it was, if not created, at least elaborated and completed by poets. In order to learn to what extent it represented common belief, therefore, one would have to be able to examine the minds of the people of that time. To what extent did their ideas accord, in these descriptions and constructions, with the personal fabrications of their poets, with their free inventions? This is hard to say. Let us not forget, however, that the poets themselves were far from general agreement, and that the local legends varied infinitely.

Religious Particularism.—Divine wills were everywhere conceived as of the same nature as human wills. Hence it was naturally admitted that since divine wills were inspired, like human wills, by individual motives and sentiments, the former might, also like the latter, be at variance. The very principle of polytheism wished it so; for if all the gods had had only one and the same will, there would have been only one and the same god. To attribute a distinct personality to each one of the gods, was to recognize implicitly that they could have different and even contrary desires. In fact, each of the Greek tribes had its recognized protectors in the divine world; and when they were associated in city-states, in confederations, even in a nation, this diversity continued. Certain gods, no doubt, were recognized and even worshipped in almost all the Greek city-states; but by no means did they everywhere enjoy the same favor. Almost every town had its preferred god, whom it looked upon as its protector, charged with defending it either against its enemies or against the gods of its enemies. Even in the remote period of the Homeric poems the gods appear to us as divided between the nations at war; and this division is perpetuated in all Greek history. Athens is bound to Athena; Argos relies upon Hera; Sparta commends itself especially to Apollo. And just as there are special gods for city-states, so too there are special gods for tribes, for families, and even for individuals. A Greek did not hesitate to invoke the protection of some one god in preference to another for an enterprise or for any project whatsoever, if he had any personal reason for counting upon that god's favor.

This, however, did not prevent some of the principal gods from early acquiring a national character; and this character became more and more perceptible with the progress of civilization. This is what happened especially in the case of Zeus, by reason of his supreme rank. There was a general tendency to make him the god par excellence; and this sentiment was naturally favored upon second thought. Never, however, did it become sufficiently strong to abolish the particularistic devotions of city-states and of individuals. To a Greek, moreover, Zeus himself did not represent an immutable will. Altho superior to the other gods, he did not differ from them in nature. The idea of natural laws, as we conceive them, was totally foreign to the masses; in that early period it existed only very vaguely, if at all, in but a few superior minds. According to the common belief, every occurrence, every phenomenon, was the result of a special determination, which could always be suspended or modified.

This religious particularism had its favorable and its unfavorable aspects. No doubt faith in the gods of the city-state strengthened patriotism; whereas piety, far from detaching the believer from terrestrial interests, attached him more firmly to those of the city-state; it exalted devotion to the commonwealth. On the other hand, it was sometimes a cause of intolerance; for to refuse to pay homage to the gods of the country was tantamount to disavowing the country. The crowd could not fail to regard the free thinker as a bad citizen, an enemy of the city-state; and accordingly it felt justified in banishing him or even in putting him to death.

(2) CULT

Priesthoods.—Like the gods, the cults in Greece were essentially local. Consequently, there was no unified sacerdotal body. The majority of the Greek cults had originally been domestic cults; it was the head of the family who offered the sacrifice in the name of his own people. This was likewise true of the phratries and of the tribes; indeed, wherever there was a social group, the head of that group was by right its natural representative before the gods. When the towns, the city-states, were organized, it was often the old domestic cults which became the cults of the new collectivities. Those which did not remain hereditary in a family, according to a fixed law of succession, were transferred to some public function. Moreover, every association acquired a priesthood of its own. Thus there were as many priests or colleges of priests as there were cults, altho at no time was there manifested the least tendency toward the formation of a national hierarchy. Let it be noted, in addition, that these priests, whoever they were, had nothing to teach, since the religion involved neither dogmas nor theology. In no sense were they doctors or expounders. Their function was limited to the performance of religious ceremonies according to consecrated rites.

Sacrifices and Prayers. Religious Formalism.—To these rites the Greeks attached great importance. The cult consisted of sacrifices, prayers, and various festivals, all the details of which were minutely regulated. Each god had his preferred offerings, which had to be presented to him in a traditional form. An oversight, an omission, was likely to cause him grave offense. The diversity of these offerings was therefore great, and they differed still more according to the importance of the favor solicited and according to the means of the suppliant. Sometimes they consisted of victims, such as oxen, sheep, goats, or swine; sometimes of cakes, grain, or flour; at other times they were composed of libations of wine, honey, or water. Human sacrifices, mentioned in the *Iliad*, seem to have disappeared almost entirely in the historic period, by virtue of the gradual mollification of customs. In general, there prevailed some idea of an equivalence between the thing offered and the favor solicited. One scarcely finds in Greece a religious ceremony which may be looked upon as a pure, entirely disinterested act of devotion.

Festivals and Games.—All the Greek festivals were related to the national religion, as were also all the solemn acts of public and private life. Some of them commemorated legendary events; others grew out of primitive rites the original character of which had become more or less effaced; a certain number perpetuated obsequies formerly instituted in honor of some hero. But whatever their origin, their rôle in the national life, and in that of the city-states, was considerable. Not only did they excite intense emotions, occasion public rejoicings, evoke common traditions of long standing, and bring into closer relationships all those who took part in them; but, more than that, they gave rise to spectacles which contributed materially to the physical, intellectual, and moral development of the various Greek peoples and of the nation as a whole.

Among the festivals of the city-states, those of Sparta and Athens, especially the latter, are the best known. Sparta had its *Hyacinthia*, its *Carnea*, and its *Gymnopædia*; Athens, its *Panathenæa*, its *Anthesteria*, its *Lenæa*, its *Country Dionysia* and, a little later, its great *City Dionysia*. We see these festivals steadily developing in organization and increasing in number and importance, according as the city-state itself grows and as its social life becomes more and more active. From year to year new forms of art are pressed into the service of

the festivals.   In the sixth century B. C. the *Panathenæa*
begin to offer the rhapsodists occasion for reciting to the
Athenian public, *in extenso,* the great poems of Ionia.
At about the same time, and in the same city, the festivals
of Dionysus introduce the dithyramb, perfected by Arion
and Lasus; and also, on the other hand, the great novelty
of the day, the first dramatic efforts of Thespis and his
successors.   On their part, the plastic arts most capable
of contributing to the glory of the cult, namely, architecture and sculpture, naturally profit by the intense religious movement excited and sustained by these great
periodical manifestations.   Moreover, the influence of the
festivals transcends even these limits.   Among all the citizens they create and develop a sense of beauty; they call
forth a most honorable spirit of emulation among the
tribes of one and the same city-state invited to participate
in their celebration; they give the wealthy an opportunity
to dispense benefactions and charities, thereby doing
honor to their own generosity; they provide spiritual
pleasures for the poor; they arouse in everybody common
sentiments of exultation and pride.   We may add, finally,
that these festivals, in attracting strangers from near and
far, spread abroad the renown of the city in which they
were held, giving it a reputation for hospitality and for
beauty which was not without advantage to the growth of
its commerce.

Still more important were the Panhellenic festivals, the
great games held at Olympia, at Delphi, on the Corinthian Isthmus, and at Nemea.   As far back as the
eighth century B. C. the Olympic contests began to attract
the inhabitants of the neighboring city-states to Pisa;
and in the two following centuries these contests acquired
a decidedly national character.   The most celebrated

athletes in all Greece gathered there to contend for the prize awarded to the winner of the foot-race, the wrestling match, the boxing bout, and the pentathlon. All the Greek peoples took a lively interest in these contests, which called for physical strength, agility, and courage; and the honors which the city-states heaped upon their victorious members bear witness to the value that was everywhere attached to these qualities. For assembled Greece these spectacles were the glorification of an ideal of virility. On the other hand, when horse-racing and chariot-racing were introduced, the princes and the landed nobles were glad indeed of the opportunity to set out their luxuries for popular admiration. To the banks of the Alpheus came not only the wealthiest citizens of Greece proper, but also the tyrants of the Hellenic city-states of Sicily, southern Italy, and Libya. Barbarians alone were excluded; and this very fact brought it about that in these quadrennial panegyres the sentiment of national unity and original fraternity could not fail to make itself felt, notwithstanding rivalries and hatreds. The truce proclaimed at that time in the name of the gods brought back to men's minds what was too often forgotten in daily life. Delphi, which also celebrated every four years its Pythian Games, offering public exhibitions of the same kind, was still richer in religious suggestions, thanks to the Temple of Apollo and to its oracle, which made it a sort of Panhellenic sanctuary. Moreover, the victories won in these contests, like those achieved on the Isthmus and at Nemea, served as a theme for lyric poetry; and this poetry, in celebrating the country and the family of the victors, reveled in clothing its eulogies in mythical narratives which gave new life and new glory to all the old legends, both local and national.

(3) DIVINATION AND ORACLES

Ideas of the Greeks concerning Divination. Seers. Oracles.—With the national religion there were likewise associated numerous forms of divination, unanimously looked upon by the Greeks as one of the most precious manifestations of divine benevolence. Among them, in fact, there prevailed a general belief that certain revelations concerning the future could be obtained either thru the observation and interpretation of signs, or from the responses which certain gods condescended to make to those who questioned them. Thanks to such celestial advice, one hoped to escape from the uncertainties and perplexities of daily life, both public and private.

The interpretation of signs was preëminently the office of seers consecrated to that service, that is to say, of specially endowed men and women. To them, accordingly, one had daily recourse for the purpose of finding out the significance of such minor incidents, interpreted as divine omens, as the flight of a bird, a peal of thunder, an unexpected meeting, or even a simple word unintentionally uttered or accidentally overheard; and in the absence of recognized seers, each individual drew personal conjectures from such omens. We should have but a poor conception of the intellectual temper of Greece if we failed to take into account these universal superstitions and their significance.

Of all the forms of divination, however, none was of so great importance as the oracles. An oracle, whatever its form, was properly the revelation made by a god in his sanctuary. All the gods did not give oracles, and all the sanctuaries did not lay claim to the privilege of prophecy. Among those that had this special privilege, there were certain ones that enjoyed a superior authority. Especially favored were the oracle of Zeus at Dodona, those of Apollo at Delphi and at Clarus, and that of Trophonius at Lebadæa, in Bœotia. Each of them had its following; but in the sixth century B. C. that of Delphi had already become the national oracle par excellence. This was due to its central location, to the amphictyonic festivals held there, to the sagacity of the priests in charge of it, to its relations with Sparta, and perhaps also to the very form of its revelations. It was from Apollo himself, infallibile interpreter of the thoughts of Zeus, his father, that these revelations were supposed to emanate. Apollo spoke thru the mouth of an inspired woman, the Pythia, who in a sort of delirium uttered confused words, which were immediately construed in a more or less ambiguous and enigmatic form by "prophets" charged with this duty. The consultants who carried away these mysterious sentences then sought to interpret their meaning, at once pleased and perplexed by this divine confidence, anxious possessors of a secret on which often their most cherished hopes depended. Moreover, an oracle of this nature was not consulted solely with regard to private affairs. The Greek city-states also addressed themselves to it officially for information or advice affecting their most serious interests. They never failed to consult it regarding the sending out of their colonies, or regarding their military enterprises; they sought its counsel in matters of law; they were especially anxious to secure its advice regarding all religious questions, as also regarding portents, epidemics, and scourges of all kinds. Many of them had special officers charged with conducting these consultations, as also with applying old oracles to new cases which might arise.

Let us not conclude from this, however, that the Greek

city-states had accepted the principle of a sort of theo-
cratic government.   The truth is, their freedom of action
was never seriously diminished.   Aside from the fact
that these consultations depended entirely upon their own
free will, there was of course always more than one way of
interpreting an oracle.   The prudent ambiguity of the divine word, which evaded all responsibility, explains why
the authority of the gods was more apparent than real.
The politicians knew how to make the people accept,
among numerous possible interpretations, the one which
accorded with their own personal views; and in the last
analysis the actual decisions were usually made on the
basis of rational motives.

(4) RELIGIOUS SENTIMENT; MORALITY

Religious Sentiment.—If now we inquire into the exact
nature of Greek religious sentiment, there appears to be
no doubt that its primary and fundamental element was
fear.   The Greek did not regard goodness or even justice
as essential attributes of divinity.   On the contrary, it
seemed to him quite natural, as we have observed, for
the gods to be jealous, irritable, and implacable in their
hatreds, and for them to use all their power to satisfy
these passions.   His first concern, therefore, was to avoid
offending any one of the gods.   But there was always
great danger of doing so unintentionally.   Excessive ambition, an effort to rise too high in the world, inordinate
success, or a too brilliant stroke of fortune, were regarded
by these suspicious lords as so many attempts upon their
superiority.   Hence the first duty of a man was to remember that he was a man.   A haughty word, or the
omission of a traditional homage, might bring down the
wrath of one of the divine powers upon an individual or

upon a whole city; and in such an event it was expected that the offended god might avenge himself by causing some public or private misfortune, a catastrophe or a scourge of some kind. No doubt the forms of the cult were looked upon as means of avoiding these terrible consequences. None of these means, however, seemed absolutely sure; and therefore, as soon as a man had reason to suspect any divine disfavor, he consulted the oracles and prophets, the depositaries of divine knowledge, upon whom it then devolved to recommend various modes of appeasement and conciliation. In this respect there was no difference between the most enlightened and the least cultivated peoples of Greece. Starting with the same beliefs, their sentiments were likewise the same.

If this state of mind did not paralyze the activity of the Greeks, it was no doubt due to the fact that their natural energy enabled them to find in these very beliefs, not only objects of fear, but also reasons for confidence which far outweighed the former in value. In general, the Greek persisted in consulting his gods until he had obtained favorable presages from them; and having once obtained them, he felt sure of success. His gods then became incomparable allies for him; and precisely because he considered them very awe-inspiring, he did not doubt that they would cause his enemies likewise to feel their invincible power. Thanks to a spiritual anthropomorphism, thus interpreted, the very conception of destiny was happily alleviated. Between mankind and this far-off power these semi-human gods interposed themselves very opportunely—these gods whom one could propitiate and with whom one could even make friends.

Did this confidence amount even to love? If by love we mean a sort of rapture of the soul rising in ecstasy toward an ideal of perfection with which it is eager to unite, it seems evident that no such thing was possible in Greece, at least not before the development of a philosophy imbued with mysticism. Nevertheless, in regarding a god as the protector and friend of the city-state in which one lived, one came to the point of loving that god as one loved the city-state itself. His legend was embodied in the local history and his worship was identified with patriotism. There is no doubt that the Athenians were as proud of the legendary exploits of Athena as they were of their own; and one will readily admit that their devotion to the virgin warrior who had always lived by preference on the Acropolis, was not essentially different from a respectful love.

Religion and Morality.—What influence did this religion have upon morals? Certain it is that the myths on which it was based had nothing in common with morality. These myths were formed to account for ancient or new rites, or to unify diverse beliefs, and for that purpose they interpreted these phenomena in the form of narratives or genealogies. Hence the phenomena in question had to be represented, now as conflicts between deities, now as unions, legitimate and illegitimate, between gods and goddesses. On the other hand, the desire to link princely lines with divine origins had led to the invention of innumerable love-adventures between gods and mortals. Hence a multitude of stories in which violence, deception, falsehood, and sensuality were given free rein. How could a religion bound up with such beliefs have failed to endanger human morals?

There are a few evidences, indeed, that these myths sometimes served as excuses for excesses, when offenders sought precedents for their own justification. On the whole, however, these were exceptional cases. In general it may be said that, contrary to what would be expected, the Greek religion, such as it was, rather served as an effective support for morality. It did not do so, to be sure, without having itself been subjected to the influence of reason. There is no doubt that morality, while progressing of its own accord, first purified religion. It spread abroad the idea that the life of the gods was not to be judged according to the rules of human conduct; it relegated their life to a purely mythological order of things, which had but a slight connection with practical reason. But then religion, thus purified, had a beneficial reaction upon morality. Since the gods were everywhere regarded as the natural patrons of the family, the tribe, or the city-state, it seemed logical to believe that everything which favored their prosperity was agreeable to them. It is to be admitted, therefore, that respect for an oath, justice, probity, obedience to law, moral discipline, even humanity, were of a nature calculated to gratify them, while contrary acts necessarily displeased them. Hence the conviction prevailed that the gods heaped blessings upon peoples who practiced justice and punished those who trampled it under foot. Thus it came about that this religion, which taught no morality, nevertheless became the guardian of the public morals.

(5) ALIEN RELIGIONS

Foreign Religions. The Mysteries.—Altho the Greek city-state had its preferred gods, it nevertheless recognized all the Hellenic gods and paid homage to them. In principle it excluded only the gods of barbarians, without, however, denying their existence; and thru the force of circumstances it was even led gradually to admit them. The city-state, intolerant as regards its own members, could not be equally intolerant as regards foreigners.

Having once allowed them to settle within its confines, it could not easily, for any length of time, proscribe their cults or ignore their beliefs; and in the long run these beliefs necessarily won some acceptance among the people who gave them a place in their midst. In the period prior to the Persian Wars, one case of this nature is particularly to be noted—the influence of the Thracian cult of Dionysus.

This cult seems to have been foreign to Greece proper at the time when the Homeric poems were composed. Of a semi-savage nature, it was characterized by ecstatic transports, processions of women across the mountains, shrieks and howls, and the immolation of animals, whose bodies were torn to pieces and whose still palpitating entrails were devoured by eager worshippers of the god. At what precise time and by what route it penetrated into central Greece, is unknown. At a very early date we find it in honor at Thebes, at Delphi, on the frontiers of Attica, in Elis, and elsewhere—an evidence that there existed in the Greek soul, notwithstanding its qualities of moderation and reason, a certain inclination toward mystic enthusiasm which must be taken into account. If sensual excitement, which found satisfaction in this cult, was not everywhere received with the same enthusiasm, at least a part of this religion of Dionysus was established everywhere, even in Attica, bringing with it an element of exaltation which was destined to make itself felt in the dithyramb, in tragedy, and in comedy.

On the other hand, and perhaps under the same influence, primitive religions enter into an entirely new stage of development at that time. This was the case with the religious celebrations called the "Mysteries." What distinguished them was their secret character. We have reason to believe that they were originally local cults, pertaining to certain families. Little by little these families admitted others to them, on condition of a preliminary initiation and of a promise not to divulge any secrets. It finally came about that some of these cults were adopted and patronized by certain states. None was more celebrated than that of Eleusis, the rites of which were held in the sanctuary of Demeter and Kora (Persephone). The Mysteries of these two goddesses proceeded almost certainly from an ancient agrarian cult. They owed an ever-increasing favor to the revelations which they made to the initiated concerning their fate after death. The official religion, it is true, recognized a god of the underworld; and poetry had spread abroad some vague notions regarding an abode of the dead; but what it told of this abode could not inspire anything but a sense of dread. Consequently many troubled minds were impelled to look elsewhere for hopes and assurances which the traditional beliefs did not hold forth to them. These hopes were given precisely to the initiated in the form of visions. Ideas borrowed from the legend of Persephone, carried away by Hades and later restored; or again the contemplation of symbols based upon the grain of wheat long buried underground and later appearing with its stalk and spike; and together with this, mysterious formulas, radiant apparitions following darkness—all these things became for well-prepared believers who were eager for reassuring promises, so many guarantees of a privileged happiness. For them there was no need of positive and precise doctrines; it sufficed for them to see and hear. In a sense it was the very reality of their cherished survival that the Mystery revealed to their eyes. The guarantee of it was given them by the initiation.

Such is the idea that one may form of the Greek religion before it had been permeated by philosophy—a religion with little coherence, for the most part; devoid of doctrine; very susceptible to the inventions of poets and very favorable to the free play of their imaginations; little by little becoming united with notions of morality of which it was originally independent; powerful by reason of its close connection with all the activities of public and private life, and by reason of its intimate association with local and national sentiments; susceptible of a certain mysticism but especially productive of outward manifestations; creator of numerous and diverse cults and festivals; inspirer of some of the most beautiful literary and artistic works that human genius has produced.

CHAPTER III

THE TESTIMONY OF EPIC POETRY

The Ancient Greek Epics.—Almost everything that has just been said about the beginnings of Greek civilization is to some extent expounded and greatly clarified by the testimony of the Greek epic poems. Only three of them have come down to us; but these three represent magnificently an epic literature which was certainly considerable. They are: the *Iliad* and the *Odyssey*, which are supposed to have been composed between the ninth and the end of the eighth centuries B. C.; the *Works and Days* of Hesiod, which is perhaps a little more recent. These poems reveal to us the entire life of that period in its three principal aspects: war, with its vicissitudes; navigation and maritime adventure; and agriculture—an admirable trilogy which idealized the passions, customs, and ideas of a singularly energetic humanity and endowed them with a beauty which permeated the entire subsequent life of the Greek people.

Heroic Legends. Heroes.—The substance of these three epics is composed of legends, that is to say, of narratives more or less fabulous but regarded in their time as historic. Nowhere is the richness of the Hellenic imagination better illustrated than in the abundance and variety of these narratives. Every section of Greece, every tribe, every large family, had its own set of legends. They were mixtures of memories, of traditions, and of free inventions; the elements of truth in them were concealed behind pure

33

fiction. But truth or fiction, these narratives were titles to nobility to be proud of. Each of the human groups which had created them had put into them what was close to its heart—the image of its past, its own character, its ideal. In them it recognized, and cherished, its very own self.

In general, an epic narrative was concentrated, so to speak, around one personage or several personages, sometimes around a family. These representative personages were the heroes. Without stopping here to inquire if they were all of the same origin, we may content ourselves with noting their general characteristics at the time of their entrance into epic poetry. The epic hero is a man of the divine race. Son, grandson, or descendant of a mortal woman supposed to have consorted with a god, he has elements at once of divine and of human nature. Being mortal, he is subject to human miseries, physical and moral; but having sprung from the blood of a god, he is much superior to the common run of men in strength, in endurance, in fleetness, in stature, in beauty, sometimes also in prudence. But altho all the heroes had some of these superiorities in common, they nevertheless differed considerably among themselves. In them, accordingly, is manifested the full variety of aptitudes characteristic of the Greek race; and this accounts for the influential rôle which these heroes played in the development of the national life. In the person of an Achilles, the Greek, to whatsoever city-state he belonged, admired all the physical qualities of which he was instinctively fond; in that of a Nestor or a Ulysses, he applauded sound reasoning, skill, and practical sense, which in his eyes were of no less value. Thus in creating its heroes Greece set up for itself, from its very infancy, living types of humanity in which it was always to take delight. Let us, therefore, rapidly survey the epic narratives which had the glorification of such types as an object, and let us seek to discover in them the more important moral concepts which they embody.

(1) WAR

General Idea of War in Greek Epic Poetry. Law of Nations.—The *Iliad* shows us two nations at war, the Achæans on the one side and the Trojans on the other. It is not a war of conquest; the vindication of the principle of justice serves as its cause. A Trojan prince, Paris, has eloped with an Achæan woman, Helen, wife of King Menelaus. Aided by the goddess Aphrodite, he has seduced her and carried her away on his ships, together with a part of her riches. The Achæan princes, confederated under the authority of Agamemnon, have come in arms to lay siege to Troy, demanding the return of Helen and her riches. The Trojan king, Priam, dominated by his son, Paris, refuses to surrender them. Such are the underlying facts to be considered.

The act of Paris illustrates the prevailing custom of that age. Thus we witness the abduction of women and the pillage of property, not by professional pirates, but by adventurous princes; and neither their families nor their subjects disavow these practices. In this instance violence is accompanied by treachery, since Paris has been received as a guest at Sparta. This violence the Achæans feel justified in punishing. A vague feeling for the law of nations inspires their outraged feelings. They have not come to destroy the city of Troy, but to secure justice for themselves. A remarkable fact is that they regard the injury done to Menelaus as a common injury done to all of them. Among them prevails a feeling of national solidarity strong enough to make them consent to place themselves under one leader. In this we perceive clearly the earliest manifestation of a Panhellenic sentiment. During the war itself the idea of a law of nations appears on several occasions: arrangements are concluded between the two parties, oaths are exchanged, on both sides efforts are made to terminate the hostilities. The oaths are violated, to be sure, but even this violation is sharply condemned by the saner men whom passion does not blind.

Let us note, however, that these principles of international law were not yet very precise nor very well understood. The Trojans of the *Iliad*, in the moments when they foresee their defeat, anticipate that their city will be burned and pillaged, the men massacred, the women distributed among the conquerors and carried away by them to become their slaves and their concubines; and we know that in other epic poems which supplemented the *Iliad*, all this was effectively realized. According to the *Iliad* itself, the combatants overcome and disarmed on the field of battle may, according to the pleasure of the conqueror, either be slain on the spot or sold as slaves. Except in case of special agreement, the dead are left without burial; and only in exceptional cases are their bodies ransomed. Finally, altho the Achæans are fighting for the vindication of the principle of justice, the most prominent of them do not dissimulate an added motive, namely, the desire for booty, on which they eagerly reckon in advance.

But it is important to note (for it is one of those things which add honor to the genius of the race) that at times a natural spontaneity outstripped the always slow normal progress of law and custom. The conversation of Priam and Achilles is equivalent to a superior and almost divine revelation. Here we see the rise, as it were, of a new dawn of humanity, the beneficent glow of which appears all of a sudden amid surviving vestiges of barbarism. The more cruel Achilles is shown to be in his treatment of the conquered Hector, the more impressed we are by the sudden emotion which takes hold of him when he sees the aged Priam embrace his knees, when he thinks of his own father, likewise aged and likewise destined to mourn his fallen son. The feeling which suddenly rises in him is the intuition of a human solidarity founded upon a common destiny, which exposes all mortal beings to the same vicissitudes and the same sufferings. Does not such a scene realize a moral attainment of incomparable value?

The Combat and the Combatants.—The war which the *Iliad* unfolds before our eyes is the siege of a city. But the Achæans are not conducting a war of siege; for that they have neither the means nor the method—no engines of war, no approaches. The siege is a blockade, which is drawn out indefinitely. The actual fighting takes place in the open. We may disregard here the small amount of military science which is manifested; suffice it to say that, simple as it all is, there is nevertheless revealed an unmistakable sense of organization. The Achæans are divided into tribes and phratries; they are drawn up, now in parallel lines, now in columns. Their leaders are mounted on chargers, and for the most part they ride ahead of their men in order to open up wide gaps in the opposing ranks.

Of particular interest to us, on the other hand, are the sentiments which animate the combatants. What this martial poetry exalts above everything else is, of course, courage. It shows us courage inspired by moral motives, such as honor, love of glory, patriotism, and desire for revenge. But since these motives do not always operate

with the same force, the firmness of spirit of which they
are the support is not always the same. It is likely to
weaken, even to fail, especially in a crowd of combatants.
Sometimes sudden panics seize them, resulting in flight,
in a disorderly and tumultuous rout. It is necessary for
the leaders to intervene, to rebuke the fugitives, to put
them to shame and to threaten them, to recount to them
all the reasons which command them to stand firm. In
this way hearts are hardened and wills are strengthened.
Reason, aided by noble sentiments, restores among the
combatants a courage of which this very power of reason
is the fundamental element.

Among the motives of action, honor holds first place.
None of these men will allow himself to pass for a coward.
Almost all of them covet praise; they love glory. Among
the leaders glory is a passion, perhaps the foremost of
their passions. To honor is added patriotism; in the
mind of the Achæans the two are inseparable. They
wish to honor their country by their valor and to uphold
the name of their fathers. Among the Trojans, patriotism is especially the anxious desire to defend their wives
and their children, their gods and their homes. It is expressed admirably in the exclamation of Hector: "the
best of the auguries is to fight for the city of one's
fathers." Moreover, the Achæans think also of their
native land, and the desire to see it again as soon as possible is one of the sentiments which inspires them.

Such an army can not lack discipline. Somewhere the
poet shows us the Achæans marching to battle in silence
and in order, while the Trojans advance tumultuously,
emitting loud and confused cries. The contrast is due,
perhaps, to a personal conception. But is not this conception itself significant? Clearly the Greek public to
whom this picture was presented appreciated the beauty

of it. It amounts to saying that in the judgment of the hearers of the *Iliad*, order, good deportment, and discipline were necessary conditions underlying the superiority of one army to another. In all the manifestations of the Greek mind these fundamental qualities will always be found.

The Army outside the Battlefield. The Council and Assembly.—When the army is not fighting, it becomes a people again. We then observe in operation the institutions referred to above. What we see is the functioning of an aristocratic royalty. At the head we find a supreme king, Agamemnon, the leader of the army. At his side there is a Council of subordinate kings, the chieftains of the confederated peoples—a Council which he calls to deliberate with him on all serious resolutions, and the advice of which he generally follows. Further down is an Assembly, a gathering of the entire people. The king communicates his decisions to it; the members of the Council sometimes support these decisions; the Assembly approves by acclamation. It does not deliberate, but it has to declare itself in all matters; its concurrence must either be won or else exacted by the prestige of authority.

Such a form of government gives very free play to discussion—deliberations of the Council, consultations of chiefs, embassies, exhortations to the troops, harangues addressed to the Assembly. Suffice it to say that here already we find a genuine eloquence, still primitive in its simplicity, but nevertheless skillful; at times vigorous, urgent and terse; more often suggestive, narrative, or even digressive; always, however, endowed with a natural elegance, always easy and supple—a well-nigh perfect example of its kind. In the *Iliad* there are almost as many beautiful speeches as there are beautiful narratives.

The Besieged City.—The *Iliad*, in its general trend, is
incontestably the poem of the conquerors; but it by no
means disregards the conquered or treats them with indifference. One of its merits is that it introduces us,
when necessary, into the besieged city and reveals to us
there the sorrowful effects of the war. It is full of a profound human sympathy.

A few celebrated scenes are particularly significant in
this respect. The most valiant of the Trojan warriors,
Hector, returns for a few moments to the city, where he
meets his wife Andromache, accompanied by the nurse
holding in her arms their only child Astyanax. Hector
is about to leave them to return to battle. The presenti-
ment of death haunts his mind. Yet this matters not,
for he has no right to shun personal danger. In vain
Andromache entreats him and weeps. Moved to the very
depths of his soul, he tears himself from her arms, embraces the child whom he is never again to see, at the
same time praying to the gods that some day the boy may
be as brave as and more happy than his father. Further
on it is Priam and Hecuba, as well as Andromache, who
witness from the walls of Troy the combat in which
Hector succumbs to the blows of Achilles and who behold the outrages inflicted upon the body of the conquered hero. Nothing could be more moving than the
picture of their anguish, their moral distress. Finally,
at the end of the poem, we are present at the burial of
Hector. One after the other, his mother, Hecuba, his
widow, Andromache, his sister-in-law, Helen, lament beside his funeral pyre. Thus from the beginning to the
end of this epic, which exalts warlike virtues, a certain
attention is devoted to pity; and this is not the least
important nor the least beautiful feature of the poem.
Hence a very noble side of the Greek soul is revealed in

this work, which serves as witness and interpreter of its most ancient aspirations.

(2) NAVIGATION AND MARITIME ADVENTURE

The Odyssey.—The second of the great Greek epic poems, the *Odyssey*, supplements the *Iliad* by presenting a very different spectacle. For the most part it is an account of the wanderings of Ulysses, roaming on the seas or detained on some far off island, seeking to return to his native land of Ithaca. As a sequel to his adventures, the poem relates his return to his home, invaded during his absence by neighboring princes who have sought to compel his wife, Penelope, to marry one of them.

The Legends of the Sea.—The basis and original elements of this poem, accordingly, are the legends of the sea, some of them supposed to have been told by Ionian sailors when they returned from their first voyages of exploration—marvelous tales in which it is scarcely possible to discern what belongs to free fancy and what is merely a distortion of misinterpreted realities. The itinerary of Ulysses seems to have been jumbled at the pleasure of the narrator. Such as it is, however, it indicates a certain knowledge of the northern coast of Africa and of parts of the western Mediterranean, especially the shores of Sicily. The voyages of Ulysses constitute an entire cycle of legends of undoubtedly diverse origins, all of them, however, abounding in the marvelous. The countries represented by the poet are supposed never before to have been visited by any human being. Their inhabitants are either giants, or monsters, or privileged peoples, or gods. The imagination which created this fairy world, as well as the imagination of the people for whom it was created, had still retained much of its childlike naïveté. The charm of the unknown worked powerfully upon these people. They had no thought of criticism or of verification; it sufficed for the poet to know how to lend probability to the improbable. The Greek narrator excelled in this, to such an extent that we of the present day still allow ourselves to be fascinated by the charm of his imaginative creations.

Navigation and the Greek Mariner.—But what moves and interests us most in the narratives of this part of the *Odyssey* is the essentially human element. Ulysses, altho a hero, is a Greek mariner of the type that was undoubtedly common at the time of the first distant navigations. We see him with his companions in his boat, the latter poorly adapted to resist wind and weather, sailing along the coast, the projections of which serve as guiding-points for him, spreading his only sail when the wind is favorable, otherwise advancing with difficulty by the propulsion of oars. He sails only by day, fearful of losing his way in the darkness of night, and draws his boat up on the sand when evening approaches. Provident and wary, knowing the dangers that menace him, he does everything he can to avoid them; and when his prudence fails him, his courage and presence of mind come to his rescue. Driven toward an unknown shore, he manages to discover a hidden opening for his boat. He does not enter the interior of a region without first exploring it as far as he can. He is constantly on his guard. He observes everything which may help to inform him as to the customs of the inhabitants. He is ever ready to fight or to flee. In reading certain scenes of the *Odyssey* we can form a mental picture of the men of Miletus disembarking for the first time on the unknown shores of the Propontis. Such an episode is in a sense a fragment of what might have been their log. Elsewhere we see them struggling with the difficulties and hardships of primitive navigation, with hunger and thirst, buffeting the winds and waves, which make play of their frail craft. We understand, we almost share, their anxieties, their terrors; we admire their endurance, their energy, their discipline. Ulysses represents all of them; but in him we recognize especially the chief endowed with all the qualities of leadership, the man on whom rests the responsibility for the common safety, who foresees everything and thinks of everything, whose courage is never daunted, whose resourceful mind is never at a loss. The *Odyssey* was truly the poem of a seafaring people.

The Return of the Navigator.—It contains, however, something more than narratives of the sea. It also describes for us, in the form of a legend peculiar to Ulysses, a very different aspect of the life of the navigator—the long absence of the head of the family believed to have perished at sea, and the drama of his homecoming. Thus it throws a brilliant light on a social state which it is of the greatest interest to consider.

In a rich, princely home a woman, Penelope, and her son, Telemachus, remain alone, awaiting year after year the return of husband and father. They alone await it; the people scarcely believe any longer in the possibility of his return. Neighboring princes covet the rich and seductive woman, whom they consider a widow, and with her they perhaps hope to secure a part of her fortune. As she rejects their proposals in fidelity to her absent husband, they establish themselves by force in the latter's home and live on his goods, which they insolently squander. The young Telemachus has neither the authority nor the strength to expel them. What is to be done? There is no public authority to protect the family; in the social order of that time the power of the state does not yet exist. Each family defends itself; outside it can seek only voluntary allies. If these allies fail it, it is reduced to its own resources.

Ulysses does, however, return; but he returns alone. What can be done against so many allied adversaries? Disguised as a beggar, he observes his enemies, secretly rallies some helpers and with the latter prepares the surprise blow which will enable him to recover his home. The entire second part of the poem is given over to an account of this preparation and recovery. It first conducts us to the rural possessions of Ulysses, introduces us in a succession of charming scenes to his devoted servant, the aged swineherd Eumæus, and at the same time sets forth the economical manner in which the hero manages his affairs. Then it conducts us to his urban home, where a series of episodes reveal the details of the domestic life, all the while describing for us the insolence of the suitors and the sentiments of the personages in the drama. The narrative is replete with moving scenes, with precise and curious descriptions. Nowhere else do we find so much instruction regarding the customs and the private life of primitive Greece; for here as elsewhere we have a feeling that the particular story related to us is to a certain extent of general applicability. Other navigators besides Ulysses must have had similar adventures in those ancient times. There must have been other homecomings, of which his was, as it were, a sort of dramatized representation.

(3) AGRICULTURE

The Poem of "Works and Days."—To these two aspects of the life of the time, war and navigation, another poem, the *Works and Days* of Hesiod, adds a no less in-

teresting description of the agricultural life. Son of
an Æolian of Cyme, in Asia Minor, the author informs
us that his father left his country, where he lived in difficult circumstances, and settled in the town of Ascra,
in Bœotia, where he does not seem to have found much
more prosperity. His legacy, probably modest, was
divided between his two sons, Hesiod himself and Perses;
and it is precisely this division which is the occasion, if
not the subject, of the poem. The poet informs us that
the settlement did not satisfy Perses, and that the two
brothers had recourse to an arbitrament, which fell short
of reëstablishing the desirable understanding between
them. Perses, if one is to believe his brother, was a slug-
gard who worked little and squandered much. In bitter,
sorrowful verses Hesiod enjoins him to put an end to the
quarrel, severely reproaches him for his laxity, reminds
him of the necessity of work and shows him how one
may profit by it. The entire poem is at once satirical,
reproachful, and didactic.

*Rural Property in Bœotia. Apportionment of In-
heritances. Disputes.*—What we see here at the very
start is the division between two brothers of a very modest
inheritance. From what the poet says it appears that his
portion was small; and that of Perses could not have
been much larger. Moreover, when Hesiod speaks of his
neighbors, we are led to understand that their condition
was very much the same. There is no doubt, consequently, that the small landowner prevailed in that part
of Greece at that time. All the advice that Hesiod gives
applies only to rather poor people. The smaller the
property, the greater the attachment to it; and we are
not surprised to see also that its ownership was jealously
disputed. But the manner in which the disputants
reached a settlement remains somewhat obscure for us.

Of course we know that they had recourse to the arbitrament of the "kings," that is to say, probably the rich family chiefs, who exercised a vaguely defined authority in the growing cities. Hesiod gives us a rather unfavorable idea of their sense of equity; he even goes so far as to call them "devourers of gifts." Are these only the malicious words of a dissatisfied litigant? Perhaps—at least to some extent. Nevertheless, if we take into account the boldness of the poet and the popularity of his work, we are led to believe that in so speaking he felt himself sufficiently well supported by the opinion of the great number. And from this we may conclude, without too much hesitation, that everything was not for the best in Bœotia in the seventh century B. C. How, then, did the working people get along in this state of affairs? The poet informs us.

Work in the Fields. The Family.—Thanks to him, we see them actually at work. His laboring man, who is Hesiod himself, has only a plow, a simple swing-plow, made by his own hands; and he has also but a single ox to drag the plow. One servant assists him in his work. With this poor equipment he cultivates the soil. His wife, on her part, occupies herself in the house, assisted perhaps by a slave. It is she who weaves the linen and woolen cloths for clothing, who prepares the food. No season of the year is lost. From the time of plowing and sowing to the harvest, every detail of useful occupations is regulated and cataloged. Some of these occupations are reserved for days of winter weather which do not permit of outdoor work. It is then that the cultivator repairs his broken tools or makes new ones. His parsimony is extreme. Poor food, carefully measured out, prevails; the slices of bread are counted. It would even seem that the mouths to be fed are also counted, for

Hesiod believes that his countrymen ought not to have more than one son. Perhaps he is thinking also of the disadvantages of the division of property among brothers. Besides, how is a piece of land already so small to be divided up?

Is this narrow life, accordingly, entirely devoid of pleasure? Such is not the impression which, on the whole, this austere poet gives us. First of all, in this laborious year there are, in spite of everything, moments of relaxation. The harvest and the vintage are the expected compensations. When either the one or the other has been good, the household joins in celebration. For this exceptional work no doubt some additional helpers have been called in. Once the work is done, there is leisure to rest in the shade, to repose beside the brook, to converse lightly—in short, to be happy. Moreover, in reading the poem we seem to divine in the author another more durable and more personal satisfaction. It is the satisfaction of one who knows his business, who is conscious of doing his work well, and who delights in his experience. The man who addresses us in these verses is a close observer of nature. In some sort he is constantly prying into it, and in the end he knows it so well that he does not hesitate to interpret all its signs. That some allowance should be made in the work for prejudices, for certain superstitions, and for bold generalizations, there is no doubt. It remains no less certain, however, that here already is to be found the initial development of an agricultural science not without value. And there can be no doubt that the person who thus described this science took pleasure in summing it up, in controling it year by year and day by day, and especially in communicating it to a public whose admiration it could not fail to arouse.

The Mythology and Morality of the Agriculturist.—
There is another feature which can not here be overlooked, because it is of direct interest to the history
of civilization. It is the consideration which is given in
the *Works and Days* to mythology and to the practical
philosophy growing out of it.

What the author of this poem demands of mythology
is not, as the poets of the heroic epic demand, that it
provide him with subjects for beautiful narratives, but
rather that it explain to him the necessity of work imposed upon mankind. He finds this explanation in the
myth of Prometheus, in that of Pandora, and in that of
the succeeding ages of humanity. These old narratives
seem to him to account for the prevailing condition of
the world. They lead him to believe that formerly there
existed happy generations of men on whom the rigid law of
work was not imposed; and on the whole his naïve mind is
satisfied with this state of affairs. It is true that he has
no hope of ever seeing the return of this golden age.
Far from it. He admits that everything in the world is
going from bad to worse. He is conscious of having been
born in an age of violence and injustice. This, at least,
is what he affirms in general. But in his practical application to the daily affairs of life, he by no means draws
all the consequences from this idea. He firmly believes
that justice is the law of humanity, since it is its privilege,
and he does not doubt that Zeus is its natural protector—
a somewhat negligent protector, perhaps, but nevertheless one whose power is definitely manifested by the
prosperity which he accords to good people and the punishments which he inflicts upon impetuous people. And
that is why he has confidence in work associated with
justice and piety; for without such confidence, everything
he teaches would be futile.

(4) EDUCATIONAL INFLUENCE OF THE EPIC POETRY

Thanks to these epic poets, Greece possessed, toward the beginning of the seventh century B. C., a sort of idealized summary of its principal forms of activity, as one can see from this brief survey. In these works it could learn to know itself, to take cognizance of its good qualities as well as of its defects. This was of very great advantage to it; for it is certain that the educational value of these beautiful poems contributed greatly to the moral and artistic development of the country. The spectacle of conflicting passions offered abundant material for reflection. Almost everything of importance which could be said regarding good and evil, regarding the qualities which do honor to humanity, and regarding human weakness, had here been said. And the majority of these teachings were presented in the most vivid and most moving form—in the form most likely, consequently, to make a deep and lasting impression on the mind. We do not hesitate to say that all of Greek wisdom originated in these works of imagination and reflection.

But from the standpoint of the awakening of an artistic sense, an essential element of Greek civilization, the epics were equally beneficent and equally efficacious. They showed, in effect, that the representation of life was the thing most likely to move men and to arouse in them the impression of beauty; and at the same time they disclosed, by admirable examples, how this effect could be produced. It appeared that literary art consisted essentially of simplification and idealization. These poems, composed of living substances, delved deeply into reality. They represented emotions, sentiments, and passions—things which constantly change and contradict themselves.

But a powerful mind had succeeded in overcoming this confusion and clarifying this obscurity. It had sketched noble figures in bold outline, strongly conceived and daringly executed, as on a stage on which they stood apart by themselves in full view. Everything else was action; and action also showed itself subject to the natural laws of art. Each poem formed an entity easy to survey at a glance. A simple yet varied mode of composition tolerated no obscurities; each part was well proportioned, and the interest of the whole was skillfully maintained and tempered. The rich inventive genius of the poet was restrained by rules of order and moderation. These were the fundamental principles of Greek art, one may say, which were thus affirmed.

Moreover, the same epic poems gave to Greece the most beautiful poetic language. In what ways, and by what gradual process, did this language become differentiated from the usual language? This would be difficult to say. The *Iliad* reveals the language to us as a finished product, already in its full perfection. Its vocabulary appears as a rich storehouse of words, well adapted not only to define the impressions of the senses, but also to express a very great variety of emotions, to denote shades of thought, and even to give voice, at that early date, to a goodly number of more or less abstract ideas. It was not, to be sure, a language to be used for every-day speech. But because it grew out of the very genius of the race, it was eminently well calculated to stir that genius. In the process of awakening thought, it suggested imitations and adaptations; it caused people to sense the value of the derivation and the composition of words. In fact, all the operations of the intelligent mind, all the emotions of the soul, were thereby rendered easier, to the great profit of the mechanics of the language. Moreover, this beautiful language was assisted by a versification which redoubled its charm. Hearing its melodious ring, the people came to feel more vividly that their language was not only adapted to the exchange of indispensable ideas, but that in resorting to rhythm and cadence, in adorning itself with well chosen ornaments, it could become capable of charming the mind, of exalting the soul, of producing delicate or profound sensations, of transporting its hearers to an ideal world. The entire intellectual and moral development of Greece in the sixth and seventh centuries proceeds directly from what had thus been learned.

CHAPTER IV

INTELLECTUAL AND MORAL DEVELOPMENT IN THE SEVENTH AND SIXTH CENTURIES BEFORE CHRIST

General Character of the Seventh and Sixth Centuries.
—The general progress of thought during these two centuries was stimulated, moreover, by other causes: the increase of the population, which gave rise to large urban communities; conflicts between parties; great commercial enterprises. Revolutions, always destructive, were also influential factors; they brought powerful individualities into play; and at the same time they created moral ties, common sentiments among men whom they united for the protection or promotion of the same interests. In the clash of passions the element of personality necessarily acquired a new force. Turned to action, the men of that time interested themselves less in things of the past and more in those of the present. Their hatreds and their friendships—these are the subjects that occupy them above all; but they are also interested in exhortations and counsels, insofar as these devices are still a form of immediate action, a manifestation of the character or of the will. But by a natural reaction, the taste for pleasure increases in this more restless life. It is favored, moreover, by the greater facility of social relations, by the gradual mollification of customs, as also by the diffusion of movable wealth and the consequent increase of luxury.

Unfortunately we do not possess, for this interesting epoch, a volume of testimony comparable with that furnished by epic poetry. Of the brilliant literature which flourished at that time, we have scarcely anything but fragments. What remains is nevertheless sufficient to bring to light three essential innovations: the successful rise of personal poetry; the creation of the choral lyric, interpreter of collective sentiments; and finally the birth of philosophy and of scientific research. To this, moreover, may be added the first steps in the perfection of architecture, sculpture, and the arts in general.

(1) PERSONAL POETRY

New Elements introduced by Personal Poetry. Iambic and Elegiac Poetry.—The epic poem was essentially a narrative portrayal of the past. If the present was nevertheless reflected in it, this was in some sort involuntary; almost never did the epic poet speak of himself. Great was the innovation, therefore, when men and women began to make their own sentiments the very subject and substance of their poetry. It was natural, or rather necessary, that this bold expansion of individuality should create new means of expression. Thus, for the grave and too uniform measure of the epic hexameter were substituted livelier and more varied rhythms. These were, on the one hand, the iambic form, with its diverse combinations; on the other hand, the elegiac distich, related to the epic hexameter, but more lively, more familiar; and finally, the simpler metrical forms of the Æolian and Ionian poets.

The Spirit of Satire. The Pamphlet. Archilochus.—Iambic poetry, which owed its success to the genius of Archilochus of Paros, produced a scandal at its birth.

For the first time poetry, in the hands of this merciless and passionate railer, became a terrible, a murderous, weapon. In his swift-moving verses, as sharp as arrows, he dared to express anything—his injuries, his furious resentments; and he expressed it all marvelously. A poet by instinct, but at the same time an accomplished performer, combining vigor with pliancy, sensibility with anger, he composed celebrated masterpieces from day to day and filled them with his powerful personality; and in these casual pamphlets he succeeded in leaving behind something that has proved durable. For not only did he give admirable expression to certain eternal passions of humanity, but his genius naturally combined with the mordant vivacity of mockery, fine observations and suggestive reflections. He was a master in the use of the proverb, the apolog, and the fable. His fancy was inexhaustible; and beneath this wealth of invention, there was a philosophy of life.

After such an example and such success, the impetus was given. The spirit of satire had won a place in Greek society. We need not enumerate here the successors of Archilochus—a Simonides of Amorgos, a Hipponax of Ephesus, and others. But we should emphasize the fact that with this kind of poetry there appeared a new tendency in the public mind. No doubt sarcasm and insolent indiscretion are the personal affair of the poet; but the people are amused by it and encourage it for the pleasure they take in it; and they show no active disapproval of these intrusions into private life, these immoderate attacks sparing neither the honor of men nor the dignity of women. Malignity prevails over the sense of propriety. Public opinion is so complacent toward slander that it becomes indulgent toward calumny. Thus we witness the development of a moral disposition which will be found again in the cultivated Athens of the fifth and fourth centuries, and without which neither the comedy of Aristophanes nor the mutual invectives of a Demosthenes and an Æschines would have been possible.

Elegiac Poetry.—Besides the iambic, there is the elegiac poetry. Whatever may have been its origin, the latter enters into history without any very specific destination. It is a sort of discourse in verse, the tone of which varies from a harangue to a simple conversation—a discourse at first sung to the accompaniment of the flute, afterwards simply recited. It seems, altho it can not be positively stated, that its natural place was in private gatherings, especially at banquets. What remains to us of the elegiac poetry of the seventh and sixth centuries, therefore, gives us some conception of the ideas and sentiments, the fears and purposes, in short, the subjects of reflection and discussion which occupied the Greek city-states of that time.

Callinus and Tyrtæus.—A few fragments of a poet of Ephesus, Callinus by name, make us to some extent witnesses of the anxieties of Asiatic Greece, menaced in the seventh century by the barbarous Cimmerians. The elegiac verses of Tyrtæus transport us to Sparta, at the time of the Second Messenian War. Some of them summarize in beautiful verses, in vigorous and patriotic accents, the things that were supposedly said at that time in the "syssitia," common meals at which the participants recalled the exploits of the brave and reassured one another in the sentiment of national duty. Other fragments of the same poet explain the laws of the country, recall to mind that they have been sanctioned by the god of Pytho, and boast of the fine order which they have instituted in the city-state, at the same time commenting upon their political and moral significance. It is a master of wisdom and of discipline to whom we listen; but in reading his verses we see in imagination the population of soldiers for whom they were written. The poet reveals to us, even better than the historians have been able to do, what these people thought and loved.

Mimnermus.—The elegies of Mimnermus of Colophon, composed in the seventh and sixth centuries, picture to us the voluptuous life of the Greek cities of Asia Minor. Some delicate and brilliant verses recall the fleeting days in which these rich city-states, menaced by the ambition of their powerful neighbors, the kings of Lydia, forgot their fears or consoled themselves for defeats by giving themselves over to pleasures. In the midst of an elegy which celebrates the charm of youth and the beauty of women, a note of melancholy makes itself heard; it is the plaint of the aging poet, who does not resign himself without regret to the universal law of life. Many of his fellow-citizens, in these city-states in which civic energy was weakening, must have thought and felt as he did.

Solon and Theognis.—At the beginning of the seventh century the same elegiac form is brilliantly represented at Athens by the law-giver and poet Solon, who on occasion also used the iambic form. This was the time when Attica was tending to usurp the place of Ionia, the latter having been subjugated by the kings of Lydia. It was adopting its manners and its spirit; it was assimilating its literature and its arts. In his youth Solon did not disdain the amorous elegy; but in the later period of his political activity he turned especially to the form which lent itself to counsel, to justification of his own laws, and to a sort of moral and civic instruction. Like the iambic, which he succeeded in softening down without completely disarming it, the elegy served to explain his intentions, to refute his critics, and to point out the dangers which menaced the state. It is in part his own biography which is set forth to us in these fragments; and it is also a period in the life of Athens. But this poetry, altho inspired by circumstances, abounded in general sententious remarks, in good lessons for all times; and that is why it was transmitted in Athens from generation to generation. Sung and memorized in the schools, it became one of the elements of Athenian civilization.

The taste for wisdom imposed itself at that time on even the most passionate natures. Toward the end of the sixth century the Megarian poet, Theognis, gives us proof of this. Involved in the civil discords of his country (Megara of the Isthmus), he manifests in his elegies the spirit of furious hatred and implacable resentment which animated the defeated aristocracy. But he, too, addressing himself to his younger friends, especially to his beloved Cyrnus, whose counselor and guide he must have wished to be, endeavors to outline certain rules of conduct; and if violence is not absent from his counsel, it is nevertheless tempered, here and there, in a manner which cannot but surprise the modern reader, by skillful precautions; and even dissimulation is not excluded. A curious mixture, very characteristic of a time of trouble and moral uncertainty.

The Seven Sages. Gnomic Poetry. The Wisdom of Delphi.—To the elegy is related the sententious wisdom which Greece attributed especially to seven privileged men, among whom the poet Solon was included. It was a rather indefinite group, to be sure, including different names at different times. The least disputed among them were Thales of Miletus, Bias of Priene, Chilon of Sparta, and Pittacus of Mytilene, all of whom lived in the seventh and sixth centuries. Under these names there spread across Greece a goodly number of sententious thoughts, either in verse or in prose, for the most part precepts of moderation, almost all of them inspired by a somewhat assertive spirit of prudence. It was the sort of wisdom which the sacerdotal college of Delphi also proclaimed, and which it summed up in certain celebrated maxims such as "Nothing in excess" and "Know thyself." It evidently responded to the experience of men who were reared in the midst of civil discord and who had witnessed numerous changes of fortune. Several poets, the best known of whom is Phocylides of Miletus, made a specialty of embodying practical reflections of this kind in versified formulas, easy to understand and useful to retain. These were properly the gnomic poets.

Melic Personal Poetry.—But during the same centuries another form of lyric poetry was ushered in, similar in certain respects to the iambic and the elegiac, but different in that it remained inseparable from singing and from musical accompaniment. Still further removed from simple discourse, it resembled our songs, admitting, as they do, of a great variety of strains and sentiments. It seems to have risen first in Lesbos; but it spread rapidly in Ionia and thruout all Greece.

The Lesbian Poets: Alcæus and Sappho.—Alcæus of Mytilene and Sappho of Eresus, in other words, both of them Lesbians, were the promoters of this form toward the end of the seventh and the beginning of the sixth century. Both made use of the dialect of their country; they also used analogous if not identical meters, and short strophes that never varied in one and the same poem, each consisting of a small number of lines or of ingeniously grouped members. A very simple air, accompanied by the notes of a sort of lyre called the "barbitos," was designed to lend to this poetry, now a delicate charm, now an additional force.

Only fragments of their work have come down to us, a few rare pieces all the more precious because they help us to picture the brilliant and tumultuous life of their city-states, divided, as they were, between pleasure, the arts, and commerce, and disturbed by civil discords.   It was no doubt for a circle of friends belonging, as he himself did, to the oligarchical party of Mytilene, that Alcæus composed his "Songs of Love" and his "Songs of Civil War"; and it was to them that he sang them. Sometimes he expressed, with as much grace as ardor, the charm of the ladies whom he loved.   Sometimes also, in the heat of his aristocratic passions, he exhaled his hatred and contempt for a Melanchrus or a Myrsilus, leaders of the democratic party and tyrants of the city-state; and he called his friends to vengeance.   His contemporary, Sappho, introduces us into a society of young men and young women who, like herself, seem to have been devoted to the cult of poetry and of music.   It was in their midst that she poured forth, in her varied songs, notably in her "epithalamia," her passionate and jealous tenderness, all the emotions of her ardent soul, to which her genius lent an immortal beauty.   One may say that some of the liveliest sentiments of the human soul have never vibrated more melodiously than on these two rival lyres.   The surviving fragments of their poetry make it clear to what extent sensibility had become more delicate, more vibrant, so to speak, in that elegant society, and what refinement of feeling was already associated with it.

Court Life in the Sixth Century.   Anacreon.—But this was not peculiar to Lesbos.   The same tastes prevailed at the brilliant courts of the tyrants and princes of that time—with a Polycrates at Samos, with the Aleuadæ and the Scopadæ in Thessaly, and with the sons of Pisistratus at Athens. We find proof of this in a few fragments of the Ionian poet Anacreon of Teos, who, driven from his country by the Persian conquest, was received as a guest in one after another of these rich homes. He knew how to please these great lords by composing songs in praise of love and wine which he sang at their banquets. Less fervent than the poets of Lesbos, he seems to have had a sort of voluptuous grace of his own, a suggestion at once of piquancy and of tenderness, which still makes itself felt in the all too few extant fragments of his work.[1]

(2) CHORAL POETRY

General Character of the Choral Poetry. Extant Fragments.—But this poetry, in a sense private, reserved for social gatherings, could not suffice for a people whose public life was becoming more and more important. For religious worship, for the national and local festivals, for the celebration of victories won in the games, for everything which called forth strong public feeling, other more powerful manifestations were necessary. Choral poetry alone, by the force of its means and the intensity of its effects, could satisfy this need. Its history, unfortunately, is but little known to us; and whatever its success may have been, the works of its most illustrious representatives in the seventh and sixth centuries have almost entirely disappeared. Since music and poetry were indissolubly associated, the progress of musical art in the following period explains why these compositions fell out of fashion; and as soon as they ceased to be sung, there was less concern about preserving them. Let

[1] It is known that the popularity of his poetry was very great. The apochryphal collection of poems called "Anacreontics" shows that this popularity persisted even to the Byzantine period.

us merely note what influence they had upon the development of Hellenic civilization.

Choral Poetry at Lacedæmon.—The first steps in the perfection of musical technique brought with them the rise of choral poetry and carried the latter beyond the period of its infancy. In the seventh century we see it appearing with conspicuous success at Lacedæmon. No city-state, in fact, was better predestined for it; for nowhere else was civic spirit so strong or religious sentiment so profound. The ancient witnesses tell us of the influence exerted by the Cretan Thaletas, one of the first masters of this new art. Among the Spartans, thoroly suffused with the idea of discipline, there was a sense of order and harmony which happily entered into the songs of their choruses, regulated by the notes of the lyre or of the flute. Terpander was to find a no less favorable reception, if we judge by one of his fragments which celebrates Sparta as the city in which military valor and melody, dear to the Muse, flourished side by side. After him, a Lydian named Alcman, who once did not hesitate to place the merit of the citharist on a par with that of the warrior, enjoyed a still more lasting favor. People of all ages took part in these musical performances: choruses of children, choruses of adults, and choruses of old men sang in response to one another and manifested the concurrence of the whole city-state in the same sentiments of honor and patriotism. Even young virgins did not hold aloof from these festivals; Alcman excelled in composing for them the choral odes called *Partheneia*. Important fragments of one of his *Partheneia* still make it possible for us to feel, in a charming manner, with what vivacity and freshness he could express their sentiments and his own.

Expansion of Choral Poetry in the Peloponnesus.—It

was not long, naturally, before the example given by Lacedæmon was followed in other Greek city-states, especially in the Peloponnesus. A contemporary of Alcman, the Lesbian Arion, of Methymna, made himself famous at Corinth, whither he was summoned by the tyrant Periander. His claim to honor lay in his having transformed into a regular choral hymn the old Dionysiac improvisations known as "dithyrambs." In order to execute his compositions, he is said to have been the first to organize a circular chorus of fifty singers. His poems could not fail to adapt themselves to this form of representation. To the poetic form thus revived and modified a most brilliant fortune fell. For while, alongside of this new dithyramb, tragedy was developing, which seems to have been merely another adaptation of the songs sung at the *Country Dionysia*, the dithyramb itself was evolving and making ready to become what it turned out to be in the fifth century, one of the most perfected forms of musical art associated with poetry.

Choral Poetry in Sicily and Southern Italy. Stesichorus.—But already another form of choral poetry was manifesting itself in Sicily and southern Italy, which is no less worthy of attention. In long compositions, the strophes of which were harmoniously grouped in triads, the great poet Stesichorus, of Himera, gave lyric form to ancient epic legends, chosen episodes from the Trojan War, the crimes and misfortunes of the sons of Atreus, the adventures of Helen, the hunt for the Calydonian Boar, and other analogous themes. And in all these old subjects, rejuvenated by song and music, enriched by ideas and sentiments which a more advanced civilization could produce, adorned by an art which had at its disposal a greater variety of colors, and assembled and condensed, finally, in more dramatic forms, acquired a lustre and a glory which exalted the imagination. The poet of Himera was destined to be one of the indirect inspirers of the Athenian tragedy, when the latter, a century later, created its immortal masterpieces.

National Character of the Choral Poetry in the Sixth Century. Simonides.—Meanwhile, from the second half of the sixth century on, this choral poetry, accepted in all parts of Greece and everywhere associated with the religious and political life, definitely acquired a national character. From this point of view nobody represents it better than the brilliant poet Simonides of Ceos (558–468), who, by reason of his long life, carries us well into the fifth century. A wandering poet, we find him now at Athens at the court of Pisistratus and his sons, now in Thessaly with the princes of Crannon or Larissa, now again in Sicily as a guest of the tyrants Gelo and Hiero. His poetry represents the flowering, as it were, of the civilization of that time; it interprets all its sentiments, it expresses its essential thoughts. Exercising his talent in almost all of the lyric forms, Simonides composed pæans, eulogies, dithyrambs, dirges, and songs of victory, to say nothing of epigrams and epitaphs, in which he succeeded in immortalizing in a few verses the memory of the brave men who had defended Hellenism and freedom against the onrush of barbarism. Endowed with a touching sensibility, with an imagination both pleasant and brilliant, with an emotional gravity fitted to religious subjects, and with a quickened sense of perfection adapted to things mundane, he was, among the poets of that time, one of the most prolific contributors to that fund of useful thought, of delicate sentiment, and of varied observation concerning human life which the two following centuries were destined to turn to account.

Influence of Lyrism.—In a general way the lyric poetry

of the seventh and sixth centuries was for Greece a great
school of reflection. If we still possessed its masterpieces,
we should understand better the various stages in the progress of Hellenic thought between the time of Homer and
that of Æschylus. It was also, to an equal extent, a
great school of literary art. Thanks to the lyric poets,
the language acquired a suppleness, a splendor, a variety
of shades, a depth and a faculty of abstraction which the
epic poetry did not possess. It enriched itself with a
new vocabulary, still more striking and more expressive.
At the same time the art of composition was perfected
thru the influence of music. The poets learned to condense their subjects, to make the most of them by means
of symmetrical groupings, to employ more intelligently
the effects of comparison and contrast. And the public,
on its part, educated by them, acquired a more exacting
taste, a more alert and more delicately a_tistic sense. In
this manner the way was prepared for the century of
Æschylus and Sophocles.

(3) PHILOSOPHY AND THE BEGINNINGS OF SCIENCE

Birth of Philosophy and the Sciences.—But the general
intellectual progress is still better attested by the beginnings of philosophy and of certain of the sciences.

The contemporaries of Homer and Hesiod had looked
upon the universe with the eyes of veritable children.
Deeply impressed by the great phenomena of nature, they
attributed to superhuman beings the play or the conflict
of forces which excited their fear or their wonder. Accordingly, they peopled the world with gods, whom they
conceived as resembling themselves in their passions, altho
infinitely superior in power. Thus accustomed to miracles, they did not think of questioning their authenticity

or of disputing them. Little by little, however, a few thinkers, far in advance of their times, began to reflect. It was in Ionia that this intellectual movement first made itself felt. Miletus, a great commercial center, enjoying relations with Chaldæa and Egypt, known as the mother-city of numerous colonies and reputed as the home of much of the new knowledge, gave the signal for it.

Ionian Science. Thales and Hecatæus.—Toward the end of the seventh century an entirely new manner of comprehending the nature of things made its appearance in the person of Thales. Engineer, astronomer, geometrician, statesman, his title to fame is that of having opened the way to a rational explanation of the great phenomena of nature. He was the first one frankly to uphold the idea that the genesis of the world was something else than a theogony; and he dared to say so. Obedient to a truly Hellenic instinct for simplification, he conceived a primordial substance the transformations of which produced an infinite variety of things, and he thought that this substance might be water. A rather crude idea, to be sure, but a singularly interesting attempt and one well calculated to excite the spirit of research. A little later a compatriot of Thales, Hecatæus, himself also statesman, tried for the first time to give a complete description of the inhabited world. Geography, which studies the surface of the earth, thus developed alongside of natural philosophy, which seeks to explain its formation and composition. And in the process of their development these new sciences brought with them mathematics, geometry, astronomy, and calculus, all of which served them as indispensable allies.

The Successors of Thales.—Once started, this admirable movement, which did so much honor to Greece, was bound to continue. After Thales, two other Milesians, first

Anaximander and then Anaximenes, both of whom lived in the sixth century, were animated by his spirit and devoted themselves to the same researches. Always falling back upon the fundamental idea of a single original substance in perpetual transformation, each of them had, nevertheless, his own personal views—a notable example of the activity of the Greek mind, ever eager for criticism and research. A marvelous emulation inspired these thinkers. Anaximander thought he was improving upon Thales in conceiving instead of water, as the origin of everything that exists, something indefinite and illimitable, which on account of its very nature would be more likely, according to him, to assume all forms by the sole effect of motion. This was perhaps merely substituting a vague idea in place of an error. Anaximenes sought to correct his two predecessors by explaining all life in the universe by transformations of air, which, by the way, he confused with vapors or mists. He at least had the merit of thus bringing to light the importance of the phenomena of condensation and rarefaction, with which he thought he could rest satisfied as explaining the formation of all things. We must not neglect to say that he, together with Hecatæus, was undoubtedly one of the first to make use of prose in a didactic work, and that in so doing he helped to press the Ionian dialect into the service of science.

Science and Philosophy in Sicily and Italy. Pythagoras and Xenophanes.—It appears that the Greek mainland was not immediately captivated by these subtle and profound researches; but they were favorably received in occidental Greece, in Sicily, and in Italy. Coming from Samos, his birth-place, Pythagoras, in the second half of the sixth century, founded an institute at Crotona in Italy, later at Metapontum. A mystic moralist as well as a mathematician, he seems to have depended upon nobody directly. For him philosophy is especially the study of numbers, which in his eyes become the symbolic representation and the ultimate explanation of all things, of all ideas; and altho he wanders into abstraction when he seeks to define the essence of things, he at least grasps their numerical relation with a precision that is entirely new. For this reason he deserves to be looked upon as one of the promoters of arithmetic and geometry, and as the creator of the mathematical theory of the musical scale. Besides Pythagoras, another Asiatic Greek, the poet-philosopher Xenophanes, a native of Colophon, made for himself at about the same time, and likwise in Italy, a name no less renowned. It is to him that tradition attributes the origin of the so-called Eleatic School. In fact, his poems convey to us the idea of an itinerant rhapsodist traveling from city to city across Sicily and southern Italy. Their subjects are varied, some historical, others satirical, and others philosophical. One senses here a fearless and inquiring intelligence. He does not hesitate to scoff at the anthropomorphic mythology; and in certain fragments revealing his entire system of thought, he affirms the unity of all life, which he identifies with God. An entirely new view, which, as we shall see further on, was destined to be taken up again and developed by the powerful genius of Parmenides.

Orphism.—But while these thinkers, consciously or otherwise, were undermining the foundations of the traditional religious belief, the ancient religions were coming to life again, as stated above, in the form of "Mysteries." Moreover, a certain philosophy was now interwoven with this movement. A few men undertook to give to religion a theology and a code of morality. Thus Orphism was

born, constituted about a new myth of the god Dionysus,
very different from the narratives of the ancient poets.
Whatever may have been its origin, it was at Athens,
toward the middle of the sixth century, that Orphism
seems to have taken form and consistency in the poems
composed by a certain Onomacritus and given out by him
as revelations of the legendary Orpheus. Here he exposed by means of mythical fictions the origin of evil,
the miserable condition of humanity, and the means of
salvation which the religion of Dionysus-Zagreus offered
to the initiated by the observance of practical rituals and
of a code of abstinence and purification. Herodotus attests with what favor Orphism was received by the sons
of Pisistratus; and there is no doubt that a part of high
Athenian society shared their sentiments. Nor do these
sentiments disappear with the period of tyranny. Orphism becomes one of the elements of Greek culture.
Its influence will be found also among several of the great
thinkers of the fifth and fourth centuries.

(4) THE BEGINNINGS OF GREEK ART

Importance of Art in Hellenic Civilization.—The picture which we have just drawn would be altogether incomplete if we failed to add at least a few words concerning the beginnings of the formative arts. No element
was of more importance than art in the civilization of
ancient Greece; none manifested more vividly certain essential traits of the Hellenic genius. And these traits are
already clearly discernible in the initial period with which
we are now concerned.

General Character of Greek Art.—From its first attempts Greek art, like Greek literature and philosophy,
looked upon the imitation of reality as a process of sim-

plification. In this it was impelled by its instinct for
beauty, as well as by a natural gift of synthesis. Far
from losing himself in a complexity and infinite variety
of details, the Greek paid attention chiefly to the whole.
This simplification applied at once to forms and to movements. In the reproduction of forms it tended to lay
emphasis upon the lines which the eye follows easily,
rather than upon those which it has difficulty in distinguishing. In the imitation of movements it used for its
effect the creation of a rhythm, which found expression
in an apparent or somewhat disguised symmetry. It was
this profound tendency, happily combined with an understanding of life, which was to result, after the first technical difficulties had been overcome, in the beauty peculiar
to the masterpieces of Greek art.

Architecture and Sculpture.—It was perceptible, from
the very start, in architecture. Of this we are able to
judge by the still existing ruins of the oldest temples.
The Greek temple is an isolated edifice of comparatively
small dimensions, the sanctuary and abode of a god, himself conceived in the image of man. It presents to the
eye straight lines, which stand out sharply against the
sky. Solid on its foundations, forming a well proportioned mass, it appears plainly from afar, fronted or surrounded by columns which serve as an elegant appendage.
In the course of the eighth, seventh, and sixth centuries,
the way of progress was in the direction, not of increasing, but rather of decreasing the impression of size and
weight. The .shaft of the columns becomes thinner and
longer; the decoration, all the while remaining unobtrusive, becomes finer and more elegant. If works of
sculpture are brought into play, they must always remain
subordinate to the conception of the architect, and never
alter the general lines or characteristic plans. Their

function is to adorn the pediments and recall the legends
of the gods. They attenuate their reliefs in the metopes
and still more in the friezes, so as not to disfigure the surfaces; and they seek scrupulously to respect the harmony of the whole.

The technical apprenticeship of the sculptor, moreover,
was much more protracted than that of the architect.
It is only in the second half of the seventh century that
Greek sculpture, related by legend to the ancient
Dædalus, enters into history with the names of some
bronzists and some workers in marble and clay. It likewise aims at simplicity and rhythm; but at first it has
difficulty in freeing itself from a certain stiffness and
heaviness due to the inexperience of the artists. The
schools of Samos and of Chios successively achieve important advances. Little by little the sculptor learns
to free the arms, which were at first rigidly attached to
the sides of the body, to distinguish better the delicate
curves of the face, and to indicate the play of muscles.
In the sixth century, when the Cretan masters, Dipoenus
and Scyllis, came to settle at Sicyon and to found and
head the school in the Peloponnesus, the process of improvement becomes more discernible. Spurred on by the
demands of the victorious athletes, the artists apply
themselves more and more to the study of the human
body. At the end of this century, Canachus of Sicyon
and Ageladas of Argos, in spite of the fact that the old
stiffness and rigidity still persisted in their work, already
possessed a rather definite knowledge of human anatomy.
At about the same time the Attic School was born. A
few pieces that have come down to us, notably the charming Corae of the Acropolis, and some funeral stelae, still
indicate that the Athenian artists were already distin-

guishing themselves by a diligent effort to achieve a certain elegance and refinement in their work.

Ceramics.—Modern archæology, in collecting painted vases, and in classifying them and determining their approximate age and origin, has done much to increase and make more definite our knowledge of Greek art. Intended for private as well as commercial uses, these vases were undoubtedly industrial products; but a certain art was quickly introduced into the ceramic industry, and the perfecting of the latter makes it possible for us today to recognize in this, as in architecture and sculpture, the progress of taste. Moreover, it is the same spirit, the same tendency, which determines them all. At first Oriental influences make themselves strongly felt; the oldest Greek vases reproduce, more or less, certain decorations dear to the Orient. The vase painter seeks to adorn with figures or ornaments the surfaces which he is called upon to decorate; he avoids leaving them bare. Then, in the Corinthian ware, we find him already leaning toward greater order and elegance, representing rows of animals arranged in horizontal strips, one over the other. The sixth century happily introduces an innovation in the form of vases ornamented with black figures; and at the same time we find at Athens a number of genuine artists, such as Ergotimus, Clitias, and especially Exechias, composing freely on amphoræ and kelebes, on bowls and pateræ, small pictures representing scenes from epic poetry, such as the exploits of Hercules and Theseus, or the adventures of Ulysses and Ajax. During the early stages of this new art the simplification of execution, due in part to its clumsiness, is still excessive; it reduces the bodies to angular, geometric forms, such as we find on the funeral amphoræ of Dipylon. But little by little this execution becomes more expressive; it succeeds better in reproducing life and motion; it gains in charm by virtue of its sincerity. Some of the latest products of Attic art in this period are already veritable masterpieces.

(5) CONCLUSION

To sum up, in the few centuries which we have just surveyed, Greece had done more than merely outline its civilization; in large measure it had already realized it. It had constituted states, that is to say, human collectivities in which individual and social faculties were able to develop under a régime of law; it had established a social order composed of citizens united by common sentiments and associated in traditional cults. Thru the voice of its law-givers it had formulated the essential principles of justice. Altho mutually independent, and too often hostile toward one another, these states were nevertheless conscious of a real fraternity, which was affirmed by the great national cults, by the increasing authority of certain common sanctuaries, and by the festivals and Panhellenic games, but especially because they all recognized, in their diverse dialects, the same original language which enabled them to understand one another. And this language had already served to express a rich literature, which was everywhere admired. In various works, in epic poems, in iambics, in elegiacs, in lyrics, and in philosophic prose, there was revealed a marvelous flowering of thought and sentiment, striking manifestations of a national genius in which intelligence and sensibility proved to be equally powerful. Invention of all kinds had emanated from this fund of wealth as from an inexhaustible but not turbulent source. A like sense of order, measure, harmony, and beauty made itself admired in all forms of art, according as they developed. At the end of the sixth century Greece had acquired a privileged rank in humanity.

PART II

THE FIFTH CENTURY

CHAPTER I

POLITICAL LIFE IN THE FIFTH CENTURY

Distinctive Character of the Fifth Century.—We have now arrived at the period in which Hellenic civilization shone forth with the greatest brilliancy; for it was precisely in the fifth century that it appeared in its full perfection. Altho in many respects, of course, it developed still further in the fourth century and even in the following period, this development did not take place without bringing about some gradual alteration of its characteristic features. The fifth century was the privileged period in which tradition and the spirit of innovation, those two great forces which are ever at work in human life, seemed almost to balance one another and by virtue of their association realized a most fortunate harmony.

The Rôle of Athens.—In achieving this realization Athens played an altogether exceptional rôle. It is true that other cities produced remarkable men at that time; but no other could point to so great a number of them, and no other brought forth so many admirable works of all kinds. Athens is the city in which the great traits of Greek civilization, those which have left their imprint upon humanity, became most prominent and most illustrious. We have already seen how this city had grown in the sixth century. The revolution which overthrew the tyrants gave it a new impetus. A democratic constitution, tempered by the influence of a still respected aristocracy, permitted it to develop its power in the period prior

77

to the Persian Wars. Its victories in these wars
and its solidarity of action (from approximately 490 to
450 B. C.) rendered its people the most glorious representative of national independence. Supported by a powerful maritime confederation, Athens became, toward the
middle of the century, under the government of Pericles,
the mistress of intercourse among the Greek peoples and
the sovereign of the Hellenic seas. In this material prosperity its genius unfolded magnificently; thru its statesmen, its poets, its historians, its thinkers, and its artists,
it succeeded in becoming an incomparable model of intelligence and beauty.

Nevertheless, its political organization proved insufficient to overcome the formidable difficulties which soon
rose before it. The force of circumstances set it at
variance with Sparta, whose power was almost equal to
its own. In a war lasting twenty-eight years (432–404
B. C.) and abounding in catastrophes, it gave evidence of
a remarkable energy, but it did not succeed in providing
against its own defects. This sharp rivalry carried it
finally into a disaster which was of fatal consequence to
all Greece. The result of its defeat was the creation
among the Greek cities of a state of irremediable division,
which culminated in the subjection of all of them to the
domination of Macedonia. For the moment let us give
our attention to that Athenian democracy the rôle of
which we have just defined.

(1) THE ATHENIAN DEMOCRACY

Achievement of the Athenian Democracy.—By virtue
of its merits and its defects, the Athenian democracy is
one of the most interesting political experiments in all
history. We have already seen how it was constituted

by Clisthenes, in 507 B. C.; but not until after the second
Persian War did it succeed in organizing itself, first under
the influence of Themistocles, then under Pericles and his
associate Ephialtes. After about 460 B. C., when the
authority of the Areopagus had declined, we may say
that it had realized its basic principles in all their significance.

The popular sovereignty was absolute. All powers
were vested in the people, that is to say, in the general
body of citizens, who exercised them directly, or very
nearly so. It was in fact the Assembly, composed of all
the citizens, which decided on everything, either immediately or in the last resort. There was no check against
its authority. If it wished to modify the laws, it instructed a commission to propose new ones, which it
accepted or rejected according to its pleasure. As for the
conduct of business, it regulated everything by decrees. It is true that a Council of Five Hundred was
charged with examining the decrees beforehand and with
revising them; but its power did not go beyond that and
consequently did not in any way restrict that of the
Assembly. The Council, furthermore, was elected by lot
and was renewed every year. In actual practice, therefore, the power of making laws, as also for the most part
the power of negotiation and administration, belonged to
the Assembly. The latter also possessed judicial power,
altho it exercised this power directly, to be sure, only in
cases of particularly grave charges involving the safety
of the state. In ordinary cases it delegated its power to
the courts; but the latter, each of them composed of
several hundred citizens chosen by lot, were after all
scarcely more than fractions of the Assembly. Nothing
could have resembled less a judiciary body, at the same
time possessing its spirit, its traditions, and the prestige

derived from special training. Moreover, the sovereign
Assembly was constantly at work. It met regularly
several times a month, and besides that whenever it was
convoked for an extraordinary session, either by a commission of the Council of Five Hundred charged with this
duty or by the Generals (*strategi*). At all times, as a
matter of fact, it had to be ready to declare its will, since
everything depended upon it.

The same principles applied to the tribes and to the
demes, and in general to all regularly constituted groups
of citizens. Each of these bodies, political or religious,
governed itself on the sole condition that it was not to
encroach upon the rights of the state. Each of them
drew up its own laws or regulations; each made its own
decisions and controled their execution. It was an established idea of the Athenian people that every collectivity was the best judge of its own interests.

Public Offices and Services.—Such a system of government did not admit of officials, properly speaking.
Every public office was only a temporary commission,
generally of one year's duration and always revocable.
In no case did a public charge belong to any one man.
Moreover, almost all functions were assigned by lot, so
that any citizen whatsoever, provided he was in full possession of his rights, had as much chance as any other of
occupying, in his turn, this or that office. This was in
line with the most democratic conception of equality. It
was also, no doubt, a precaution taken against personal
or collective influences; and perhaps, too, it was thought
that this chance designation was least likely to inflate
with pride the persons on whom it fell. Only a few special
functions calling for a very definite type of ability—
for example, those of *strategi*—were entrusted to elected
citizens; but even they were named only for a strictly

limited time, and the people always reserved the right to recall them or to replace them as soon as their services were found to be no longer satisfactory.

Aside from these reserved functions, it is clear that one could not expect to find any special competence in the persons on whom the lot fell. As a matter of fact, their functions were reduced to executive measures in which there was scarcely any variation, or which were clearly defined in the decrees to be executed. A little practical sense, accordingly, was all that was required to carry them out correctly. What, then, was the custom in case of work calling for technical knowledge? In such instances the people or the interested collectivity chose commissioners, upon whom they conferred definite powers. In both cases, however, they were bound to render an account at the expiration of their charge or commission; for the principle of personal responsibilty applied to everybody. Naturally, individual responsibility varied in importance according to the nature of the duties imposed.

Government. The Orators.—If in this organization the people governed everything, who, one may ask, governed the people? For it is certain that no assembly in the world has ever governed effectively. The Athenian people passed on proposals which were laid before them, but it was necessary for these proposals to be presented and explained to them and to be discussed before them; and every policy, in order to become one, had to be conceived and executed by a small number of capable men. In other words, the Athenian democracy could not have functioned without the intervention of persons whom it called "leaders of the people" (*demagogs*)—a designation which would now have no unpleasant significance if it had always retained its true

meaning. These "leaders of the people" had no means
of influence other than persuasion. Athens, therefore,
could not get along without orators, and there more than
anywhere else the skillful orator had a chance of gaining
political power and influence. His task was both difficult and perilous. Addressing an Assembly which had
neither well established traditions nor precise knowledge
regarding most of the matters that came up for consideration, he had to instruct his hearers, to set forth clearly the
advantages and disadvantages of the projects under discussion, and to point out their relation to general views,
and also to arouse sentiments favorable to his ideas.
Thus he entered very seriously upon his responsibility ; for
if his proposition violated some law, he exposed himself to
a charge of illegality, entailing the loss of his civic rights
and a ruinous fine. And even without that, he risked at
the very least the loss of his reputation or some perfidious
imputation on the part of his adversaries before a crowd
quick to suspect evil designs.

The Administration of Pericles and His Successors.
—The administration of Pericles showed by a striking example what use a superior man could make of these
institutions; but it also revealed the dangers to which he
was exposed. Combining an extensive training and
knowledge of affairs with an inborn prudence and perspicacity, power of reflection, and quickness of judgment,
in addition to a spirit of decision, a commanding character, and a power of eloquence, he exercised a sort of
personal domination over the Athenian people for a
period of thirty years. Enlightened and guided by him,
the Athenian democracy gave proof of logical progress
in ideas and of constancy in action. It succeeded in out-
lining a policy at once energetic and prudent, inspired by
ambition, it is true, but by an ambition which was not

lacking in grandeur and which was restrained, when necessary, by a sense of moderation. It was distinguished especially by a knowledge of everything which embellished human life. It was truly a beautiful spectacle. But this domination, entirely personal and always in danger, sometimes had to defend itself by questionable means; and it culminated in a misfortune which revealed its fragility. Moreover, it remained an exceptional condition; and altho we may justly do honor to the Athenian democracy because of it, it would be an excess of indulgence to judge that democracy solely by a success of such short duration.

After the death of Pericles there is no doubt that the Athenian people were still successful in turning their remarkable qualities to account. In the course of the Peloponnesian War their constancy was much to be admired. At that time we see them facing severe trials with no signs of weakening, skillfully taking advantage of certain circumstances, valiantly reorganizing their forces after the disastrous Sicilian Expedition, and for a long time resisting implacable and formidable enemies —in a word, disputing the victory to the last moment. But what they manifestly lacked was wise management and moderation in the conduct of affairs. Replacements of persons in office—which are not peculiar to any form of government—had special consequences there, leading, as they did, to sudden changes of foreign policy and to risky enterprises. Besides this there were defeats suffered by the generals, internal revolutions, as well as discontent and defections on the part of the members of the maritime confederation. These, then, are the defects and reverses which it is necessary to balance with the merits and successes. Both are in large measure explained by the qualities, good and bad, of the Athenian constitution. A few observations will set this forth more clearly.

Civic Spirit.—It is certain that the participation of all the citizens in the government had the effect of developing and maintaining a civic spirit among the popular masses. It was almost impossible for a man called daily to deliberate upon matters of common interest not to sense their importance. A considerable part of the citizen's leisure time was taken up by public life. As a member of a deme, of a tribe, of one or several religious associations, and as a judge, magistrate or commissioner, and in any case in the Assembly or occasionally in the Council of the Five Hundred, the Athenian felt himself an active member of a collectivity with the prosperity of which his own welfare was closely bound up. Obliged to listen to the proposals or the reports of commissioners and to the speeches of orators, and to form an opinion on each subject brought up for discussion, he could scarcely fail to acquire a certain adeptness in public affairs, a certain practical knowledge of men and of things. Thus his political intelligence was formed and his attachment to the city-state was strengthened. Such a people, well directed, was necessarily more capable than any other of wisdom and of patriotism.

But no quality, natural or acquired, has ever brought it about that the masses could do without an intellectual aristocracy or protect themselves always against their own mistakes. The democratic evolution had left no instrumentality at Athens to counter-balance the will of the people. On the other hand, it was difficult for the democracy, organized as it was, to have real statesmen as leaders. An extensive and solid education was rare at that time; and those who had the best chance of gaining one often found themselves removed from the conduct of

affairs and thrown back into a disdainful or blindly
hostile opposition.

The Athenian Conception of Liberty.—This situation
was due chiefly to the manner in which liberty was conceived by the Athenian people. It was not based for them,
as it is for us, upon the notion of the rights of men, that
is to say, on respect for the human personality. Indeed,
how could such a sentiment have existed in a society which
regarded slavery as a natural fact? Liberty, not alone
for the Athenians, but for the Greeks in general, was a
privilege, the privilege of the citizen. It consisted essentially in participation in the government and in equality
before the law. It did not involve any positive limitation
of the rights of the State. With respect to this the
Athenian people had no precise idea. To them it seemed
just for a man to be condemned to ten years of exile without having been permitted to speak in his own behalf, even
without having been placed directly on trial, simply because he was suspected by a majority of his fellow-
citizens; or again, it was not unusual for a citizen to be
banished or condemned to death because his religion involved ideas other than those of the masses, and he
professed them. Equality, on the other hand, was understood and practiced in a singular manner. The rich,
or those who were regarded as such, were subject to
contributions, not regulated and proportional, but arbi-
trarily imposed under the name of *liturgies* and often
excessive. Accused by persons who made a business of
it, and scarcely able to count upon the impartiality of the
popular tribunals, they often found themselves obliged
to purchase the silence of their adversaries. Such
abuses, even if we assume that they were not of very
frequent occurrence, could not fail to create in the
classes most affected an animosity which was always

dangerous and became even more so at the time of crises. They had the effect of keeping these classes in a perpetual state of distrust and discontent, and often even transformed them into conspirators.

Difficulties of Constitutional Opposition.   Revolutions.
—What contributed the most to this state of affairs, however, was the difficulty met by an opposition party in carrying out any effective plan of action.   No doubt every individual, by means of certain arrangements, could freely express his opinions before the Assembly; but even supposing that one obtained a hearing, his chances of success were often slight.   The majority of modern democracies find their equilibrium in the play of political parties, which succeed one another in the control of the government; but this is possible only if the government consists of a grouping of coördinated and well defined powers. As we have just seen, however, the only real power at Athens was that of the Assembly; there was no supreme magistracy, nothing analogous to a cabinet of ministers for directing the conduct of affairs.   Under these conditions no oratorical success assured a party even of the minimum of continuous action which it would have required to gain its ends.   It was necessary to win as many victories as there were deliberations.   How, then, was it possible to pursue a far-sighted policy based upon a crystallized public opinion, a policy which could be realized only gradually and to an extent which only time and experience could determine?

All this explains the attitude of the Athenian aristocratic party in the fifth century.   Until about 450 B. C. we witness this party, supported by the personal authority of some of its leaders, such as Cimon, trying to combat a policy which tended to make the people as such omnipotent.   Between 450 and 430 B. C. it is against

Pericles personally that the same party directs its attack; at every turn it combats his proposals, up to the sentence of exile pronounced against its leader, the statesman Thucydides of Alopece. Once he is out of the way, everything is reduced to oratorical skirmishing, pamphleteering, and attempted impeachments. But according as the opposition becomes more aware of the small value of the constitutional means of action, it resorts more and more to other means outside the constitution. It was at this time that the "societies of friends," or *hetairia*, were organized, at first mere gatherings of malcontents, which circumstances combined to make the hotbeds of conspiracies. Then come the sorrowful crises of the Peloponnesian War; and thereafter on two occasions, first in 411 B. C. in the midst of the difficulties and moral depression following the disaster in Sicily, and again in 404 B. C. after the capture of Athens by Lysander, the oligarchical reaction breaks forth with violence. It is the explosion of a long suppressed exasperation, the vengeance of a humiliated class which gives free vent to its resentment. Because it did not succeed in doing full justice to all the elements of the city-state, the democracy, without suspecting what was in the air, produced this tyranny, which suddenly broke loose.

The Democracy and the Maritime Confederation.— Another mistake the democracy made was in organizing the maritime confederation. When the Greek inhabitants of the islands, freed from the Persian yoke, had come to Athens, they were received there as allies and consequently as equals. The occasion was opportune for constituting a Hellenic confederation, which in the long run would perhaps have been able to attract to it almost all the peoples of Greece. In order to do this, however, it would have been necessary for each city-state in this confederation

really to preserve its independence.   Nothing of the kind
happened.   The Athenian people, accustomed to unlimited power, could not for an instant entertain the idea
of a federal government in which they would have had
only a limited share of influence.   Thus we have the
spectacle of a city-state, that is to say, a popular assembly, governing other city-states from afar, and not
only compeling them to pay taxes which it alone determined, but calling before its tribunals all the federal
cases and intervening in their party disputes.   Thus the
Athenian democracy was transformed into an imperial
power, obliged to maintain itself by the employment of
military and naval forces which its subjects paid for
but which it alone commanded.

Physiognomy of the Athenian Democracy.—These
inner defects appeared, of course, only little by little.
A critical analysis necessarily brings to light certain
features which the ordinary movement of life concealed,
especially during the brilliant period in which Athens
found itself developing from day to day.   We may be
sure that the majority of the Athenians of that time were
proud of their city-state and, on the whole, content to
live in it.   Surely most of them found it agreeable to
feel that they were being governed as little as possible.
The one-year magistrates had no difficulties to contend
with, no exacting duties to perform.   How could they
have abused so limited a power—one, moreover, which
they were to relinquish so soon?   Consequently, they lived
without constraint, each to his own taste, without any
obtrusive interference to fear.   Here, then, was a great
indulgence from the point of view of the customs as well
as in the application of the laws.   People were content
to make light of things that were punished elsewhere.
Discipline at Athens acquired the good-natured form of

raillery. We may recall, as a sort of summary, the characteristic judgment which Thucydides attributed to Pericles:

Our constitution (he has him say) is called democratic, because it is made, not for the advantage of a few, but the good of the great number. Moreover, our laws assure equality to all as regards private interests. As for each man's reputation, it is determined by his individual merit; one values a man, with a view to public service, less according to his condition than according to his own worth. Poverty, if one is capable of serving the city well, offers no obstacles to the humblest citizen; on the other hand, there is no espionage whatsoever on one another; nobody accords a neighbor a cool reception because he indulges in certain pleasures. We have no ceremonies here, which, without being penalties, are none the less disagreeable to undergo. Thus private life is exempt from chicaneries without our having, for that reason, any less fear, any less respect, for the laws, so far as the citizens are concerned.[1]

The orator who thus expresses himself is supposed to be speaking in the name of the state at a public ceremony; he can present things only in the most favorable light. But the gravity of the historian does not harbor the thought that there is nothing serious in this official optimism. The appreciation laid in the mouth of Pericles, moreover, conforms to the impression left to us by all of the existing testimonies. Notwithstanding the important reservations expressed above, there is no doubt that the democracy at this time had not yet realized among the Athenians many of the conditions which in any human society favor the development of the best qualities of the mind and the will. Athens had the distinction of being the first to experiment, with brilliant

[1] Thucydides, II, 37.

partial success, with this form of government, of having illustrated, so to speak, some of its best aspects, and, in so doing, of having given future generations a useful example and valuable instruction.

(2) POLITICAL LIFE IN THE OTHER GREEK CITIES

Other Greek Democracies.—Of the other Greek democracies little is known. None of them, however, seems to have been distinguished from the type of the Athenian city-state by the possession of any very original institutions. Those of the islands of the maritime confederation, at Samos, Chios, and Lesbos, were directly inspired by the examples of the Athenian people and naturally felt the effects of what took place at Athens. The same parties were in conflict, the same passions were aroused, and the same revolutions occurred—with very slight differences. In Greece proper the most important democracy, after that of Athens, was the Argive democracy; but Argos, always closely watched by the jealousy of Sparta, and, besides, only moderately active and occupied more with agriculture than with commerce, remained without expansion or colonization.

In Sicily, on the other hand, the intellectual activity as well as the business activity was great. Cities such as Syracuse comprised a population in many respects similar to that of Athens. But the necessity with which the Greeks of Sicily were confronted, of defending themselves against the incessant menace of the Carthaginians, compeled them to maintain a military force which was a constant danger to liberty. The victorious generals, at the head of mercenary armies animated by no civic pride, had very little difficulty in taking advantage of the party conflicts for the purpose of gaining power for

themselves. They played the rôle of protectors of the
poor, and partly by deceit and partly by force they set
themselves up as tyrants. When their excess finally led
to their overthrow, they generally retired in favor of other
ambitious men or of a revolutionary democracy, whose
acts of violence prepared the ground for a new tyranny.
Few and short were the periods of internal peace and
stability. The same observations apply to several of the
Greek city-states in southern Italy.

Oligarchies.—From the political point of view, on the
other hand, one can not set any great value on the contribution of the Greek oligarchies to the development of
Hellenic civilization. The most important of them, that
of Sparta, while displaying its peculiar qualities of
energy, discipline, and constancy, succeeded neither in
making its preponderance acceptable abroad, nor in re-
lieving at home the rigors of a legislation which in consequence of the steady decline of the number of its citizens
slowly led it to its ruin. Sparta was alarmed by this
fatal weakening, and as a result engaged all the more in
the maintenance of its supremacy in the Peloponnesus.
Jealous of the increasing power of Athens but incapable
of supplanting it, and wrapped up in traditions and prejudices which prevented it from admitting salutory influences from abroad, this city consumed itself in efforts
which, to be sure, secured it a temporary victory over
its rival, but at the same time exhausted its forces without producing anything truly great or useful. Its
military power, its internal tranquility, its individual
virtues, were able to deceive some Athenian malcontents.
The latter extoled its laws in hatred of the democratic
régime which they impatiently endured; they admired, not
without reason, some of its kings and generals. It is
no less certain, if the fecundity of a people is to be meas-

ured by what it has done for the good of humanity, that Sparta, as a city-state, remained unproductive in the fifth century. Distrustful of everything which it could not understand, Sparta was the great obstacle to the unification of Greece; and we may say that by its very successes, far from furthering national expansion, it prepared, with its own downfall, the destruction of the other Greek states.

Tyrannies.—As for the tyrannies, if in the fifth century they had any share to claim in the development of Hellenic civilization, it was only in the occasional protection which they were able to afford to literature and the arts. But politically they were the very negation of order and progress, since they proceeded from the destruction of the laws and maintained themselves only by trampling under foot the principles which properly constituted the city-state. Where the will of one man prevailed without restrictions, the term citizen no longer had any meaning. At that time, even in cases when the tyrant did not use his personal power as a means of gratifying his basest passions, those persons who were under his domination, having no assured rights and being forced to look upon obedience to the will of a master as the sole guarantee of their security, were nothing more than subjects. If such a régime had become generally prevalent, Greece would not only have fallen from the position of superiority which it owed to its conception of law and liberty, but would have been degraded to the level of the nations which it justly described as barbarian.

CHAPTER II

CULT AND THE GREAT RELIGIOUS MANI-
FESTATIONS IN THE FIFTH CENTURY

Development of Cult in the Fifth Century.—If the
reader recalls what has already been said in regard to the
place which religion occupied in the life of the Greek city-
states, he will not be surprised to learn that the brilliant
rise of Hellenic civilization in the fifth century was accompanied by a no less brilliant development of cult.
It was, in fact, the increasing intensity of their internal
life, the consciousness of their power, and the abundant
resources of some of them, which at that time made it
possible for the religious ceremonies to achieve a new
glory by utilizing to advantage the general improvement
of the arts.

The Panhellenic Festivals.—Unfortunately no writer
has given us a complete description of the great celebrations of Olympia and Delphi, and of Corinth and
Nemea, in the fifth century. We can picture them to
ourselves only by piecing together scattered testimonies,
which completely overlook interesting details. They
permit us, however, to imagine their beauty and better
to understand their moral effect.

It was in the fifth century that the sacred precinct of
Olympia, where until then only a few ancient monuments
were to be seen, was provided with the majority of the
edifices the ruins of which still cover the ground there
today. At that time was built the great Temple of

Zeus, in which was placed the celebrated statue of the god, one of the masterpieces of Phidias. At that time, too, were erected almost all the sanctuaries which the various Greek city-states gave themselves the honor of dedicating to him, either in commemoration of their victories or simply as evidence of their piety. Delphi presented a similar spectacle. From year to year there was a steady increase in the number of these votive statues, not to mention the offerings, altars, and treasures. Each of the Greek peoples had some favor to ask of Apollo, some evidence of recognition to present to him. Every one of these sacred places, where so much wealth and so many admirable works of art were amassed, thus became a focus from which the national genius radiated in all its glory. By the impression which they make even to this day upon the modern visitor, one may judge what impression they must have created when their marvelous decorations of art were still there to be seen in all their splendor.

There, at the time of the periodical festivals, thronged the sacred embassies which conveyed the homages and offerings of the Greek city-states and their colonies; and with these deputations came the ever increasing multitude of onlookers. Never had rivalry been more intense among those who took part in these competitions. Before this immense gathering an unparalled emulation inspired the athletes to display, in the various gymnastic exercises, those physical qualities which the Greeks looked upon almost as virtues. It is well known how the glory of the victors, acclaimed by an enthusiastic multitude, was afterwards celebrated in their native states. And what aroused the ancient Greeks even more than the games in the stadium were the chariot races, which at that time seem to have acquired an importance com-

mensurate with the increase of wealth.   The victories of
the Sicilian princes, Hiero of Syracuse and Theron of
Agrigentum, those of the King of Cyrene, Arcesilaus,
and others, are known to us thru the poems of Simonides,
Pindar and Bacchylides, who celebrated them in magnificent verses.   The Thessalian nobles, on their part, proud
of their renowned horses, ardently disputed the prizes in
these Olympian or Pythian, Isthmian or Nemean contests,
which according to the expression of Horace "raised
mortals to the rank of gods."   Moreover, the aristocrats of the republic themselves, notably those of Athens,
were far from showing lack of interest in these prizes.
Various writers make known to us the names of rich
Athenians who, at different times, had sought and obtained
them.   In particular we may mention the renowned Alcibiades, who was one day proud of displaying an unusual
pomp at Olympia and carried away as many as three
prizes at a single festival.

The intellect, moreover, also played its part in these
festivals.   In the fifth century, in fact, we witness the
introduction of the use of recitations.   Without mentioning the rhapsodists, the masters of oratory and dialectic,
whose instruction was at that time an entirely new thing,
the philosophers and historians attended in order to
deliver lectures or to read a few pieces before the benevolent listeners whom they were sure to find in these great
assemblages.   In this way useful exchanges of ideas were
brought about.   Men became acquainted with one another and with the new things of the day; and the relations thus established tended in some measure to relieve
the excessive particularism of the Greek city-states.

*Festivals of the City-states. Preeminence of the
Athenian Festivals.*—Like the Panhellenic festivals, many
others restricted either to the different states or to

cities or market-towns, were sanctified, so to speak, by some beautiful religious legends, and increased in importance and splendor in the fifth century. Among them, those of Athens deserve especially to be mentioned; for not only were they everywhere recognized as the most pleasing to the eye, the best ordered, and the most worthy of the gods, but it was also to them that the largest number of foreigners was attracted. Moreover, the admiration which they called forth caused them to be imitated in many places. It was notably at Athens that the theatrical performances acquired the character which gradually came to be adopted everywhere. From the middle of the sixth century the state had taken over the direction of them; and the example set by Pisistratus and his sons was followed by the democracy of the fifth century. The Assembly regarded it as one of its most serious duties to insure the good organization of the official ceremonies. It regulated them by means of decrees, the execution of which was effected by the tribes. Upon the latter, as a matter of fact, it devolved to designate those of their richest members who were to bear a portion of the expense and to take charge of the necessary preparations. The persons thus designated became morally responsible to their tribe for the success of the ceremony, and to a certain extent they were responsible also to the people as a whole. They incurred the disfavor of the public if they exposed themselves to a charge of parsimony or of negligence. Since all the festivals, or nearly all of them, had the form of competitions, the instinctive desire, strong in the Greeks of that time, to surpass others, entered into play among them all. Men outdid themselves in order to outdo their rivals.

Some Great Athenian Festivals.—These Athenian festivals were numerous. There was scarcely a month in the year which did not have its celebrations of one kind or another. The most important of them, and at the same time the most representative of the civilization of the fifth century, were the *Panathenæa*, the *Anthesteria*, the *Greater Dionysia*, the *Lenæa*, and the *Eleusinia*.

The *Panathenaea* was in a sense the national festival of Athens, that in which the city commemorated the anniversary of its birth and paid solemn homage to its ancestral goddess. We have already mentioned the rhapsodic recitations which in the sixth century became one of the principal elements of this festival and helped to preserve the character of the ancient epic poetry as an institution always rich in influence and instruction. But what undoubtedly constituted the principal attraction in the fifth century was the procession, the memory of which is immortalized in the celebrated frieze of the Parthenon. Thanks to the conception of Phidias, and perhaps also to his chisel, we still see here the idealized representation of the city-state, its people marching in good order to bring to the goddess their homage and offerings. Here we behold old men of the nobility, vigorous ephebes mastering their ardent steeds, and virgins and women in the natural grace of their postures and movements. Nothing could impress upon our minds more strongly the great wealth of order, of innate harmony, and of serene beauty contained in the Athenian religion.

The *Eleusinia* were of an entirely different character and manifested another aspect of this religion. The procession which went on foot from Athens to Eleusis, to the sanctuary of Demeter and Kora (Persephone) renewed the rites of an ancient agrarian cult the primitive significance of which was profoundly modified. The sentiments which animated the initiates and those who aspired to the initiation, have been defined above. They all went to seek, in this sacred place, hope for another life. In the rites which they observed were features in which the former rural nature of the festival was clearly discernible; but the new ideas had done away with all this and everywhere had injected added beauty. This was to be seen in the column of armed ephebes who accompanied the procession; it was apparent especially in the new monuments the rise of which Eleusis witnessed in the fifth century, in particular the Hall of Initiation (Telesterion), one of the architectural masterpieces of the time.

The *Anthesteria*, the *Dionysia*, and the *Lenæa* all centered their attention upon one and the same god, Dionysus, who at that time, in the Olympus of the fifth century, had become a personage of the first importance. The truth is, numerous cults were to some extent founded upon another cult in order to give him this importance; and under a single name homage was paid to various gods and goddesses whose identity was no longer distinguished. This explains how a single cult could present very diverse aspects. Joy was mixed with sorrow; drunkenness, sensuality, and ribaldry with enthusiasm, with a noble and generous exaltation, and with pity. It was this mixture of elements which rendered the cult so remarkably productive of creative inspirations. In the *Anthesteria* there existed curious and naïve rites which are especially interesting for the history of religions, but which we may here overlook. It is the *Dionysia* and the *Lenæa* which attract our attention above all, for with these festivals are associated some of the foremost manifestations of the Hellenic genius.

Dionysiac Lyrism of the Fifth Century.—One of the most brilliant of these manifestations was the dithyramb, the origins and first developments of which we have already outlined. This lyric form appears in full bloom again in the fifth century, and we find it associated precisely with the cult of Dionysus at Athens. The testimonies inform us that it was sung at the *City Dionysia* by choruses which competed among themselves. On the other hand, we know that the most celebrated poets, Bacchylides and Pindar, preceded by Simonides, composed poems for these competitions, some fragments of which have come down to us. Toward the end of the same century, moreover, the innovators in musical art, Philoxenus and Timotheus, adapted the same form to their new conceptions. At that time the dithyramb rivaled the nome, which, more serious and more purely religious, had always been associated with the cult of Apollo; and in this sort of rivalry between two forms and two divine patrons it seems that Dionysus tended to get the upper hand. These lyric representations charmed the Athenian public. To meet their desires Pericles had the Odeum constructed, the first theater to be consecrated especially to musical performances. Since music and song were looked upon as essential parts of the common education, everybody in Athens had at least some conception of them. Moreover, in the competitions between the tribes there were, besides the choruses of adults, also choruses of children, who likewise took part, so the ancient testimonies give us to understand, in the ceremonies of the *City Dionysia*.

The Drama: its Diverse Forms.—Nevertheless, among the elements of the Dionysiac festivals none was equal in value to the drama. It was in its theatrical productions, indeed, that Athens in the fifth century revealed most clearly the originality of its genius. In the two essential types of the dramatic form, tragedy and comedy, it produced works which immediately became models and

which since that time have not ceased to command
admiration. Both created in the preceding century,
tragedy and comedy had not been slow to win public
favor and to secure the patronage of the state. From
536 B. C. on, the latter instituted competitions among
the tragic poets, among whom Thespis stood forth con-
spicuously at that time. At the beginning of the fifth
century the comic poets, in their turn, were invited to
compete for a prize especially reserved for their art;
and from that time on, it seems, these two competitions
took place annually, tragedy at first being properly a
part of the *Dionysia*, and comedy of the *Lenœa*. This
distinction, however, was soon modified. Without entering here into the details of a regulation which varied,
and which scarcely pertains to our subject, let us simply
recall the custom observed at the *City Dionysia* during
the second half of the century. Every year the archon-
king, in charge of the official cult, had to choose from
among the poets who entered the competition, on the one
hand, three authors of tragedies, each of whom contributed three plays (to which was added one play of a
special kind called a satyr drama); and, on the other
hand, three authors of comedies, each of whom had to
furnish only one play. To each of these six competitors
he assigned a chorus furnished by one of the tribes, the
latter, as we have seen, having designated a choregus,
whose duty it was to equip and train this chorus at his
own expense. As for the actors, the manner of choosing
them, of assigning rôles to them, and of remunerating
them, was subject to various modifications of which we
need not speak here. The production of these fifteen
plays required three days. Ten judges, designated by
lot by means of a rather complicated system of drawings,
had to pronounce upon the relative merits of the com-

petitors. Only the one person who was ranked absolute first, either in the tragedy competition or in the comedy competition, was proclaimed the victor. These few facts show clearly how much pains the people took to have everything in this organization perfectly regulated with a view to encouraging the production of the most beautiful works.

Essential Character of the Theatrical Performances.—The fact is, the Athenians did not go to the theater to find relaxation for a few moments. For them a performance was a rare thing, occurring only two or three times a year. It was a part of one of their great religious festivals. A considerable crowd attended it. All the classes mingled there, and on these days everybody concurred in the same sentiments. Before the performance a great expectancy held the public mind in suspense; one knew that one was about to see something new, the work of the most remarkable intellects of the time. Everybody hoped that the awaited spectacle would do honor to the city-state before the strangers who had come to witness it, and that it would be worthy of the god to whom homage was being paid. And in the course of the performance it was inevitable that in a gathering so large and so impressionable, but composed for the most part of persons of mediocre culture, there should occur sudden outbreaks of general emotion, of irresistible enthusiasm, which removed the doubts of the more exacting and discriminating minds. Under these conditions the impressions received were necessarily more naïve, more profound, less individual and less reserved, than are ordinarily those of the spectators of our day. But in order to analyze them a little more closely, it is manifestly necessary to consider the tragedy and the comedy separately.

Tragedy and its Subjects.—What was, therefore, a
Greek tragedy? As regards subject, it was a piece or
section of the national history. For here there was no
necessity of distinguishing, as we might be tempted to do,
between history, properly so called, and legend. For the
majority of the Greeks of that time this distinction would
have had no precise meaning. In general, however, it was
from the heroic age that the tragic poets borrowed their
subjects; they drew them from either epic or lyric
poetry, or from local traditions. At all events, the
people had the feeling that these subjects were related
to their race, sometimes perhaps to their own city-state.
The people themselves formed the theme of the drama,
since it represented the adventures of their ancestors,
authentic or imaginary. And when these narratives-in-
action opposed Greeks to barbarians, a national ideal
appeared to them and filled them with pride—an intellectual and moral superiority, a sense of justice, a natural
dignity and humanity. Naturally when Athens was at
war with Sparta, it was less a Greek ideal in general than
a specifically Athenian ideal that interested the public of
Athens and caused its patriotic sentiments to vibrate.
That is why in those periods of crisis and mutual hatred
the poets chose legends which were calculated to bring
out the contrasts between the two city-states to the advantage of their own. Moreover, the tendency to discover
in the past similarities to the present, to emphasize them
by allusions, and to draw lessons from them, was not
peculiar to those times of war. It resulted from the
fact that the history of a people necessarily leads, at
different intervals, to situations in which analogous sentiments manifest themselves.

But the subjects of the tragedies, besides being national, were also religious. The action which the poet

developed before the eyes of the spectators would have
responded but poorly to their expectations if it had failed
to show them the accomplishment of a divine will.   The
incredulous, if such there were among them, constituted
only an insignificant minority ; for to the masses assembled
in the audience the intervention of the gods in human
affairs was not at all a matter of doubt.   Moreover, this
public was pleased to have the divine power manifested by
striking examples.   Since it was ever conscious of the omni-
presence of this power in real life, and .since its most
constant concern was to divine the wills or the passions of
the gods, on which depended the good or bad fortune
of men, no spectacle could interest it so much as that of
great misfortunes and their supernatural causes.   It
devolved upon the poet to make these causes clear to the
public, while at the same time they remained hidden or
obscure to the personages involved in the play.   Every
tragic performance thus conceived became for the spectators an occasion for meditation upon human destiny
or, at the very least, for suggestive emotions.

In order that these emotions might be profound, it was
expedient for the drama to bring great destinies into play.
The ancient heroic families, whose dramatic adventures
had been popularized by the epic poets, were precisely
what was necessary.   Thru the effect of the reversion to
the past, and thanks to the genius of a few poets, the
men and the events of these legendary ages had acquired
more than human proportions.   Moreover, tradition attributed to them passions, crimes, exceptional prosperities
and hardships.   Everything related to them bore witness
to the hidden power of fate, the secret force of ancient
maledictions, the futility of calculations pretending to
elude the decrees of the gods, the blindness of ambition,
and the snares concealed behind hopes.   Such is the field

of choice for a tragedy intended to distract the mind from vulgar thoughts and to place men in the presence of the gods. Nevertheless, everything properly human was no less in evidence there. In action or in suffering the souls of men were revealed in striking traits. Here we see powerful wills striving for the execution of difficult undertakings and facing the most formidable dangers; we see them standing firm against grief, placing all their forces at the service of immoderate ambitions, and delivering themselves with frenzy to the pleasure of vengeance; but sometimes also waxing tender, opening their hearts to pity, or recognizing in the destruction of their illusions the disregarded laws of justice and moderation. In these spectacles, however simplified they were by an art which delighted in clearness, there was a profundity of religious and moral perspective which has scarcely been equaled anywhere else.

Scenery of the Tragedy.—We can not fully describe here the mounting of the Greek tragedy of the fifth century; it is necessary, however, to recall certain essential features of it, notably the simplicity of the scenery, the small number of actors involved, and the presence of a singing and dancing chorus. The Athenian theater never knew the abuse of material means. It appealed to the eye only so far as necessary, leaving much to the imagination of the spectators, which the poetry was called upon to stimulate. Since the actors were only three in number, one often saw only two personages on the stage at one time, never more than three. All tumult, all confusion, was thus naturally excluded. Reduced to dialogs, the action could nevertheless be impassioned, even violent, if the subject demanded it. But such violence, materially simplified, was by its very nature spiritualized, as it were; and it was still more so as a result of the association of song and recitation. In the second half of the century, especially, the parts sung acquired more importance in the rôles; and the vocal melody, accompanied by the flute, served to convey more vividly the anxieties of the soul. Thus one drew further away from reality, but succeeded better in expressing everything that it contained. The same may be said in regard to the chorus. Having originally been a sort of collective actor, often playing the principal part, it acquired more and more the rôle of a spectator, sharing in the action by the expression of sentiments of sympathy or antipathy, but without taking any real part in it. In this way it became especially well qualified to judge the action, to mark its various phases, and by its songs to express the sentiments which the poet wished to arouse in his audience—fears or hopes, admiration or reprobation—unless it served to refresh the audience by brilliant interludes. If we add to these characteristic features the slight complication of intrigue, we can not fail to be struck by the great simplicity of the whole. As often happens, however, it is probable that the power of the effect produced was inversely proportionate to the multiplicity of the means employed.

Educational Value of the Tragedy.—In any case, the influence of the tragedy upon Hellenic civilization in the fifth century was great. It was especially at the theater that many Athenians learned the history of their country; there, at least, it was duly impressed upon their minds, since it was actually unfolded, as it were, before their eyes. And this history, under the legendary and idealized form which it took in the tragic dramas, supported their religious sentiment, developed all the instincts, all the ideas, which lie at the foundation of moral culture—the sense of duty, of honor, of devotion, of moderation, and of humanity. On each and every one in the audience there was imposed, in the presence of these spectacles which represented an idealized life, the recognition of ideal values so often obscured in the conflict of interests and in the complexities of daily reality. Finally, (and this follows naturally), the instruction of the tragedy was also æsthetic in its nature. How could masterpieces such as the plays of Æschylus, Sophocles, and Euripides have failed to sharpen the perception of beauty in a public naturally gifted in that direction? How could they have failed to make it feel the charm of a composition capable of holding the attention, of producing contrasts and surprises, and of arousing fear and pity by means of unexpected catastrophes? How could they have failed to refine in this public a taste and intelligent understanding for poetic language, now bold and terse, now rich in shades of meaning, adapted to express tenderness quite as well as rage or hatred, as delightful in the expression of joy as it was touching in the expression of sorrow?

The Comedy of the Fifth Century. Its Characteristics. —If from this tragedy of the fifth century we pass now to the comedy of the same period, the contrast seems striking. To religious earnestness are opposed drollery and profligacy. That a public susceptible of the noblest and deepest emotions, capable of passionate interest in that lofty philosophy of life, nevertheless enjoyed plays abounding in obscene pleasantries and the grossest forms of abuse, is a fact which in the first place bears witness to the versatility of the Greek mind, but which is also to be explained by the history of this dramatic form. The comedy was born in the rustic festivals pertaining to the cult of the god of wine, at the *Country Dionysia*. At first it was only the festival of humble vine-growers, consisting of joyous songs, of symbolic processions, of dances and masquerades. Dionysus was known as a lover of drunkenness, of laughter and gaiety, and of sensual pleasures. One paid homage to him by imitating him. When this rustic carnival became a literary form at Athens, patronized by the state, it had to preserve its original character in order not to deprive the god of the things that pleased him. This religious reason covered everything; it explains why no person was offended by words and actions which anywhere else would have been looked upon as intolerable. It must be borne in mind, however, that the comedy, once admitted to the public competitions, did not long retain this original element. Not only did it take the form of a work of art by imposing upon itself certain peculiarities of composition, but it sought to play a political and social rôle, to intervene in the conflict of opinions, and to pass judgment upon things and upon men; and it became a moral force which in certain respects might be compared with the press of our day, due allowance being made for inevitable differences.

The Element of Comic Fantasy.—That which first of all strikes the modern reader in each of the extant plays of Aristophanes, the most remarkable representative of this Attic comedy of the fifth century, called the "Old Comedy," is the place occupied in it by pure fantasy. Everything here seems to belong to the domain of fairies —the action, the place, the people, and the situations. The drama may take place on earth, even at Athens; this is the case with the *Acharnians*, the *Knights*, the *Clouds*, the *Wasps*, the *Lysistrata*, the *Plutus*, and the *Women in Parliament;* but it may also be transported from the earth to Olympus, as in the *Peace;* it may hover between earth and the sky, as in the *Birds;* it may descend to the infernal regions, as in the *Frogs.* Certain personages are gods, more or less travestied; others are animals, simple allegories; others, finally, are men and women. None of them, whatever they are, is subject to probability or to reason. Fantastic projects, comical eccentricities, marvelous adventures—such are the ordinary features of the plays which they fill with their mad and exuberant bustle. In conjunction with them, as in the tragedy, figures a chorus. The latter likewise, according to the caprice of the poet, may be composed of beings of any kind, not only of human personages grotesquely dressed, but of various animals, of personified conceptions, such as the Clouds, inhabitants of Hades, including the dead. Altho the chorus succeeds in saying very wise things, it is also capable of disporting itself foolishly, of emitting shrieks and howls, of bounding here and there, of insulting and attacking the personages of the drama, and even the public. Between the principal scenes of the play one sees it indulging in licentious dances. Finally, as a last characteristic feature, it was at certain times customary for the poet to discard the fiction which he had created and to cause this chorus to speak in its own name. But all this should not lead us to believe that this unbridled fantasy degenerated into confusion. Thanks to a skilled art, on the contrary, all these elements of disorder were harmoniously organized; and it is truly one of the most surprising things to find again here, in this free dramatic form, the qualities of order and moderation natural to the creations of the Greek mind.

The Satiric Element.—Moreover, with the boldest fantasy there was constantly mingled an element of satire and consequently of reality. The representation of the customs, ideas, and infatuations of the day offered the comic poets a rich field of exploitation. How many elements of truth were to be found in the majority of the characters, alongside of enormous improbabilities and drolleries! It was a source of perpetual amusement for the sharp-witted public to recognize in the play some of the types familiar to it—the foreigner with his strange-sounding language, the peasant with his prejudices and eccentricities, the petty tradespeople, the shopkeepers in the agora, the hucksters of both sexes, the braggarts, the blusterers, the simple-minded and the sharpers—an entire world of people very familiar to those who bustled about the city, whether at the Piræus or in the environs. The spectators laughed at them and learned while they laughed —just as one always learns by observing life. When it was a question of the small fry, the raillery of the comedy was neither severe nor malicious; sometimes it even re-vealed them as very sensible in their simplicity. But when the attack was on men in the public view, politicians, sophists, philosophers, fashionable authors, or others, it assumed the aspect of a pamphlet in action. And this was not merely incidental to it; on the contrary, it very often made these biting satires its principal object. From the time of Cimon the example in this respect was set by Cratinus; and his successors imitated him. All the lead-ers of the people saw themselves derided one after an-other—Pericles more than any other, and after him Cleon, Hyperbolus, and Cleophon. Such plays of Aristophanes as the *Acharnians* and the *Knights* are above all personal attacks. In the last-mentioned comedy, as in the *Wasps*, the people as a whole were taken to task, severely admon-ished for their conduct or ridiculed for their stupidity. Other plays tended to decry philosophy and especially Socrates, or to lampoon the dramatic innovations of Euripides. These plays offered severe criticism, which was often profoundly unjust, sometimes slanderous, and al-ways animated by violent prejudices, but nevertheless sug-

gestive insofar as it called attention on many occasions
to defects which were not imaginary. On the whole, we
may say, the comedies were well calculated to awaken reflection and the spirit of criticism.

Dramatic Performances outside of Athens.—The taste
for the theater at that time was not peculiar to the
Athenians. Many Greek city-states, and even market
towns, had their more or less regular performances. But
as regards the tragedy, it seems that nowhere else was
there produced a dramatic form essentially different from
that created by the Athenian masters—not even at
Syracuse, where Æschylus achieved a measure of success
similar to that which he achieved in his own country. The
same does not apply, it is true, to comedy. A great poet,
Epicharmus, created at the court of the tyrant Hiero,
and for the people of Syracuse, a form of comic composition quite different from that which held favor at Athens.
The few fragments of his works which have come down
to us merely serve to show that he combined a keen sense
of reality with a genuinely philosophic turn of mind.

CHAPTER III

SOCIETY AND CUSTOMS

General Aspect of Greek Society in the Fifth Century. The Classes.—Having surveyed the religious and political life, we have now to consider the social life, that is to say, the relations of men to one another, their manner of living and their customs. In this respect there were great diversities among the Greek city-states. The Dorians differed considerably from the Ionians; Sparta contrasted sharply with Athens. But the fact is that today Athens alone represents in history what is commonly called Hellenic civilization; and that is why, in a survey such as the present, it is permissible to consider it alone.

(1) THE ATHENIAN ARISTOCRACY

The Eupatrids.—Athens in the fifth century, entirely democratic as it had become by virtue of its laws and its spirit, still had a noble aristocracy the importance of which, from the standpoint of civilization, remained considerable. It consisted chiefly of the so-called "eupatrids." These were the descendants of the old families, who for a long time had held possession of the greater part of the land and for a number of centuries had predominated in the government. Proud of their more or less legendary traditions, they carefully preserved their domestic cults, the hereditary priesthoods of which could be held only by their members, even when some of these cults had been appropriated by a deme or a phratry. In spite of the total loss of their political privileges, these eupatrids owed to the antiquity of their lineage, to these religious functions, and also to their superior culture, a reputation which survived the destruction of their power. Moreover, a goodly number of them still possessed important estates, to say nothing of the movable wealth which they had been able to acquire by utilization of the land. In general, it was on these estates, rather than in the city, that their principal establishments were located. There they lived in plenty, surrounded by servants and a clientele of poor people who had not renounced the habit of claiming their patronage. In this way there was perpetuated, at least in the rural demes, something of the former moral influence of this class.

The Family.—It was among the eupatrids, naturally, that the old customs persisted most constantly, and their influence brought it about that the mass of the people, by a natural spirit of imitation, got rid of these customs only by very slow degrees. The head of the family exercised in his home a sort of patriarchal royalty, much mitigated, of course, by the gradual improvement in the manners and customs. In theory, at least, it devolved upon him to command and to administer. The wife was subjected by law to a legal tutelage, which was transferred, in case of her widowhood, either to the oldest son, if he had reached his majority, or to a near relative. In reality, however, she played her part in the domestic administration; usually it was she who directly gave orders to the slaves and superintended the work of the servants. Many of the necessaries of life, food as well as clothing, were still produced in the home with her active participation or at least under her personal supervision. In the city she generally led a secluded life, scarcely ever went out save when accompanied, and visited or received only women or relatives. It is scarcely necessary to say, however, that the restrictions laid upon her freedom of action by custom and by law did not prevent any woman from exerting an influence the extent of which depended only upon the value of her personal character.

Education.—The education of the children was looked upon as an essential duty of the parents, and the law itself laid an obligation upon them not to neglect it. But otherwise the State did not intervene. Custom alone regulated the ways and means. The education of the girls depended especially upon the mother; and in general it was apparently reduced to the acquisition of the most elementary knowledge and to moral development. Forced to maintain a rigorous reserve, and frequently married off at a very young age without being consulted, they developed their intelligence chiefly by experience and a power of observation which sharpened their natural acumen. The faults which are frequently imputed to the Athenian woman in the comedy and even in the tragedy—frivolity, gossiping, childish curiosity, indiscretion, lack of candor, a spirit of intrigue—were undoubtedly due, in large measure, to the insufficiency of this education.

The education of the boys was more carefully regulated, but was likewise, on the whole, rather simple. Raised up to their seventh year by the women, they were then conducted by their pedagogs, slaves charged with guarding them, into some private school; for in Athens there was no public school. There they were taught to read, to write correctly, and to figure; they were made to learn by heart the works of the national poets; they were initiated in the elementary practice of singing and of playing the lyre. If the "grammarian" who gave this instruction

was truly a teacher, he needed nothing more to awaken
the minds of the children and to arouse their interest in
beautiful things; for what lessons were not to be found
in the *Iliad* and the *Odyssey*, in the *Works and Days*, and
in the songs of the lyric poets?   The imagination of the
youthful Greek developed in the midst of the ancient
legends; he acquired his initial experience of life among
the heroes; Achilles and Ulysses were the objects of his
first admiration.   The school, however, did not keep him
very long.   Yet it is clear that in the well-to-do families
the growing youth prolonged his education by perfecting
himself in music, by reading whatever there was to read
at that time—the poets who were not taken up in school,
as well as the first works of philosophy, history, and
geography, the manuscripts of which were then already
circulating in the Greek world.   Nevertheless, the need
of perfecting this knowledge and of organizing it more
effectively was one of the reasons for the success of the
sophists, of whom we shall have something to say further
on.   Toward the middle of the century they introduced
two innovations, dialectic and rhetoric.   But hitherto
the old education had sufficed, in all its simplicity, to
mould men of high value.   At the beginning of their lives
it had provided them with a basis for sound judgment,
a strong moral and patriotic tradition, and a total fund
of knowledge which was sufficient for them.   They were
receptive toward experience and revealed a freshness of
mind accompanied by genuine prudence and acumen.

To this development of the mind was added training of
the body, to which all of the Greeks continued to attach
the highest value.   The child went to the palæstra just as
soon as his age permitted him to do so; and there under
the direction of an experienced "pedotribe" he indulged
in a series of graduated exercises which endowed him with

strength, agility, physical endurance, and courage, as
also with a sense of discipline and of rhythm. A goodly
number of young men passed later from the palæstra to
the gymnasium, where they were given practice in athletic
exercises. The highest social classes were probably the
ones which furnished the most athletes properly so called;
for aristocratic names abound in the lists of victors at
the great Panhellenic games. We may add that the practice of horsemanship was also much in vogue among the
well-to-do families.

This twofold education produced, accordingly, both
robust bodies and cultivated minds; those who received
its benefits as fully as possible were truly men, in the
broadest sense of the word. It is surely due in part to
this advantage that the Athenian aristocracy was able to
resist for so long a time the causes of disintegration
which menaced it. It provided the Athenian army with
its cavalry, and often with its leaders; and sometimes,
in spite of distrust, it even gave leaders to the democracy.
The State did not relinquish its claims upon the future
citizen until the end of his adolescence. Having passed
his eighteenth year, he entered the class of the ephebes.
Then he learned the military profession; for every
Athenian citizen was a soldier. For two years he was
bound to a service which made a vigorous and trained
hoplite of him; and at the end of these two years he
entered into the full possession of his political rights and
took the oath of arms.

Occupations and Pleasures.—Once he had become a full-
fledged man, what was the nature of the rich Athenian's
life? An important part of it was given over to his participation in public affairs, liturgies, and official com-
missions with which he was charged, sometimes against
his will. Another part was devoted to the administration

of his estates. An active master had to supervise the management of these, even when he entrusted the immediate direction to a chosen slave whom he made his superintendent. In order to derive any profit from a rather unproductive soil, it was necessary for him to keep an eye on everything, to oversee and regulate the process of cultivation, to make constant improvements, and to watch very closely the sale or the utilization of the products. Nevertheless, there remained hours of leisure for the landed proprietor, and these he cultivated particularly; for was not leisure one of the privileges which set him apart from those who were attached to a profession? Hunting, horseback riding, and bodily exercises occupied him agreeably one after the other. The hours of rest were given over to intercourse with friends, to walks, to conversation, and some of them to reading; for we know that in the fifth century the book trade was beginning to develop and that already private libraries were being formed. Among cultivated people the exchange of ideas was becoming more and more active and interesting, according as knowledge increased and as a thousand new questions concerning science, morality, and politics came up for discussion. There was much friendly conversation at Athens. The people were very fond of social gatherings, and most of the rich homes were bountifully hospitable. Banquets were very frequent; and since custom did not permit women in good standing to take part in any function in the company of men, the latter enjoyed a freedom at these banquets of which they took full advantage. In these joyous reunions the wine-cups were filled generously, and even licentiousness was not considered degrading. There was music, singing, sometimes dancing; drinking songs followed, each of the revelers having to contribute in turn. To this were often

added various diversions, such as pantomimes and acro-
batics; one listened to the sweet melodies of the flute.
Moreover, it was not uncommon for the participants in
these reunions, while preserving something of their gaiety,
to have recourse to half-serious, half-playful discussions,
wherein the piquant grace of the Attic mind found an opportunity to assert itself. We find charming examples
of this in certain well-known works of Plato and
Xenophon.

Altogether, whatever may have been the defects and the
prejudices of this aristocracy, it was none the less an
elite, a particularly necessary and precious thing in a
democracy. The influence which it exerted in the fifth
century upon the arts, upon letters, and upon customs,
was certainly beneficent. It kept the public mind on a
very high level, and it gave the city-state some of its
most remarkable men in all branches of activity.

(2) THE POPULAR MASSES IN ATHENS

The Middle Class and the Lower Classes.—This superior class, however, constituted only a small minority
of the population. Below it from the point of view of
general esteem, but above it from the point of view of
effective power, was the populace, that is to say, a
large middle class and the lower classes, both living
partly in the city itself and partly in the surrounding
country.

The Country Population.—Attica, in spite of the increase of its urban population in the fifth century, always had a large number of small landowners, who cultivated their own land with the help of a few day-laborers
or slaves, and who were sober, economical, hard-working
people. Their attachment to their deme and to the

piece of land from which they derived their subsistence was equalled only by their fondness for the old customs and traditional ideas.   Scarcely ever coming to the city except to go to market or to attend one or another of the great festivals, they participated but irregularly in the public deliberations, still less in the functions of the State, and in those of the tribunals.   In the things of the spirit they were but slightly interested, for they had neither sufficient instruction nor sufficient leisure to occupy themselves with them.   Thanks to the genius of the race, however, and to the influences it exerted upon them, they were lacking neither in acumen nor in taste.   They constituted the conservative element in the republic, strongly devoted to the democratic institutions, but often distrustful of the leaders of the urban democracy and of innovations of all kinds which the city looked upon with favor.   Moreover, it was no doubt to them that the comedy made its appeal, in the dramatic performances which they came in large numbers to witness, when it ridiculed the men of the day or those affectations or liberties which ran counter to the accepted usages; but this did not prevent it from amusing also the townspeople at the expense of this worthy countryfolk, whose rusticity it jocosely exaggerated.

The City Population.—The city, as a matter of fact, comprised a quite different population.   There people of all sorts met and mingled, to say nothing of the foreigners who flocked thither in ever-increasing numbers.   There one saw manufacturers of arms, of furniture, of divers utensils; employers and workers in many industries who combined the good taste peculiar to the Athenians with technical skill.   They included architects, painters, sculptors, goldsmiths, potters, blacksmiths, curriers, weavers and fullers, dyers and perfumers—in short, all those who produced the many articles, renowned for their excellence, which Athens either exported or kept to supply its own wants. There were located the shops where many of them worked, assisted by free artisans or skillful slaves, while others looked only after the general management and left the immediate supervision of the practical operations to some intelligent freeman in whom they had learned to place their trust. These workshops, however, were restricted in size. Usually there were only ten or twelve workers, often less, rarely more than twenty or thirty. The equipment was very simple; consequently, there was nothing which resembled our modern factories. Altogether, there was no working class such as exists today in almost every country. On the other hand, there were a number of small employers, scarcely distinguished from their employees, who had very nearly the same mode of life, the same habits and customs.

Like industry, commerce had undergone a rapid development in Athens in the fifth century. In particular, the exports of oil and the imports of wheat had given rise to a large business activity, productive of wealth. Nevertheless, it was rather the small or medium-sized business which occupied the major part of the urban population. Often the stall or store adjoined the workshop, and the products were sold by the same persons who made them; but there were also numerous dealers or retailers who sold their wares in the market-place. In order to satisfy the needs of these various kinds of commercial activity, but especially those of big business, there arose in the fifth century a new class of men of affairs, the bankers, who negotiated either the exchange of money, rendered necessary by the diversity of the monetary types in circulation, or the operations of credit, indispensable to exporters. The bankers also set up their tables in the open market in the center of the city, so that they might always be at the service of clients. But as for the most important transactions, these were conducted at home. And it was around the agora, too, that the barber-shops were located, where one learned the news of the day—inexhaustible sources of scandal and gossip.

Taken as a whole, this populace was notable for its vivacity, its ready intelligence, its sprightliness, its piquant sayings, as also for the mobility of its humor. Not entirely free from coarseness, it nevertheless possessed, in a remarkable degree, a taste for the beautiful, a natural acuteness, and an instinctive aversion to all empty ostentation. It was able to appreciate the works of its artists and poets; it prized simple elegance as well as clever raillery. Accustomed to the transaction of business, it was not lacking in judgment when it had means of informing itself. The danger to which it was exposed was that of allowing itself to be seduced by arguments more ingenious than substantial, by clever speeches to which it delighted in listening, and by everything which touched its sensibilities or charmed its imagination. But after all, between the often backward aristocrats and the two progressive innovators the populace constituted, in general, the best force of equilibrium which was opposed to revolutions and guaranteed a certain continuity to the policy of the State.

The Population of the Piræus.—The same observations do not apply to the population of the Piræus, which was more turbulent and less hampered by traditions. There too, no doubt, were great business men, heads of important commercial houses; but the majority of them were metics, that is, resident foreigners who did not form part of the citizen body. The bulk of the inhabitants of the Piræus consisted of those engaged in work connected with the port, employees of the docks and ship-yards, brokers and sailors, with whom were mixed a motley crowd of people from across the water—Greeks from the Ægean islands and Asia Minor, from Sicily, Italy, Syria, Egypt, and Thrace; merchants and sailors from Pontus and distant colonies; barbarians from different Mediterranean shores—each bringing thither his language, his customs, and his superstitions. In daily contact with these men from foreign lands, the Athenians of the port were themselves imbued with a new spirit, becoming more indifferent to the established order, more open to changes, and more adventurous. They constituted the restless element in the republic, thru the medium of which many foreign things were little by little introduced into the city.

General Aspect of the Social Life in Athens.—On the whole, no Greek city resembled the great modern capitals more than Athens, altho it was a comparatively small city. One found there the most varied tendencies, all kinds of minds, and all types of characters—a thousand divergences which not only added something agreeable and piquant to the social intercourse, but which at the same time, by calling forth comparisons, stimulated the intellect, sharpened judgments, and gave the freest play to all the faculties. And that is why Athens attracted foreigners so strongly. Nobody failed to feel at home there; all Greece was represented there—or, better said, all the values of the Greek mind were as if mustered and concentrated there.

Slavery.—Even slavery at Athens was not entirely what it was elsewhere. Altho the Athenian law did not recognize any rights as belonging to the slave, it nevertheless protected his life; and in a considerable number of families the domestic slave, if he was fortunate enough to belong to humane masters, and if he himself was industrious, honest, and submissive, could lead a very tolerable existence. The ancient tragedies introduce to us wet-nurses who in some measure have become confidantes, almost humble friends, of their mistresses. Moreover, a goodly number of the slaves employed in industry, commerce, agriculture, and in the banks, succeeded by their intelligence in making themselves indispensable, in gaining the full confidence of their masters, who then made them superintendents, managers of workshops, and sub-directors; and later, having won their freedom, the former slaves often associated with their masters in business. Nevertheless, the natural vices of the system prevailed. Not only did the public slaves who worked in the mines, and those on whom the most ardous tasks were imposed in the rural districts, have much to endure; but all of them, without exception, if their masters were brought to trial, could according to the law be surrendered by them to the opposing party in order to be put to the question. All were liable to cruel or degrading punishments—to the whip and to various forms of torture. Moreover, being dispersed thruout the country and nowhere in a position to organize their forces, as was later the case in Rome, it was impossible for them to revolt. Their only recourse when they felt themselves at the limit of their endurance was to take to flight at the risk of being hounded like beasts and of finding refuge nowhere. Finally, force, if not interest, too often compeled them to become the accomplices, or the victims of the vices, of their masters. The historian has no right to conceal this distressing aspect of the most brilliant civilization known to the ancient world.

CHAPTER IV

INTELLECTUAL ACTIVITY AND WORKS OF ART

(1) PHILOSOPHY AND SCIENCE

Intensity of the Philosophical Movement in the Fifth Century.—In this society of the fifth century intellectual activity was very great. We have already seen to what extent the enigma of the world had interested the Ionian physiologers in the sixth century. Multiplying their efforts to explain the formation and life of the universe, they had brought together a number of observations which were the first elements of physics, astronomy, meteorology, and biology; and at the same time they had inaugurated the science of geography and perfected the fundamental notions of mathematics. The fifth century developed the scientific work of the sixth century in all its forms, and it also prepared the ground for that of the fourth century, the renown of which very nearly obscures its own. In the field of science it is natural that those who come last surpass their predecessors; but if one measures genius less by complex results, in which it is not easy to discern the part attributable to each individual, than by creative power, it would seem that the great thinkers of the fifth century, Parmenides, Heraclitus, Empedocles, Anaxagoras, and Socrates, were not inferior to a Plato or an Aristotle.

Parmenides and Zeno.—The Ionians, trusting in the
123

evidence of the senses, had not sought to rise above the
data with which these senses provided them. None of
them questioned themselves regarding the fundamental
conception of existence. It fell to the honor of Parmenides
of Elea to discover the importance of this problem, already perceived but not thoroly investigated by Xenophanes, his immediate predecessor and possibly his
teacher. Without inquiring whether it did not transcend
the scope of human intelligence, he applied himself to the
problem fervently and derived from it the elements of a
metaphysics deeply impressed by the great acuteness of
his mind. The Ionian hypothesis led to the admission,
for the purpose of explaining the transformations of
matter, that the latter could be divided into extremely
small particles, escaping by their very minuteness our
imperfect senses. But reason refuses to conceive either
a cubic or a linear measure, which can not, theoretically,
be divided in two. Infinite divisibility seems to be, therefore, the necessary consequence of this conception. But
what became of the idea of continuity then? For if the
particles are distinct, there must be a separation between
them; and in order that they may move about, this separation must be a vacuum. But without continuity, how is
it possible to understand the mutual actions and reac-
tions of these particles? Moreover, this reasoning applies to motion as well as to matter. By resolving motion into infinity we destroy its very essence. It was
in the name of logic, therefore, that Parmenides was led
to deny the existence of a vacuum, that of the divisibility
of matter, and finally that of motion. Reducing these
conceptions to illusions of the senses, he affirms that inherent unity of being which is indivisible and immovable
—except that subsequently he explains the sensible illusions and coördinates them as conceptions of the imagina-

tion. The very boldness of this idealistic protest against a reality which he declared to consist merely of appearances, was destined to arouse in its author a dogmatic ardor which was clearly manifested in his teachings. He set forth his system in a poem of which several fragments have been preserved—a mixture of magnificent visions and obscure abstractions, in which there is revealed a superior personality struggling both with the material difficulties of a language still intolerant of demonstrations of this kind and with the incredulity which common sense opposed to his uncompromising idealism.

Parmenides undoubtedly wrote in the first years of the fifth century. Zeno, his pupil, made himself even during the lifetime of his teacher, and after him, the propagator of his doctrine. But less anxious to develop it than to defend it, he seems to have applied himself especially to refuting, by means of subtle dialectic, the ideas opposed to it. The arguments which he presented against infinite divisibility and motion have remained celebrated. Again in Plato and Aristotle we find evidence of the astonishment which these arguments aroused in Athens when Zeno had gone there to seek a curious audience. We can not doubt that they created a taste for discussion the influence of which soon made itself felt in all cultivated circles.

Heraclitus.—Nevertheless, at that same time the Ionian doctrine found an illustrious continuator in the person of Heraclitus of Ephesus. Persisting, like his predecessors, in the conception of a primary substance subject to a series of transformations, he had been led to believe that this substance was fire, which he considered the most subtile and the most changing element. The greatest innovation in his system, and that which gave it a particular beauty, was the eternal rhythm which he made the

law of these transformations. In admirably vigorous and
concise prose, in sententious phrases the very obscurity of
which conferred a sort of majesty upon them, he told
how fire was transformed into air, air into water, and
water into earth, and simultaneously, by an inverse process, how earth was changed to water, water to air, and
air to fire—a perpetual oscillation, an indefinite succession of apparent deaths which were in fact so many births,
coördinated movements "upwards" and "downwards,"
from which resulted a universal harmony composed of
equivalences and compensations. One readily understands
that such a thinker, to some extent dazzled by his own
vision, acquired the reputation, by his oracular style, of
being an interpreter of a wisdom inaccessible to the
masses.

Empedocles and Anaxagoras.—Nevertheless, neither of
these two world systems, the one founded upon reason,
pure and simple, and the other upon a brilliant hypothesis,
could satisfy free minds which were rendered acute for
criticism. Deprived of practical means of experimenta-
tion, they sought to make up for it by ingenious probabili-
ties; and yet in this effort their thought, altho boldly
disengaging itself from the ancient mythology, always
took, by the force of habit, a more or less mythical turn.
So it happened that almost at the same time a Sicilian,
Empedocles of Agrigentum, and an Ionian, Anaxagoras
of Clazomenæ, renouncing, like Parmenides, the conception of a substance susceptible of indefinite transformations, nevertheless attempted, like Heraclitus, to ascribe
to the life of the universe an immanent order which took
account both of its variations and of its regularity.
Both thought that its principle was to be found in a
rotatory movement, the action of which they defined with
the help of various combinations. Empedocles distin-

guished four elements—water, earth, air, and fire—which were no longer for him, as they were for the Ionians, successive and temporary forms of a primary substance. Rather did he conceive them as eternally separate and distinct substances; and his poet's imagination saw them coming together or drawing apart, one after another, under the influence of two other elements of a mythological nature, hatred and love. From this, thru the various phases which he described in verses now brilliant and now painfully didactic, resulted an endless cycle of integrations and disintegrations. In this grandiose and complex work, as in the broad intelligence of its author, all the sciences of the time, even medicine, found their place, as did also a number of superstitions borrowed from Pythagorean or Orphic mysticism. Following a different course, Anaxagoras, possessed of a more positive genius, conceived matter as a sort of dust formed of all the irreducible substances which enter into the composition of bodies; and he taught that the principle which set them apart by a rotatory movement was an element radically distinct from all the rest, the only one which was never mixed with the others. This element he called Reason (Nous), meaning thereby, no doubt, a sort of impersonal intelligence, an obscure force, the nature of which he does not seem to have defined exactly, possibly owing to the fact that he himself did not have a very clear idea of it. So much is certain, at least, that he represented it as a creator of order and organization. Himself learned and possessed of a passion for observation, he reviewed, in a work written in Ionian prose, the principal phenomena of nature, making it a point to interpret them rationally and boldly discarding all the mythological explanations which were still current around him.

    The Atomists. Leucippus and Democritus.—In opposition to this conception of a guiding principle there developed the conception of Chance, represented by the Ionians, Leucippus and Democritus of Abdera. For them the genesis of the world became a purely fortuitous thing. They imagined infinitely tenuous, indivisible particles meeting in empty space, and called these particles atoms. All identical in nature, these atoms differed, according to them, only in volume, weight, and form. Carried along in incessant motion, it was necessary, in order that the hypothesis might be conceivable, for the atoms to collide with one another, to aggregate, and thus to enter into multiple combinations, whence resulted all the bodies existing in nature. Considered by itself, this system, while professing to explain the enigma of the world, manifestly did little more than propose a new hypothesis no less enigmatical. But in revealing under the infinite diversity of effects the possible simplicity of the causes and the means, and especially in rejecting everything that still savored of mythology in science, it turned men's minds in the right direction. Democritus, moreover, did not adhere any more than Anaxagoras and Empedocles to a synthetic theory; like them, he applied himself to diligent observation of the facts, eagerly desirous of relating them all to his doctrine.

The Sceptics.—In the presence of these divergent attempts, none of which led to decisive proof, it was inevitable that scepticism should gain entrance into a certain number of minds. In some instances we see it appear in a modified form of relativity. Such was the case with the celebrated Protagoras of Abdera, who taught that absolute truth does not exist, meaning thereby, no doubt, that every assertion is dependent upon the nature of the human mind in general, and further upon the scope of each intelligence in particular. In other cases this

scepticism went much further, if we are to believe the
evidences of it in the Sicilian, Gorgias, according to which
it would seem that the latter taught absolute and systematic doubt.   It is confirmed, therefore, that the discussions of the philosophers did not take place without in-
jecting some trouble into the world of the intellectuals.
On the whole, however, it was a trouble which had prolific
results; for these conflicts of ideas vivified in a singular
manner the activity of the mind and even led men frequently to resort to first-hand observation.   The incontestable fact is that these efforts of philosophy were
accompanied by a general progress of the sciences.

Hippocrates.—Medicine, in particular, was distinguished at that time by a man of the first order, Hippocrates of Cos.   Altho it is difficult today to determine
with accuracy what is properly attributable to him in
the collection of writings which bear his name, the importance of his rôle is none the less indisputable.   On
the one hand, all the evidences of antiquity agree in award-
ing to him the title of "the father of medicine"; and on
the other hand, the majority of the writings referred to
are in any case imbued with his spirit.   We owe it to him
that medicine ceased to be a simple traditional practice, a
rather confused mixture of sane experience and superstitions, and began to follow resolutely the course of observation and to enlarge the domain thereof.   To define and
classify the forms of disease, to relate them to various
temperaments, to study closely their phases, to note
scrupulously the peculiar effect of each remedy and the
slower effect of a prescribed regimen, to discern the influence of waters, of air, of temperature, of climate—
such, in a broad way, was his work.   All told, it was the
organization of a method; and from this method resulted
all the subsequent progress.

(2) THE SOPHISTS.   RHETORIC AND DIALECTIC

Rhetoric.—Alongside of scientific philosophy, and to a certain extent under its influence, there were developed at the same time two branches which aimed at more practical results; these were rhetoric and dialectic.

By instinct the Greek was a talker, an orator, and a dialectician. The *Iliad* and the *Odyssey* bear witness to the fact that a certain art of composing a speech, and consequently of reasoning, existed as far back as the time of Homer. In the following centuries political eloquence gained considerably in experience. To be sure, it was not lacking in the statesmen of the seventh and sixth centuries, any more than it failed the men who directed the Athenian democracy at the time of the Persian Wars; only at that time nobody was yet prudent enough to formulate its rules in writing or to make it the object of regular teaching. It was toward the middle of the fifth century that some Sicilians got the idea of codifying the rules, especially for the use of pleaders. In the first treatises edited by the practicians, a Corax and a Tisias, rhetoric is presented as the art of winning a case in court, good or bad; and it consisted of a body of practical precepts and examples by means of which the student learned how to lend plausibility to any advantageous argument, whether it was true or false. There was something about it that greatly attracted people. Then came another Sicilian, the same Gorgias to whom reference has just been made, a man of an entirely different type of mind, a philosopher as well as a practician, who appropriated their idea and made its fortune. Not only did he perfect their process of argumentation to a remarkable degree by virtue of his great discernment, but at the same time by freeing rhetoric he showed it capable of embellishing all the forms of public speaking. His ambition was to create an oratorical style equivalent in prose to that of the poets, with its appropriate ornaments, its rhythm, and its effects of skillfully handled words. The examples which he gave of such a style called forth an admiration which was not due to mere infatuation; for altho his manner, in its extreme form, led to a rather puerile verbal mechanism, one can not deny that it was of a nature calculated to provoke in strong and sane minds a concise analysis of ideas, which made it possible to clarify such ideas and to render them effective, either by weighing them off against one another or by relating them by means of ingenious parallelisms.

Dialectic.—This rapid development of rhetoric naturally called forth a corresponding development of dialectic, to which the Greeks were not less inclined. The above-mentioned arrival in Athens of Zeno of Elea seems to have been an event of epoch-making importance in this regard. His method was no less calculated to fascinate the Athenian youth than was the paradoxical novelty of what he said. It was a rapid, condensed, entirely logical argumentation, which addressed itself only to reason, and which in a few words confounded his adversaries. It amused the Athenians greatly to see his opponents entangled in his quibbles, and many could not resist the temptation to imitate him. He interested them all the more in that he touched upon essential ideas, the very principles of knowledge, with the result that the most legitimate curiosity, the search for fundamental truths, was awakened in those who listened to him, as well as a taste for this sort of word-parrying—lively, brilliant, paradoxical, and well adapted to the natural subtlety of the race. All that young Athens needed in order to enter resolutely upon this new course was a number of teachers imbued with the same spirit. The occasion was good; they came to the city from all sides.

The Sophists.—The young people of the upper classes, desirous of taking part in the public life or simply of enlarging their intellectual horizon, until that time had had too many things to learn by themselves. Hence they now welcomed those who offered to teach them. Thus it came about that the term "sophist," previously applied to anybody who possessed a rare and special knowledge, was thereafter applied to persons who made it a business to communicate their learning to others for pay.

Among these sophists of the new kind, some were philosophers, others, in greater numbers, were teachers of rhetoric, others in still greater numbers were grammarians and philologists, some were mathematicians and technologists—to say nothing of those who pretended to universal knowledge. In this group were men of attainment, such as Protagoras of Abdera, Gorgias of Leontini, and Prodicus of Ceos, to mention only the most celebrated; and there were also some charlatans. These sophists were forced by their very profession to lead a nomadic life. Athens, the center of the intellectual movement, no doubt attracted and held them more than any other city; none of them, however, seems to have been permanently established there. They found it to their advantage not to allow the curiosity of their public to grow dull. Generally they condensed in a few lessons, for a definite price, what they proposed to teach; and they announced, or allowed people to believe, that these reduced courses were sufficient to make educated men of their hearers. Therein lay the greatest defect of their profession. Learning became a sort of commodity which could be sold by the piece at a fixed price. Such instruc-

tion, distributed and received at random, could be neither
very serious nor very profound.   And yet, these brilliant
lecturers, full of new views and suggestions, propagated
ideas and knowledge which otherwise would have remained
the share of only a few men.   A certain amount of philosophy, political theory, ethics, and various sciences,
was thus spread abroad, at first in the upper classes, but
afterwards in the general public.

State of Mind in the Second Half of the Fifth Century.
—As one may surmise, this influx of new ideas did not fail
to produce a certain confusion in men's minds.   Many
intelligent men in the second half of the century did not
know just where they stood in matters of religion or
even of morality.   The Greek mind had need of examining itself, of eliminating many antiquated things, of laying aside also, at least temporarily, certain investigations
for which it was not yet ripe; and also, on the other
hand, of finding certain solid truths and elaborating a
method for their development.   This was a task as difficult as it was necessary, since it called for an intelligence
sufficiently pliant and acute to penetrate all questions,
and at the same time sufficiently firm to avoid losing itself in them.   These rare qualities were combined in
Socrates.

(3) SOCRATES

The Man.   His Vocation.—He was, however, a man
of only very modest condition; but his natural genius, his
desire for knowledge, and his ardent love of what is true
and good, made up for everything else which he could
possibly lack.   Early abandoning every personal occupa-
tion, and satisfied in his poverty, he thought he heard an
inner voice confirming the vocation which led him to seek

the meaning and the purpose of life, in order to guide
his own conduct and that of others.   Hence this vocation
appeared to him as the order of a divine will.   But far
from deriving any sense of pride from that, he proposed
less to teach than to learn; for he wished to instruct
others only by instructing himself.   There is no doubt
that he had read much, listened much, and also meditated
much; and sometimes it seemed as if he were lost in his
reflections.   But it was especially by causing those who
knew, or who had the reputation of knowing, to express
their thoughts, that he exercised his mental powers.
Endowed with a most critical mind, he was never deceived
by appearances.   Very quick, he perceived how much
illusion there was in the desires of the majority of men,
and in the calculations which led them to act; and on the
other hand, lending ear to those who gave themselves out
as teachers and guides, he became aware of the inaccuracy
of their ideas.   From this he concluded that ignorance of
oneself was the most common evil, and that the necessary
condition of good conduct, as also of happiness, was to
know oneself well.

His Method.—Possessed by this idea, he created for
himself a method which became one of the most precious
acquisitions of the human mind.   It consisted fundamentally of a patient search for truths, which too often
escape the sluggish mind deceived by vain words—a search
which he conducted by means of analysis, comparison, and
induction.   The form he gave it was so simple that at
first it concealed its own profundity.   No oratorical ex-
positions after the manner of the sophists were involved;
he thought that a man who merely speaks always has a
chance of erring and of being only imperfectly understood.   In place of the continuous speech, accordingly,
he substituted a logical series of precise questions—a

slow but sure course whereby one never advanced a single step before reaching an agreement on the preceding idea, which had first to be made perfectly clear. In reality, the questioner, who was Socrates himself, as a rule could scarcely have failed to form an opinion in advance, at least provisionally, regarding the subject under discussion; but far from affirming this opinion from the very outset and upholding it at all costs afterwards, he subjected it faithfully to a control which he endeavored to make as rigorous as possible. Altogether, he felt satisfied only if his questions led his interlocutor to declare as his personal conviction the idea under discussion. It seemed then that the latter had discovered it of his own accord in the recesses of his mind, where until then it had remained latent. That is why Socrates jestingly called his method *maieutic*, that is to say, the obstetrical means of bringing forth ideas from men's minds.

Plato and Xenophon show us in their Socratic dialogs how he practiced his method every day and everywhere. From the early morning he could be seen walking up and down the public square. He deemed every occasion good to stop people and engage them in conversation. It mattered little what their social condition or their age was; artisans, merchants, politicians, sophists, young people, and full-grown men—all had to stop to be thus questioned by this indefatigable inquirer. Nor was it easy to escape him; for his lively humor, his insinuating and insidious grace, the charming irony with which he avowed his ignorance and demanded instruction, rendered flight almost impossible. Everybody in Athens knew him; and every day his influence increased. Without being a schoolmaster, without professing anything whatsoever, little by little he gathered followers around him, especially young people interested in dialectic; and the latter became his pupils without being formally known as such.

His Essential Ideas.—This method quite often led those who practiced it, and Socrates himself first of all, either to a feeling of doubt or to an avowal of ignorance. By no means, however, did he acquiesce in scepticism. On the contrary, from his conversations there emerges a doctrine which may still be defined, even today, by its essential features.

It was founded upon a new conception of philosophy. Cicero ingeniously characterized it by saying that Socrates "brought philosophy down from heaven to earth." Rejecting all speculation regarding the origin of things, regarding motion, regarding the nature of existence, which perhaps disturbed his religious instinct and in any case seemed to him too ambitious for human intelligence, he established the principle that the proper task of philosophy was the study of man and his immediate interests. If this attitude had ultimately prevailed, it would have had the grave consequence of arresting the development of the physical and natural sciences. But its immediate effect was fortunate for the reason that it resulted in concentrating the efforts of a few powerful minds on questions of prime importance— questions which the ill regulated activity of the sophists had scarcely more than superficially touched upon.

How did Socrates conceive this study of man? For him the object of all human existence was happiness; so that the science of happiness seemed to him the essential object of life. But he firmly believed that no happiness was possible outside of virtue, and that virtue, on the other hand, almost sufficed in itself to procure happiness. According to him, what prevented the majority of men from making themselves happy by means of virtue was their illusions and their prejudices. He was convinced that, if they once saw to what extent moral goodness is profitable, they would practice goodness quite naturally. All his efforts, therefore, tended to clarify these fundamental notions by showing the precise nature of each of the virtues, such as wisdom, temperance, courage, justice, candor, loyalty, disinterestedness, devoted friendship, and abnegation, and by discovering in each of them this same character of social and personal utility. On the other hand, he pointed out how much illusion and ignorance there was in the opposite vices and defects, especially in ambition and in the desire for wealth. Contrary to the traditional morality of the time, he even went so far as to deny that it was ever permissible to render evil for evil. In fact, thanks to the nobility of his character, some of the most splendid of modern Christian ideals emerged from the depths of Greek civilization.

And it was also a new religion, perhaps without his wishing it to be so and without his being very clearly conscious of it. The earlier philosophy, in revealing in the life of the universe the play of great natural forces, had in fact destroyed the entire structure of the traditional mythology; but by its very nature it was almost inaccessible to the majority of minds. It was properly a philosophy of scholars. On the other hand, it offered nothing to religious minds to take the place of what it had destroyed. Socrates, however, while rejecting the coarser elements of the mythology, remained loyal to the traditional cult and to certain fundamental parts of the common belief. If he admitted neither the conflicts nor the passions of the gods, nor anything at all that degraded them, he did not suffer anybody to doubt their intervention in human affairs. He believed in their justice, in their goodness, and in their perfection, as firmly as he believed in their power. Thus without break-

ing with polytheism, he manifestly tended toward a sort
of monotheism.   His philosophy therefore contains the
essential elements of a religion closely bound up with
morality and consequently of a nature calculated to satisfy minds which could not do without the supernatural.
Inevitably destined to become more distinct and to undergo further development with his successors, it heralded
the end of one of the great epochs of human thought.

(4) THE GREAT POETS OF THE FIFTH CENTURY

Reaction of Philosophy.—This profound intellectual
activity naturally had a more or less appreciable reaction
upon the majority of the contemporaries.   It is interesting to trace the evidence of this in the works of the most
important of them, especially in those of the most illustrious poets of the period, which was so rich in poetry.
But that would be to detract somewhat from the credit
due them; for these great minds were not merely echoes.
Each of them, indeed, was a philosopher in his way by
virtue of having his own conception of humanity and of
life; and this personal philosophy is no less worthy of
attention.

Pindar.—Among them the Theban, Pindar, is probably
the one who by education, environment, and traditions of
the kind to which he owed his glory, remained most foreign
to philosophical speculations properly so called.   The
basis of his ideas still belongs to the sixth century; his
moral sentiment is very nearly that of Solon, Theognis,
and the sages.   Nevertheless, he is distinguished from
them, not only by the brilliance with which his lyric
genius embellished his thoughts, but also by a loftiness and
a profundity which denote a more extensive and more
penetrating reflection.   Whether he is correcting the

legends in order to adapt them to a saner morality, whether he is representing the divine power by images which enlarge it magnificently, or whether again he is reminding the princes, in celebrating their victories, of the laws of human destiny, we feel in listening to him that he sees things from a higher plane and that he thinks more forcibly. The intellectual heir of an earlier age, he, too, nevertheless partook largely of the inspirations which at that time permeated the entire Greek world.

Æschylus.—The same influence is much more perceptible in the Athenian Æschylus, his contemporary. If the latter is with good reason looked upon as the creator of the Greek tragedy, it is perhaps due not so much to the material improvements for which the theater was indebted to him or to the more discerning structure of his plays, as it is to the moral value which he was able to give to his dramatic action. In each of the pathetic situations with which the legends provided him, his strong meditative mind perceived a question propounded to the human conscience. Consequently, the conflicts among the gods, like the play of passions which filled the souls of the heroic characters, were for him merely poetic motives calculated to excite pity, admiration, or fear. Each of his tragedies contains a moral problem. Accepting the old beliefs as to the jealousy of the gods, the ineluctible power of fate, the hereditary transmission of ancient maledictions, and the collective responsibility of generations, he delighted in showing the human will in some manner following a sorrowful course thru the midst of these mysterious forces, which dominated it without smothering it. And it was truly a philosophy which he thus developed—a philosophy without any precise doctrine, raising more questions than it was able to answer, and yet directed in a general way toward the idea that wrong-doing calls inevtiably for punishment, and toward the condemnation of pride and of violence.

Sophocles.—Sophocles, who, after Æschylus exerted a not less profound influence upon the Athenian soul, was inspired by the same general ideas. But those mysterious forces which he, like his predecessor, recognized, seemed in his dramas to fall into the background; altho always present, they were more concealed. Moreover, the sentiments of his personages and their characters were unfurled, so to speak, more freely. On the one hand, it seemed as if they had fallen under the influence of the dialectic of the time, for they resorted more to the processes of reason, either to justify their resolutions or to combat or disprove arguments opposed to them. This reasoning was always in conformity with their character and their passions, but it was vigorous, well conducted, substantial and skillful. On the other hand, an entirely new psychological variety manifested itself in these plays. A delicate and forceful art opposed the characters to one another, finding in these contrasts the means of illumining them more vividly and of turning them to better account. At times the poet did not hesitate to reveal, even among the most heroic of them, signs of human weakness—regret, hesitation, or the awakening of precious memories in hours of distress. Going still further in his *Oedipus Rex*, he drew a picture of one and the same man, first at the height of his power, venerated as a god by an entire people, and himself full of confidence in his fortune and in his genius; then, after the most soul-stirring vicissitudes, suddenly beaten down, fallen to the lowest depth of misery, humiliated by the abhorrence of others and by the sense of his own degradation. The truth is that the rich and supple imagination of Æschylus lent itself well to the understanding and expression of everything human. Nothing escaped his faculty of dramatic creation, neither violent passions, nor the mildest sentiments, such as kindness, grace, filial love, devotion, and delicacy. We may say that he was one of the most complete representatives of Attic civilization at a time when the latter concentrated in itself, so to speak, the best of Greek civilization.

Euripides.—At his side shone his rival, Euripides, who was a few years younger, and whose work, by its profound differences, reveals so vividly the evolutionary forces which were then operating in men's minds. Whereas in Sophocles the influence of philosophy was scarcely more than formal, in Euripides it had penetrated to the very depths of his soul and had created there an inner duality. He was at once a thinker and a poet, and his two natures sometimes had difficulty in agreeing with each other. There is no doubt that this state of mind was common to a certain number of his contemporaries; but what in them remained obscure, came clearly to the surface in his dramas. As a poet Euripides, like Æschylus and Sophocles, accepts the ancient legends and everything of the supernatural contained in them; and not only does he accept them, but he makes use of them with all the powers of his genius. Better than anybody else he utilizes in them the elements of pity and fear with which they were filled, and he makes out of them the most deeply moving tragedies that have ever been produced. Moreover, he renders them all the more touching in that he consciously reduces the heroes and heroines to the stature of plain mortals. It was truly the humanity of his time that he presented to the view of the Athenian people; and when the latter, after some resistance, became accustomed to this new manner, it is easy to understand that they became passionately attached to it, that they even preferred it to any other manner, since they found in these plays a picture, as it were, of the life which they knew by experience. Behind these creations of a marvelous imagination and sensibility, however, we are conscious of the unfailing presence of the thinker. He observes life as a moralist, weaving into the dialog his personal reflections, now subtle and bantering, now grave and slightly saddened, always rather strangely placed in the mouth of one or another character who seems temporarily to forget his rôle. And he observes it also as a sceptic, emphasizing at pleasure the improbability of certain traditions, protesting against the immorality of others, making it clear that he refuses to take account of them. From this results a composite work, equal in its qualities to the most beautiful works of its kind, nevertheless disconcerting in places, of a nature calculated to excite contemporary thought to the utmost, and revealing most clearly to us today the diverse tendencies that gave it birth.

Aristophanes.—Almost as much may be said of the comedy of the time, already defined, and of its principal representative, Aristophanes. In his case, too, behind the charming poet and the clown, there is the thinker, capricious and fantastic, to be sure, but also clear-sighted and arch, one whose ingenious and fair-minded views are mixed with prejudices. His mind is full of contrasts and contradictions; he is a defender of the religion which makes light of the gods; and he is an enemy of innovations but himself an innovator. Altho fond of the language of Euripides, and prone to imitate him, he also criticises him. No doubt entirely capable of appreciating the dialectic of Socrates, he caricatures him nevertheless. Nowhere is there revealed more clearly than in his work the mobility of the Athenian mind, accessible to all influences, never unfolding itself without reserve, employ-

ing its natural pliancy to conciliate all things that were
at odds, and adapting itself well enough, after all, to a
diversity of opinions which amused it but at the same
time did not profoundly disturb it.

(5) THE HISTORIANS

Herodotus.—At the same time that the intellectual and
moral experience acquired in the fifth century was thus
brilliantly manifesting itself in poetry, it was also providing history with the means of producing works of high
value. Until then, historical writing had still been in
its infancy. In groping about it fell back upon the
genealogies and local chronicles, in which the most prominent place was given to mythology and to the mythical
families with their store of legends. Geography, its
auxiliary, does not seem, on its part, to have progressed
very much since the time of Hecatæus and Anaximander.
But a new curiosity was awakened by the effect of the
Persian Wars. At that time the Greeks as a people had
had an alluring, altho confused, vision of everything contained in the depths of the vast Orient, until then very
little known. They could only accept with favor anything which would serve to reveal more of it.

An Asiatic Greek, Herodotus of Halicarnassus, undertook this task and succeeded very well with it. An indefatigable traveler, whose desire to see and to know led
him successively to Egypt, to Asia, to almost all parts of
Greece, to Sicily, and to Italy, where he finally settled
down and probably died, he succeeded in carrying out
a most profitable inquiry—questioning men, visiting
monuments, informing himself about everything, about
customs, laws, forms of government, and religions, without preconceived ideas or prejudices, but with a singular

mixture of acuteness and credulity, of insatiable curiosity
and religious discretion. And from everything which he
had seen, read, and heard, he produced by the power of
his genius, by his keen sense for beautiful things, by his
talent as a story-teller, and by the charm of his style, a
truly admirable work. In an immense frame, as in a sort
of moving panorama, he gave his readers a picture of the
life of twenty different peoples. How much instruction
was offered in this encyclopedic collection, wherein the
variety of human types, the multiplicity of religions, and
the history of diverse institutions, were so interestingly
set forth! Scarcely did the contemporary tragedy itself
present so rich a collection of human documents.

Moreover, by virtue of their national interest and their
pathetic episodes, these bounteous narratives, which dealt
chiefly with the Persian Wars, constituted also a veritable
drama, one of the dramas, indeed, which was destined to
stir most deeply the sons of the victors at Marathon and
at Salamis. A religious idea dominated it, identical with
that which inspired both Æschylus and Sophocles. Like
them, Herodotus believed in a jealous divinity always
ready to repress excessive pride or ambition, and always
quick to cast down any one who was rising imprudently.
Neither with him nor with them, however, did this belief
tend to discourage useful activities. Having risen from
the need of explaining certain great catastrophes, it left
to politics all its importance, assigning to it merely the
duty of observing moderation in everything.

Thucydides.—Nevertheless, however beautiful this work
was, it did not give full satisfaction to the taste for moral
analysis and profound reflection, which at the end of the
fifth century was developing more and more in minds
which had been touched by philosophy. It was especially

for the latter that Thucydides wrote at that time his *History of the Peloponnesian War.*

A member of the Athenian aristocracy, a politician, and a general, he was able to combine with the most remarkable natural endowments, the advantages of an extensive education and experience in the things whereof he was to write. From his first teachers, among whom we should perhaps count the orator Antiphon, he derived his taste for a style which, abandoning the free and rather smooth phraseology characteristic of the Ionian prose writers, sought to condense ideas and to turn every part of them to account, even at the expense of ease, of grace, and sometimes of clarity, but always to the advantage of a scrupulous precision.

In order definitively to break the bonds which still attached history to epic poetry, it was necessary to eliminate the fabulous and legendary elements from the former altogether. This is what Thucydides did. Casting a backward glance, at the beginning of his narrative, at the development of Greek civilization, he does not hesitate to explain it rationally on the basis of still existing primitive customs in Greece. Thus vanished the fiction of the golden age. But Thucydides reveals even firmness of judgment as regards the supernatural element in setting forth contemporary events. Without denying the power of the gods, he says nothing of their intervention in human affairs, believing with reason that there was no profit either for the historian or for his readers in pondering over mysterious causes of which they could know nothing. What seemed to him useful to consider in events in general was not that which escapes human calculations, but, on the contrary, that which had been foreseen or might have been foreseen. For the proper field of history, according to him, was to make usual foresight possible in the future by taking advantage of past experiences.

This view naturally led him to the investigation of remote as well as immediate causes; and it was precisely in this way that he proceeded in explaining the rivalry of Sparta and Athens. As for the direct causes, for him these were not only the few incidents which had kindled the flames of war, but also the moral disposition of the two city-states, their conception of their respective rôles, and the consciousness which they had of their power. This same method we find in all the details of the narrative. Chance, which can never be entirely excluded from human affairs, was here reduced at least to a minimum. Never had a similar effort been made to explain rationally everything which can be thus explained.

Moreover, far from failing to recognize the personal influence of certain men, he endeavors to examine and analyze the character of each of them. Thus it is that he introduces such persons as his Pericles, his Nicias, his Alcibiades, and his Cleon—figures strongly characterized and no doubt carefully drawn from life. In order to set forth their designs, their anticipations, their avowed motives or their illusions, he attributes to them speeches imitated from those which they had actually delivered, but composed primarily with a view to making them known; and whenever he sees fit, he supplements them, always discreetly, by introducing some reflections of his own. Then, too, while detaching them from the crowd, he takes care not to isolate them from it. Knowing better than anybody else the power of opinion, he feels obliged to take account of all the movements perceptible to his readers. His history not only records the sentiments of the peoples in conflict, but it tells of their successes and their revenges as well.

We may add that this thinker was possessed of a strong and vivid imagination, skilled in representing moving realities by means of a few well-chosen touches. A considerable number of his narratives are admirable. The impression they give is all the more vivid in that it seems to rise from the facts themselves, to such an extent does the narrator conceal and efface himself. We detect no apparent effort to create effects, no obstrusive reflection. The things themselves are evoked before us; and we see in them precisely what it is necessary for us to see in order to be the most deeply moved by them.

Altogether, thanks to Thucydides, the historical curiosity which Herodotus excited and unquestionably developed by the immensity and variety of the picture which he placed before the eyes of his readers, became more intense, more concentrated, and more profound. The narration of ancient or recent events, formerly the subject of epic poetry, then brought closer to reality by geography, ethnography, observation of customs, and critical analysis of the sources, became properly a subject of science by allowing itself to become more and more penetrated by reflection. Thucydides heralded and prepared the way for Aristotle.

(6) ORATORY—PERICLES

What We Know of the Oratory of the Fifth Century.
—Along with history and philosophy, oratory was, in the fifth century, one of the most remarkable manifestations of the Greek genius. It is not, of course, to be confused with rhetoric, to which we have referred above; for

rhetoric is only a theoretical science of which oratory sometimes condescends to make use, but with which it can also dispense.   Unfortunately we know the orators of this time only from what others say about them.   They would have been afraid, in publishing their speeches, of being confused with the teachers of rhetoric.   For them a harangue was above all a mode of action.   If a few hearers had not noted down their impressions, we would now know of them nothing more than their names.

Pericles.—Under these conditions it will suffice to mention here the most illustrious of them—all the more so because he is the man who gave his name to the entire century, and because in a certain sense he summarizes it in his person.   No figure, as a matter of fact, is more representative of Athens in the fifth century than Pericles. Insofar as an ideal can be realized, he realized that of the people who had taken him as their leader.   There was in him a natural authority, which clung to his character as well as to his talent.   His eloquence was the reflection of both.   To the stateliness of his appearance and bearing corresponded the nobility of his mind. Reared with philosophy, the friend and patron of Anaxagoras, he had the gift of distinguishing general ideas, while at the same time the accuracy of his views did not suffer thereby.   There was nothing small or base either in his character or in his conceptions, nor yet any exaggeration.   A man of action and initiative, he could also calm the excessive ardor of the crowd—so we are told by Thucydides—and again he could encourage it in moments of weakness.   An instinct for greatness inspired his policy and made itself felt in his words; but this instinct seemed penetrated by a sense of moderation.   As a rule, his eloquence was earnest, simple, full of revealing light and of reason; an Attic grace was blended with a

charm which produced conviction. But sometimes the
intimate force of his powerful nature was also revealed;
and then of a sudden his arguments burst forth with a
wealth of overwhelming words which upset everything
and were comparable with claps of thunder. It seems
evident, accordingly, that his eloquence had a freedom of
manner and of movement which is not to be found in the
speeches, so strongly condensed, attributed to him by
Thucydides. And this leads us to believe that the
same may be said of the speeches of his rivals and
his successors, whatever might otherwise have been his
superiority to them.

We may add that this great orator had a sense of
beauty in the highest degree, as is evidenced by the rôle
he played in promoting the artistic movement among his
fellow-citizens. To speak of the artists, of whom he was
at once the patron and the most enlightened admirer, is
in a sense equivalent to continuing to speak of him.

(7) THE ARTS IN THE FIFTH CENTURY

General Character of Art of the Fifth Century.—It
was at this time, as a matter of fact, that Greek art
reached its apogee. Greece, the creator of science,
liberty, and humanity, revealed itself at the same time
as the creator of beauty; and in all the formative arts
it produced masterpieces which have never been surpassed.
The sixth century, as we have seen, had little by little
perfected technic, without which the most gifted artist
is powerless. After the progress mentioned above, in
architecture, in sculpture, and even in painting, the masters of the fifth century had nothing more to learn as
regards anything pertaining to the routine of their
profession. Thereafter the hand was docilely obedient

to the mind. The latter, freed from material difficulties and restrictions and mistress of its means, could give itself over wholly to inspiration. To this end, however, it did not feel authorized to despise reality. Like the great dramatic poets of the same time, the artists adhered to the imitation of nature, the rich and living diversity of which they succeeded in interpreting as well as did the poets, and with quite as much idealization as the latter. In general they were less interested in that which was purely individual, the curious detail and the particular trait, than they were in that which was typical. This accounts in some measure for the nobilty, the grandeur, and the simplicity with which their works are replete.

Circumstances, moreover, favored this development and this tendency. The Persian Wars had given Greece a sense of its own moral force and the firmest confidence in its future. Full of grateful recognition toward its gods which had saved it, it set about to restore their destroyed sanctuaries and to build new ones. Its heart was set on embellishing them with all the means at its disposal. The art of the sculptors and painters, of decorators of all kinds, was invited to coöperate with that of the architects. And besides the temples, public buildings, among them, the prytanea, porticos, and gymnasia became more numerous, as well as works of public utility, such as ports, arsenals, magazines, roads and bridges, to say nothing of private residences. The great city-states and the princes rivaled one another. Athens and Corinth, Syracuse and Tarentum, Elis and Delphi, Delos and the cities of Ionia, gloried in the works which they commanded of the best known artists. A general emulation was expressed in rich offerings, statues, and dedicatory monuments. And almost everywhere it was collective sentiments which the artists were called upon to express in figured representations.

Architecture.—What Greece accomplished at that time in the domain of architecture is truly admirable. The Greek temple is indeed one of the products of the human genius which comes closest to perfection; and the Parthenon at Athens may be looked upon as its highest development. It was between 450 and 430 B. C., under the auspices of Pericles, that this marvelous edifice was erected upon the isolated rock of the Acropolis, the joint work of the architect Ictinus, who drew the plans for it, and of the sculptor Phidias, who not only adorned it with his masterpieces, but also directed the work on it and supervised the execution of it in all its parts. Never, perhaps, has a monument better expressed the soul of a people and its conception of beauty. Large enough on its rocky eminence to dominate the city, there was yet nothing colossal about it. It was especially by the harmony of its proportions and by the fine and delicate grace of its lines, that it was distinguished from the very beginning. Slightly elevated on its base, exposing to view its peristyle of Doric columns with their robust and charming curvature, and proudly supporting its archi-trave, which crowned it without seeming to weigh it down —it appeared from a distance as the most suitable abode for a goddess in whom strength was combined with reason. Viewed from close by, it satisfied the most critical scrutiny by the beauty of its materials, the finish of its workman-ship, and the discreet blending of colors which enhanced the effect of its general design. Moreover, it fascinated the visitor by its admirably sculptured pediments, by the reliefs on the frieze which encircled it, as also by those on the metopes placed at intervals between the triglyphs

of the architrave.　There, in effect, were unfolded divine
or human scenes in logical groups, in forms full of life,
grace, and majesty—national legends of which Athens
was proud, allegories which recalled the city's own exploits, idealized representations of its most beautiful
religious ceremonies.　Thus the temple, in a sense, spoke;
it expressed a thought, a devotion, a group of sentiments,
at the same time manifesting the most properly Hellenic
conception of art.

This type, moreover, was on occasion skillfully modified
by the architecture of the fifth century, depending upon
circumstances.　On the same Acropolis, the Erectheum,
so different from the Parthenon, the Propylæum, the
small Temple of the Winged Victory, and, elsewhere, the
Temple of Zeus at Olympia, and the Telesterion at
Eleusis, show sufficiently with what subtile inventive
power it varied its plans, and diversified its means and
effects, in order to adapt itself either to the conditions
of the surrounding country or to the particular purpose
of the edifice.　Certainly it lacked neither freedom nor a
certain suggestion of fantasy.　What one never finds in
its work is a suggestion of disorder or bad taste.

Sculpture.—As in the case of architecture, so also in
the case of sculpture, the mechanical progress made in the
sixth century led, from the beginning of the fifth century
on, to a mastery which reached its climax thirty or forty
years later.　It manifests itself by an exact determination of proportions, an increasingly certain knowledge of
anatomy, a greater perfection of form, a proper sense of
movement, and, in more restricted measure, by the study
of the human physiognomy, altho in this respect, too,
the art of the time was concerned more with what was
typical than with individual details.

A certain antiquated manner is still found in the first

period, in the work of Calamis and Myron, and in the case
of the unknown creators of the pediments of the temple
at Ægina and the sculptures of the Temple of Zeus at
Olympia, remarkable as these last works already are.
It disappeared with Polyclitus of Argos, this industrious
creator of admirable statues of young athletes, in which
is revealed the full beauty of the human body harmoniously developed. In the second half of the century
Phidias, Alcamenes, and Pæonius produced incomparable
masterpieces. Under the chisel of these masters the
subject almost seems to become spiritualized. These are
no longer merely perfect forms which they produce out
of marble; they are truly gods, whose majesty is expressed in the dignity of their postures and in the nobility
of their features. Admirable draperies envelop them;
and sometimes, in order to heighten their beauty, the
artist combines with the whiteness of the marble the luster
of gold and the polish of ivory. Skillful, when necessary,
in expressing motion, the sculptors of this time used it
only with discretion, satisfied merely to suggest it in the
calm poses which they liked to represent. Works which
today have disappeared, such as Phidias' statue of
Zeus at Olympia, his Athena in the Parthenon at Athens,
and the Aphrodite of Alcamenes, called forth in antiquity
a unanimous and lasting admiration. We still feel this
admiration in the presence of the mutilated marble pillars
of the Parthenon.

To the impression produced by each of the figures considered alone is added that which is produced by them as
a whole. The principle of balance and symmetry, which
Greek art had sought from its very beginnings, is realized
there in its perfection. It is a symmetry without stiffness or monotony, which seems to result spontaneously
from the subject represented, and which is skillfully con-

cealed under the great wealth of inventions; it is a symmetry which is not intended solely to please the eye, but
which speaks to the mind, by making itself the ally of
allegory, by giving a clearer significance to the scenes
represented. If art is an adaptation of reality to reason
and to sentiment, it would seem that it has never produced
anything which conforms better to its definition.

Painting.—Whereas a certain number of the most beautiful sculptures of the fifth century are preserved for our
admiration, the ancient paintings have long since disappeared. Hence we are compelled to rely upon descriptions
in representing them to ourselves. It is true that a few
painted stelæ and an abundant series of figured vases
add a precious contribution to this indirect information,
but in spite of everything they give us only an imperfect
idea of the pictures executed by the great artists of that
time. Accordingly, we can say of them here only a few
words.

Alongside of the great sculptors of the fifth century,
we see a succession of painters whom antiquity ranked
with the great artists. The leaders among them were
Polygnotus, Micon, Apollodorus, Zeuxis, and Parrhasius.
All the testimonies indicate that the work of these masters
attained a rare perfection. It was impossible, moreover,
that it should have been otherwise, when the contemporary
sculptors showed themselves so skillful in reproducing
form and movement. These great painters, therefore,
were likewise creators of life and beauty, and they also
contributed to the development of the æsthetic sense of
their day. It even seems that, by reason of the means
peculiar to their art, they had carried further than the
sculptors the interpretation of human emotions in representing the moving play of the features, as also of the

poses and gestures. Like the sculptors, nevertheless, while laying hold of the infinitely varied aspects of life, they knew at the same time how to disengage from it, and to make prominent, those traits most worthy of attention. From what we are told of their work we can not doubt that they obeyed the same principles in everything; they, too, associated symmetry and balance with variety, and realized movement without exaggeration or confusion.

The Industrial Arts.—At any rate we can judge the influence which the fine arts exerted in the fifth century upon the industrial arts. Our museums have collected quantities of painted vases, miniature figures, medals, gems, jewels, coins, even utensils, which bear witness to it. Nothing, perhaps, is better calculated to make us feel how thoroly the Greek civilization of that time was imbued with the artistic sense. We may mention, in this regard, the red-figured vases, the most beautiful of which are as remarkable for the elegance of their design as for the grace of their form. Various scenes are represented upon them, now borrowed directly from contemporary life, now imitated from the pictures of painters renowned at that time. In both cases, technical skill is allied with personal accent. Each of these works is a more or less original invention, almost always bearing witness to a refined taste, and often graceful or charming. And even in the products of the second order it is seldom that one does not find something of these qualities.

If we remember that these attractive objects could be found in the public markets thruout almost the entire Mediterranean basin, we understand better the part which Greece played as the educator of humanity.

(8) Greek Civilization at the End of the Fifth Century

In all forms at once, therefore, Greek civilization had developed magnificently in the course of the fifth century. In some of these forms, especially in certain creations of literature and of art, it had even reached its culmination. On the other hand, the human type realized in some of its better representatives was truly worthy of admiration for a happy equilibrium of physical qualities and moral qualities, for its broad and intelligent interests. Profound love of country did not exclude in the cultivated Greek an already vivid sense of human fraternity; the conception of laws was reconciled in his mind with that of liberty, and respect for the past with legitimate aspiration for progress. A truly spiritual religion began to free itself from the ancient mythology and to do away with the most burdensome supersitions of the past. In particular, an ideal of beauty was formed which continued to grow and to revive incessantly in various forms.

Does all this mean that Greece thereafter had nothing more to acquire, and that it was fatally condemned to more or less rapid decay, like a plant exhausted by its very blooming? Events were destined to prove that this was not the case. Its genius was still far from having manifested all its resources; and the fourth century was to complete in many ways, and in a glorious manner, the magnificent work of the fifth.

PART III

THE FOURTH CENTURY

CHAPTER I

POLITICS, BUSINESS, CUSTOMS

Survey of the History of the Greek States in the Fourth Century.—The Peloponnesian War had seemingly settled the question of hegemony in Greece to the advantage of Sparta. But in reality such was not the case. Athens, altho defeated, had not yet reached the point of resignation; and Sparta, altho victorious, showed itself incapable of asserting its unwieldy and ineffective preponderance. In 395 B. C. a coalition was formed against Sparta. This was followed by another war; after which a peace imposed by the King of Persia, who profited by these rivalries, reduced Greece to a condition of decadence and general weakness (386 B. C.).

During this decomposition of the nation a new ambition, that of Thebes, sprang up unexpectedly. While Athens was endeavoring to reconstitute its maritime confederation, Thebes was seeking to dominate central Greece and the Peloponnesus. Two remarkable men, Epaminondas and Pelopidas, achieved some brilliant successes for the Theban arms. Victorious over Sparta in the battle of Leuctra (371 B. C.), the Thebans brought that city to the verge of ruin, organized Arcadia and Messene against it, and even pressed forward into Thessaly and Eubœa. But the death of Pelopidas, and a little later that of Epaminondas, who perished at Mantinea in 362 B. C., led to the collapse of this short-lived ascendency. The power of Sparta was shaken no less profoundly, while Athens, on the other hand, witnessed in 355 B. C. the dissolution of the confederation which it had momentarily reëstablished. None of the Greek states was any longer in a position to claim supremacy.

But precisely at that time Macedonia, which had scarcely emerged from a semi-barbarous condition, was organizing its forces under the initiative of its young king, Philip II (359–336 B. C.). He was at once a statesman and a soldier. Ambitious, and having at his disposal a strong and enthusiastic army, as well as a considerable wealth for that time, he succeeded in the course of a score of years in overcoming everything which stood in the way of his plans. His victory at Chæronea (338 B. C.) over the combined forces of Thebes and Athens, made him the master of Greece. Assassinated two years later, he bequeathed his methods of action and his plans regarding Asia to his son, Alexander. It is well known how the latter realized them. Having compelled all Greece to recognize him as a ruler, he undertook the conquest of the Orient; and by a series of prodigious successes he achieved this in a few years. When he died at Babylon, in 323 B. C., he had founded an immense empire and had opened up the Orient to Greek civilization. A new period was ushered in. First of all, let us endeavor to characterize more fully what we have just surveyed in a few words.

The Weakening of Public Spirit in the City-states.— In the preceding century each of the principal states of Greece had pursued its own independent policy, to which it devoted itself entirely. A sense of confidence sustained the energy of the citizens and redoubled their power. In the fourth century this confidence decreases steadily from day to day. Strong and firm resolutions now give way to hesitation, indecision, discouragement, and, consequently, disagreement.   The inadequacy of resources is everywhere felt as an obstacle to large enterprises.   A certain languor, quite natural after so much fighting and destruction, invades the soul of the people.   Above all they want peace, which thereafter seems to the majority of them the greatest of all blessings; it is peace which they wish to preserve at any price, even to the extent of closing their eyes to more or less imminent dangers.   Moreover, this frame of mind is favored by the improvement of material prosperity.   The development of commerce and industry causes men to feel more keenly the need of tranquility, which will permit them to enjoy life.   Under these conditions the weakening of civic spirit was very unfortunate.   Private interests tended to predominate over the public interest.   Everybody thought chiefly of leading an easy life, of growing rich, and of enjoying as many pleasures as possible.   Movable wealth, which accumulated in the hands of the most clever or the most fortunate, created a class of capitalists, among whom the taste for luxury increased from father to son.   How could all this have failed to modify the habits of life?   These changes are well known to us especially as regards Athens; but there is no doubt that what was true of Athens was also true of the majority of the Greek city-states.

Mercenary Armies.—First we may note a rather characteristic fact—the growing distaste for military service. More and more the citizens manifest the desire to evade what until then they had considered their first duty and their honor.   More and more it becomes customary to resort to mercenaries for the recruitment of armies; each republic enrolls for pay the troops of which it has need. Moreover, available mercenaries are not lacking.   At this time there is found in Greece a sort of errant multitude, composed of all those whom the almost incessant

civil discords had thrown into exile. Besides these out-
casts, there are those whose miserable condition forces
them to seek a means of livelihood; and there are also
adventurers, tempted by the prospect of pillage or simply by a taste for the hazardous and the unknown. In
this way groups of professional soldiers are constituted;
and to command them there appear captains of bands,
professional officers, who on their own initiative organize
small armies and offer their services to whomsoever is
willing to pay for them. The majority of military ex-
peditions are conducted with these mercenary armies, while
citizen armies, growing ever less numerous, play only a
limited and secondary rôle. The activity of the citizens
turns to other channels.

Politics. Parties.—But from the fact that the people
were less engrossed in matters of public interest, we should
not conclude that they renounced politics. Far from it.
A republic does not have to have great plans, nor need
the majority of its citizens think only in terms of the
common welfare, in order that the conflict of opinions
may continue. Foreign affairs, even when one has renounced vast ambitions, offer none the less an ample subject for discussion, especially among people who like
to talk and are accustomed and pleased to listen to
speeches on both sides of every subject. Furthermore,
in view of the uncertainties of the general policy, internal
dissension could not but increase. The old parties took
new names, without disappearing for that reason; their
number even increased in the process of dismemberment,
according as groups were formed which were less attached
to definite programs than to particular men. The spirit
of rivalry among the leaders of these groups was intense,
and it manifested itself in two ways: on the one hand, in
the public deliberations, where ideas were opposed or de-

sires came into conflict; on the other hand, in the civil
actions which these rivals brought against one another.
Thus politics became a contest in which well-known orators
stood opposed to one another, and in which hatreds and
implacable enmities were given free rein.   And for the
majority of the citizens this contest was the most soul-
stirring of spectacles, involving, as it did, the honor and
often the very lives of the contestants.   It is not surprising that a part of the life of the Athenians was devoted to such oratorical combats.   Nothing was more
likely to give them the air of pursuing a useful activity,
even when these speeches were not translated into action.

In spite of all this, from the political point of view
Athens was still one of the least disturbed of the Greek
city-states.   It knew no internal revolution until the time
of the death of Alexander.   This was not the case elsewhere.   The *Politics* of Aristotle furnishes numerous
proofs of the fact that few of the Greek states were
free from civil disturbances at that time.   Each form
of government, in those small and turbulent communities,
tended to exaggerate its principle; democracies allowed
themselves to lapse into demagogy, aristocrácies into
oligarchy; and often both forms terminated in tyranny.
This is what we see in Sicily, Italy, and Thessaly, in several of the Greek colonies in Asia Minor, and in numerous
states of Greece proper.

The Business World.—One thing which saved Athens
from factional conflicts was perhaps the importance which
business activity had acquired there at that time.   Indeed, in the fourth century this city was one of the great
trading centers of Greece.   In this respect the policy
inaugurated by Pericles in the preceding century had
borne all its fruits.   Athenian industry, devoted especially
to the manufacture of articles of luxury, such as furni-

ture, arms and shields, vases, ornaments and jewelry, exhibited a remarkable activity and ingenuity. It was commended for the good taste, elegance, and finish of its products. Its numerous workshops, operated under the direction of artisans who were veritable artists, turned out products which were in demand far and wide. The export and import trade, which was the counterpart of this production, sustained an active and lucrative commerce. Nothing is more instructive in this regard than the advocates' pleas of that time, notably those which have come down to us under the name of Demosthenes. The cases dealt with by the latter reveal the nature and importance of the affairs with which these business men were occupied; and at the same time they acquaint us with the men themselves. It was a mixed world of metics and of citizens, of honorable merchants and of others less honorable. Their vessels sailed to Sicily, Egypt, and Pontus, to bring back wheat for the consumption of the population of Attica; from Panticapæum they returned with salt-provisions, skins, and wools; in passing they took on wines at the islands, and various products of Asia Minor and of Syria, which they either exchanged along the route or conveyed to the market of the Piræus.

In order to insure to this traffic the necessary guarantees, a body of laws was gradually evolved wherein was manifested the practical sense indispensable to business; and from day to day these laws were adapted to the requirements brought to light by experience. Athens had also witnessed the birth, and was now witnessing the rapid development, of banking houses, the necessary auxiliaries of commerce and industry—banks of deposit and banks of credit, the operations of which are frequently described in the speeches which we have mentioned. At their head we find active and intelligent men of affairs, such as

Pasio and Phormio, formerly slaves but later freed, becoming associated with their masters in the conduct of business and rising to be persons of note. These bankers receive capital, either to insure its safekeeping, or to invest it in various enterprises, such as the exploitation of mines or commercial speculations; they also lend money at interest, open accounts, grant credits, facilitate payments by correspondents—in a word, serve as intermediaries in the majority of business transactions. Some of them even play a political rôle. Pasio, for example, seems to have used his capital to help Timotheus in certain military operations. From this time on, therefore, Greece realized that coöperation between capital, industry, commerce, and banking which is the prerequisite of all material progress.

Customs.—Some changes in manners and customs could not fail to result from this new condition of society. A certain relaxation of moral discipline was bound to make itself felt in consequence of the rapid enrichment of a few, of the development of urban life, of the more and more frequent relations with foreign countries, and of the affluence of the resident aliens. The latter were no longer only sophists, philosophers, or artists who came to make themselves known; they were people of all kinds and of all values, some attracted by commercial interests, others by curiosity, by the beauty of the city which the fifth century had made so worthy of admiration, by the renown of its schools, or by the pleasures to be found there. The old Athenians, attached to the local traditions, became less and less numerous every day. The young generation took more liberties; the old generation itself lost some of its gravity in losing a part of its authority. Athens began to resemble Corinth. Courtesans came there in large numbers and mingled in society, making their grace appreciated and in some cases their wit; and naturally their seductive powers did not fail to cause family troubles, sometimes even violent disruptions.

Against this relaxation, of course, protests were raised. A little further on we shall have to speak of philosophy and its new tendencies. But to this reaction by instruction was added the reaction by example, by hereditary sentiments, and by the natural force of practical reason. Hence in society as a whole there arose more differences, perhaps, among men; and in each social group considered by itself, more divergences, more inward conflicts. The interest of the psychological spectacle offered to the observer increased all the more. The types of human nature presented to his eyes, being more complex, demanded closer consideration and more delicate analysis. This accounts for the fact that the literature of the fourth century is unlike that of the fifth. It is the reflection of a social organization which every year was growing more and more different from that which had preceded it. It is the result of new habits of mind; it reveals sentiments in the process of transformation. Consequently, in the evolution of Hellenic civilization, it represents a well defined epoch.

CHAPTER II

ORATORY, DRAMA, HISTORY

(1) THE ORATORICAL ART

General Survey.—These varied interests and this play of passions were to find their expression in the art of oratory, and at the same time to furnish the latter with splendid material. The masters of the preceding century had developed oratory to a high degree; they made it conscious of its resources and had provided it was a carefully studied technic. Already great orators, in turning the methods of their predecessors to account, were showing themselves capable of rendering these methods more flexible. The orators of the fourth century continued what their predecessors had so well begun; they made the public address an instrument well adapted to express all sentiments in appropriate form, to follow all movements of thought, and thus, according to the exigencies of the subject, either to instruct or to move the hearers.

Pleas of Litigants in Civil Cases.—A truly new form of eloquence appears in the civil law pleas which have come down to us. Those of Lysias, composed at the beginning of the century, are models of the art, which is purposely concealed. Written for speakers in various conditions of life—who according to the Athenian law had to deliver their pleas in person—these speeches aim to imitate the language, as well as the manner of talking and reasoning, natural to each speaker; and in these recitals, in this brief and precise argumentation, in the ingenuousness of certain details, there appears a certain subtle gift of imitation which is of very great charm. With Isæus, whose preserved speeches bear upon the question of inheritance, a concise but always simple logic, with nothing strained or labored about it, deals with more or less complicated matters which are to be clarified. It leads the mind of the judge to its end in view, at the same time making good use of momentary rests, in order better to recover the argument and then to press it more effectively. Of Demosthenes, and of a few others whose work is associated with his, we also possess, besides the great political addresses, a collection of speeches relating to property disputes, litigations among heirs, and commercial and banking affairs; and in these, too, we find a simple, brisk eloquence, varied in tone and vigorous when necessary, bearing witness to a graceful art which combines ease with force. Finally, in the important fragments of the speeches of Hyperides, notably in one describing the low practices of a sharper, we may admire, in addition to the same qualities, a fine sense of humor combined with a light and piquant grace. It is to this class of literary works that we must look, certainly not for an exemplification of all Atticism, but for one of the most seductive forms of Atticism in the fourth century, imbued with moral observation and singularly well adapted to expound spiritually the things of every-day life.

Political Eloquence.—Nowhere, however, did the art of oratory shine forth so brilliantly as in politics. The more confused the general state of affairs became at that time, the more urgently eloquence was called upon to overcome hesitations and to determine ends and means. For this purpose it used all its resources. The fourth

century in Athens was the century of orators. The
names of Æschines, Lycurgus, and Hyperides, and especially that of Demosthenes, have remained illustrious,
and their speeches which have come down to us have not
ceased to be admired.

The fact is that, whatever final opinion one may form
of the men and events in question, works such as the
Philippics, or again the speeches of the two adversaries
On The Embassy or *On The Crown*, have a lasting value
in themselves; and this is true not only because of their
merit as models of oratorical style or composition, but
still more by reason of their being disputative studies of
both sides of one and the same political situation, in
which there are manifested, under prejudices and violent
passions, rare qualities of practical intelligence, of a
strong and penetrating reflection, and of a broad human
experience. Praised or criticized for their general tendency, they have at all times been read and pondered
with profit by historians, by statesmen, and in fact by all
highly cultured persons; and all have found in them lessons
of psychology, of sound reasoning and of historical
analysis, as well as fruitful suggestions and noble inspirations.

Particularly in the case of Demosthenes, undeniably
the greatest of the Greek orators, eloquence makes use of
all the qualities which do honor to Greece—clear and
skillful arrangement, forcefulness of thought, logical
reasoning, the art of grouping and interpreting historical
facts, as also that of relating effects to their causes, of
discovering motives behind actions, of placing men upon
the scene, and of providing an interesting narrative; and
besides all this there is an accuracy of expression, a
strong and grave simplicity, an unobtrusive nobility, and,
of a sudden, admirable flights of fancy. There are pas-

sages in the *Oration on the Crown* which are equal in moral value to some of the most beautiful pages of Plato.

Together with these fiery orators we have also to mention Isocrates, but as belonging to another group of minds. He represents at once a tendency more closely approaching philosophy and an art that makes itself more prominent. Celebrated as a master of rhetoric, he endeavors in carefully prepared oratorical works to apply all the devices which had little by little been invented to give a finished elegance to the written and the spoken word. By the careful structure of his composition, by the harmonious balance of his phrases, by the expert development of his periods, by the precision and variety of his rhythms, by the choice and invention of his words, and finally by the arrangement of his antitheses, he convinced even the most sceptical listeners. Moreover, in this brilliant form he set forth general ideas which responded to the sentiments of many of his contemporaries. Fascinated by a noble but unrealizable ideal, namely, peace among all the Greek city-states and national unity against the barbarians, he made this policy the subject of fictitious addresses, pamphlets, and imaginary legal arguments, by which he aimed to exercise an influence upon public opinion or upon the statesmen of his time. Whatever illusion he created for himself in this regard, his work nevertheless remains as evidence of the lofty sentiments and the genuinely human intentions which do honor to the Hellenism of this period.

(2) THE DRAMA AND THE PORTRAYAL OF CUSTOMS

Observation of Customs and Characters.—This century, so favorable to oratory, was no less conducive to

the observation of customs and characters, and in part
for the same reasons.   The great diversities which appeared more and more among men with the dissolution of
the older social order and the increasing predominance
of individualism, called for psychological analysis.   We
have just seen how it penetrated into oratory and made
a large place for itself there, now in an easy, familiar
form, now in grave or impassioned eloquence.   It was imposed to no less an extent upon the philosophers and
historians, a goodly number of whom manifested at that
time the same taste for the study and representation of
these moral varieties.   They appear in the Socratic
dialogs, of which Plato and Xenophon have left us living
specimens.   Especially in the writings of Plato we see
passing before our eyes an entire series of quickly sketched
personages, each with his own physiognomy.   Moreover,
notably in certain parts of the *Ethics* and *Politics* of
Aristotle there are fine and precise notations which reveal
the characteristic traits of the different ages or those by
which the human passions are distinguished from one
another.

The most illustrious exponent of this philosophy,
Theophrastus, made himself known in this form of writing
by the little books of *Characters*, which served as a model
for La Bruyère.   As is well known, it is a collection of
portraits representing types less than individuals, each
of the types being characterized by a group of traits
which no doubt have never been combined in one and the
same man, but which form part of one and the same
definition.   There is ingenuity in the selection and grouping of these details, a form of ingenuity which is not,
and does not purport to be, anything more than an acute
form of observation.

The New Comedy.—Under the influence of this taste a

new form of comedy was born at that time, very different
from that which had delighted the Athenians of the fifth
century. The latter, with its exaggerated buffooneries,
its exuberant fantasy, its absurd inventions, its violent
attacks on the men of the day, and its biting satire at
the expense of all innovations, had now outlived itself. It
was no longer suitable for a society which was becoming
more and more polished every day, and which was at the
same time taking more and more account of the things of
real life according as it discovered their interest. Already Euripides, even in tragedy, had called attention
to everything which daily life contained in the way of
dramatic material; and it was precisely this material
which the comedy of the fourth century, after a period
of apprenticeship and transition, learned to utilize to
excellent advantage.

In the last third of this century this new form reached
its perfection in the hands of Philemon and Menander.
What they place upon the scene is, in a general way, the
society of their time. In the frame of an intrigue borrowed from incidents of contemporary life and developed
by means of a few ingenious combinations, they group
together and put into action characters whose sentiments, eccentricities, and manners form a living picture
of the social environment in which they lived. Above all,
their art takes pride in naturalness and in truth. Their
aim and desire is to make the spectators recognize themselves, or at least their neighbors, in these fictitious characters. The public taste demands that the very incidents
shall have nothing impossible, nothing too extraordinary,
about them; hence they are often simply divers occurrences which one might think were taken from a chronicle
of the day. And precisely because these plays imitate
life very closely, they incite people to think in the process

of affording them amusement. They bring up practical problems, make an appeal to judgment, and offer useful lessons to those who would reflect.

This delicate art completes in the happiest manner the simpler and broader art of the preceding century. It takes more account of little things, but guards against being absorbed by them. Menander causes men of all kinds to pass before us—misers, babblers, braggarts, gossips, fickle and inconstant lovers—in short, characters of mediocre value, yet good to observe for one who is interested, according to Menander's own formula, in everything human. He reveals to us carefully portrayed individualities who adhere to their age and to their station, and to the temporary emotions and sentiments rooted in their very natures. We meet rich people and poor people, servants, freedmen, and slaves; likewise, mothers, wives, young girls, as well as adventuresses and courtesans. Nothing gives us a better idea of the nature of Greek society at that time. It is revealed in its true character and in its diverse forms, with its faults and even its vices, with its good qualities, its elegance, its charm, and its humanity—the last word used here in its broadest sense as the one which best describes this society with which we are concerned.

As a form of art, moreover, this comedy exerted an influence quite different from that which had preceded it. The so-called "old comedy," that of Aristophanes and his contemporaries, was too exclusively Athenian to be easily transported to a foreign theater. On the other hand, nothing prevented the comedy of Menander, in which human life was pictured in its general aspects, from adapting itself to various forms of society. This accounts for the fact that it could later serve as a model for Plautus and Terence. The latter writers, in turn, found imitators

in the countries of Roman civilization; and thus this
same comedy furnished to modern literature the type of
the comedy of intrigue, the comedy of manners, and even
the character comedy. The plays of Molière, whatever
may have been the originality of the latter's genius, are
related thru well known intermediaries to Menander. We
note here, with regard to tragedy as well as to the other
forms of literature, the influence of Hellenic civilization
upon our own.

(3) HISTORY

History and Public Taste in the Fourth Century.—
Like oratory and drama, history in the fourth century
could not fail to modify to some extent the traditions
which it inherited. Its principal representatives at that
time were Xenophon, Ctesias, Ephorus, and Theopompus;
and the popularity which all these men enjoyed proves
that historical writings found numerous readers at that
time. What has just been said explains this popularity
and enables us to understand what the general desire
was in this matter. The Greek people were becoming
more and more curious about the spectacles of life; they
called upon the historians to reveal life to them in its
multiple aspects, and the historians, as is natural, sought
to give them what they wanted.

Xenophon and the Influence of Socrates.—In the works
of Xenophon, history appears to us thoroly permeated
with the Socratic spirit. When still a young man,
Xenophon had felt the influence of Socrates all the more
profoundly for the reason that the ideas of the latter were
in close accord with his own natural tendencies. The
teachings of this master, and the personal experience
which he himself afterwards gained, were combined in a

dogmatic morality which came to embody all his conceptions. This morality is revealed in dialogs in his *Memorabilia* (*Recollections of Socrates*); it pervades the whole historical narrative which forms his *Cyropædia;* it appears and makes its presence felt everywhere, even in those works which he wrote properly as a historian, the *Anabasis* and the *Hellenica.* In the *Anabasis*, which gives account of the expedition of the younger Cyrus against his brother, King Artaxerxes, and the retreat of the ten thousand Greek mercenaries who had taken part in it, he brings out especially the value of discipline, of prudent courage, and of physical endurance. These are the services which could be rendered, in the midst of the most severe trials, by calmness, reflection, and confidence in divine guidance and protection; and the interest of the work lies in the judicious recording of the sentiments which these trials called forth, whether among the soldiers or among the few personages whom circumstances detached from the crowd. The same applies to the *Hellenica*, which recounts the series of events which agitated Greece from approximately 411 to 360 B. C. With whatever justification one may reproach the author for his prejudices, for his partiality, and too often for his lack of knowledge of men and of things, one can not deny him the gift of being able to interest and please his readers. This is so not only because of the elegant simplicity of his style, revealed in a certain natural grace which charms and attracts, but also because this pleasing narrator is a moralist who calls attention to the quality of actions and emotions, and in so doing invites us to judge them.

Other Historians of the Fourth Century.—The actual writings of Ctesias, Ephorus, and Theopompus are known to us only thru a few extant fragments and a few short quotations. The testimonies are rather numerous, but not sufficient to make up for the lost works and to enable us to judge them. What we do know of them, however, makes it possible for us at least to recognize in these writers, too, some characteristic traits of their time.

Ctesias, who had lived for some time as physician at the court of Susa, excited the lively interest of his readers by the information which he had gathered there. The Greeks of the fourth century were particularly interested in Asia, for their political and commercial relations with that continent were steadily increasing. Ctesias caused himself to be received, rightly or wrongly, as a witness who had come to inform them about many things of which Herodotus had been able to give them only an imperfect idea.

Both Ephorus and Theopompus, before becoming historians, had been pupils of Isocrates, who himself, it is said, induced them to deal with historical subjects. The oratorical art, in the person of this renowned teacher, therefore claimed history as a part of its domain. Ephorus and Theopompus, notwithstanding profound divergences in their natures, seem to have been strongly inspired by this thought. The task which Ephorus set himself, in writing his *Universal History*, was that of bringing together in a comprehensive work all the facts which others had amassed before him. Such a plan did not involve very much personal research. The success he achieved was due to the happy use which he made of these diverse materials, to a clear arrangement which permitted the reader to follow the course of events, and which at the same time grouped these events in such a way as to facilitate the understanding of them, and to the interesting nature of this vast historical survey, which revealed, with a remarkable narrator's and writer's talent, the entire past of Greece from primitive times to the middle of the fourth century. As for Theopompus, a brilliant and fervent orator, it was to the questions of his time that he devoted himself in his *Hellenica* and *Philippica*, the former comprising the last years of the Peloponnesian War and the hegemony of Sparta down to 394 B. C., and the latter covering the entire reign of Philip of Macedon. Brilliant speeches, dramatic narratives, even ingenious fabrications, formed the substance of the work. The men of the day were brought forward and judged according to the personal sentiments of the historian, who did not attempt to disguise either his antipathies or his prejudices. Whatever objections may be raised against this manner of comprehending history, there is no doubt that his work was singularly lively and suggestive, abounding in portraits and in moral descriptions, and consequently very well calculated to satisfy the curiosity of the public for which it was intended.

CHAPTER III

PHILOSOPHY AND SCIENCE

The Thinkers of the Fourth Century.—While the literature of the fourth century, like that of the preceding century, continued along the line of historical, dramatic, and oratorical works, altho inspired by a somewhat different spirit, speculative thought also advanced and achieved remarkable progress. Two names summarize its history, those of Plato and Aristotle; the former dominates the first half of the century, the latter the second half. Both men played very important parts in the history of Hellenic civilization; for their spiritual authority was powerfully exercised, not only in their time and thruout all antiquity, but indeed also down to the very present day.

(1) PLATO

The Philosophy of Plato as Religion.—Socrates has been represented above as the initiator of a religion permeated with philosophy. Plato, his pupil, who was superior to his teacher in knowledge and genius, put his whole soul into this religion. In the conversations of Socrates it was still only in a state of rough outline. The teachings of Plato gave it form and enabled it to perpetuate itself after him, without having to undergo any very profound modifications.

For a long time, almost from the beginning, philosophic

178

thought had felt obliged to free itself from the traditional religion. This emancipation had been effected, even before Socrates, in such a way that philosophy was seemingly on the way to abolish religious sentiment itself. But in reality this was not the case. On the contrary, the religious sentiment was very strong in Socrates. He endeavored to transform rather than to destroy—a singularly delicate and difficult undertaking. What elements of the popular belief was it necessary to eliminate? What did it seem best to preserve and to adapt? It would seem that he did not succeed in arriving at a definite answer to these questions. Plato devoted his whole life to the matter.

Closely associating morality and religion, as did Socrates, and at the same time subjecting religious belief to reason, Plato did not hesitate openly to reject every element of the immoral or of the absurd that the ancient mythology contained. He even did so with a vivacity reminiscent of the satirical boldness of Xenophanes. Nevertheless, this censure did not go so far as to proscribe the polytheistic conception; it sufficed for Plato to introduce into it a notion of order and of hierarchy which gave satisfaction to the monotheistic tendency of his thought. Firmly attached to the idea of divine intervention in human affairs, he did not object to imputing this intervention to distinct powers, on the sole condition that these powers should be subordinated to a superior authority and represented as coöperating with one another in a common endeavor. Precisely to define the nature and functions of these minor gods, however, was not, according to him, either possible or necessary; and likewise, by a complacency of imagination—an element that seemed to him unessential—he disregarded this task of definition and devoted himself to tradition and the

ancient revelations, without, however, attributing to
these latter elements any absolute right to assert themselves.   This was equivalent to giving mythology its due
share, while at the same time reserving to free thought
its due liberty.   The essential thing seemed to him to be
the affirmation of a universal order conformable to
reason.   Thus from this restricted polytheism, in which
the ancient beliefs found their rightful place, the idea
of a divine sovereignty, characterized at once by perfection and by power, was definitely detached.   It was not,
however, an absolutely unlimited power; a certain dualism
was still present in the thought of the philosopher, who
believed it necessary for the explanation of evil.   According to him, the divine power, while wishing only the
good and seeking to realize it by creation, was able to
create it only in matter, that is to say, finitely and imperfectly.   Thus the way was opened which for a long
time was to be followed by all philosophy which seeks to
explain the paradox of ideal and real.

Manifestly this theology tended, perforce, to throw off
all national character.   This is a fact to which it is important to call special attention.   In freeing itself from
the ancient mythology and the poetic fables, it broke the
bonds which attached the beliefs of Greece to their native
soil.   The religion of Plato was no longer the religion
of a definite people; there was nothing to prevent it from
becoming a universal religion.

Moreover, it lent itself to this development all the
better for the reason that it completed in essential ways
the vague or insufficient data of tradition.   Plato was,
in fact, the first to undertake to demonstrate method-
ically the immortality of the soul by a series of proofs
which seemed to him to supplement one another.   Under
the influence of Pythagorean and Orphic suggestions,

which he interpreted and transposed to suit his purpose, he originated a doctrine which he developed especially in the *Meno*, the *Phædrus*, and the *Republic*. He asserted that the soul of man, in acquiring a body, carried with it more or less vague memories of a previous life, in which it had had the intuition of substantial realities which the intelligence alone could comprehend. And he taught that the soul, according as it succeeded more or less in reviving these memories by reflection and by the power of reasoning brought into contact with sensitive impressions, prepared for itself a more or less happy lot in subsequent existences. To this doctrine he added—drawing inspiration from Orphism and the Mysteries, but freely adapting these borrowings to his own ideas—the conception of a judgment of the dead, of punishments and rewards, and of a cycle of transformations, to which he assigned as a consummation, as the supreme end to be achieved, a return to the pure contemplation of God. It was in this way that his philosophy sought to answer the troublesome questions which men had been asking themselves even before his day; and altho his answers made no claim to absolute certainty, they were at least supported by reasoning and suggestions with which many minds desirous of spiritual reassurance were able to content themselves.

Moral Value of the Platonic Religion.—This religion was closely bound up in the metaphysics of Plato with his morality. According to him, as a matter of fact, the things we know by the senses owed their reality only to their participation in pure essences which he called Ideas, and which could be known only by Reason. But the highest of these Ideas, that which he sometimes seemed to identify with God himself, was the Idea of God. He thought, therefore, that every effort of the soul should tend toward the fullest possible possession of this Idea—which was tantamount to saying that the purest cult, the one most worthy of God, and also the best for man, was virtue. But this virtue, as he conceived it, could not be reduced to ordinary honesty, to the mere conscientious observation of justice, to the practice of courage or temperance, or to simple obedience to the laws. The new element which he introduced into it, the principal element in his eyes, was constant aspiration toward the Ideal. He pictured virtue as a continuous ascension, whereby the soul, detaching itself and drawing further and further away from the world of the senses, was always rising higher and higher, to the point of rendering itself, in so far as humanly possible, similar to God himself. Moreover, it seemed to him that this progressive development of spiritual life, directed in its course toward the Supreme Good, was at once the necessary condition and the surest guarantee of happiness. It is in this respect that Platonic philosophy surpassed in a singular manner all the other forms of ancient morality, and that it still remains, after more than twenty centuries, one of the noblest assertions of the tendencies of the human conscience.

The Philosophy of Plato as Science.—But if it presents itself from this point of view as a veritable religion, no one can fail to recognize the fact that it is also to be looked upon, with at least as much right, as a science, or rather as a synthesis of many sciences. The school founded by Plato in Athens in 387 B. C., called the Academy, was indeed one of the most active centers of study and learned research in all Greece prior to Aristotle. Plato himself considered mathematics indispensable to philosophy. He devoted himself with indefatigable ardor to the science of numbers, to geometry, to astronomy, and also to the understanding of nature. A continuator of Pythagoras, Empedocles, and Heraclitus, he wished to neglect nothing pertaining to their researches, and he sought also to develop what they had discovered. The conception of the universe set forth by him in the *Timæus* reveals a mind rich in varied branches of knowledge, employing all the materials previously amassed by Hellenic science, and at the same time sufficiently resourceful to adapt them to his personal views. Here, however, we have to consider, above all, what he did for logic, psychology, and political science.

It is to him especially that we owe our knowledge of logic prior to Aristotle, as practiced by the Eleatics, the Sophists, Socrates, and the Megarian School. There is no doubt that Plato, in practicing logic himself, in giving it, in his dialogs, the form of a dramatic action, sharpened it, made it more flexible, and disciplined it—in a word, perfected it. With him the so-called Socratic method, as defined above, acquired all its efficacy. We see it appearing in numerous forms, with as much adroitness as surety. Definition, analysis, comparison, induction, and deduction—each played its part in these vigorous and refined, sometimes even subtle, argumentations. But the Platonic system of dialectics goes well beyond that; it does not stop, as did the Socratic logic, with definitions; it is no longer even a simple method of reasoning. It embraces a complete education of the mind, an entire intellectual discipline, which proposes to accustom reason to detach itself more and more from concrete things, in order to render it capable of elevating itself to the highest degree of abstraction, where, for Plato, the supreme reality is to be found.

His psychology is in a sense a reflection of this logic. Altho it does not form a very well defined entity, nevertheless a few traits of it stand forth prominently and enable us to characterize it. The distinction of the three parts of the soul, which he calls reason, generous sentiments, and sensual appetites, far as it may come from satisfying the exigencies of exact observation, is none the less a first attempt at analysis and classification, the value of which must be admitted. With this fundamental distinction is coördinated that of desire and the will, which is only a corollary of it. But it was especially in the study of the operations of the intelligence that Plato manifested his perspicacity. Nobody had as yet undertaken with such care to give account of the nature of knowledge and of the diverse forms in which it appears. It is well known how he distinguished between these forms by means of a double scale, placing, on the one side, inferior knowledge, which he sub-divided into conjectural opinion and judgment, and, on the other side, superior knowledge, which is at first reflection and in its perfected form becomes science. It is to the elaboration of this last conception that he is especially attached. To him is due the credit for having defined this last degree of knowledge, which is the full possession of the object, completely permeated by intelligence. And if perhaps he did not define with sufficient clarity the limits of the domain accessible to the human mind, he at least saw how far it ought to extend.

As for his politics, it was by no means summed up, as is too often believed, in the construction of a utopia founded upon communism. The state portrayed in his *Republic* is not, for him, a real state; it is a sort of suggestive hypothesis which he uses to bring out clearly the defects of the majority of human communities and the passions that divide them. Better than anybody else before him, he saw and demonstrated how close the relation is between the character of a people and the form of its government; better than anybody else he succeeded in bringing to light this fundamental truth, that sound political customs are what make sound governments; and in clear-cut traits he defined the conditions from which result the solidity or instability of institutions. In short, the *Republic* is full of profound observations, which have become precious acquisitions for political science.

Influence of Plato.—All in all, it is in Plato's work that philosophy is revealed for the first time as the synthesis of all the sciences. It is true that none of the parts of this great body of knowledge was as yet either sufficiently developed or even delimited with the desirable accuracy. This important synthesis therefore called for a series of revisions, which demanded long and patient analyses. But the genius of Plato had perceived everything from a lofty perspective. After him it was necessary for observation and experience to do their work in order to control, correct, reform, or develop his views one by one. To his pupil, Aristotle, is due the honor of having begun this work and of having thus marked out some of the courses which scientific inquiry was destined to follow in the future.

(2) ARISTOTLE

Rôle and Character of Aristotle.—Very different from Plato, the marvelous teacher in whom the Athenian genius had found one of its best interpreters, was Aristotle of Stagira, in Macedonia, who had none of his sensibility or of his poetic imagination. He was a born observer. A sense of exactitude, a desire for accuracy, and a passion for research were combined in him with a penetrating discernment and force of thought. It is because he succeeded in subjecting the study of facts to a sound and logical method that he appears to us as the most excellent representative of the scientific spirit in antiquity, or, better said, as one of the fathers of modern science.

Principles of His Method.—Without entering here into the details of his metaphysics, it is necessary to recall at least some of the fundamental principles which explain his method. According to him, every determinate thing proceeds form four causes: 1, the substance of which it is made; 2, the form which modifies this substance and determines it; 3, a movement whereby the transformation from the substance to the form is effected; 4, an end which is the reason for this movement. In the case of substance, that which is to be called into existence has at first only a potential existence; the motive cause, in effecting the transformation from the indeterminate to the determinate, realizes this existence in fact. This realization tends toward a term which is the best possible state for that thing, its final cause. From this it results that observation, with Aristotle, is dominated by the idea of finality. According to this principle, one truly knows any given object at all that exists, or its parts, only if one has discovered its purpose or end. It is in this respect that science, as Aristotle conceived it, differs most from modern science, the latter, since Bacon, having systematically discarded all inquiry into the end or purpose of things. But the truth is that the difference, essential as it may be in theory, is much less important in practice. For, on the one hand, Aristotle in his numerous observations generally does nothing more than indicate the relation of the effects which he notes to their efficient causes; and, on the other hand, the science of life can not study an organ without seeking to discover what purpose it serves.

The Study of Nature.—It was perhaps in the vast domain of natural science that the genius of Aristotle revealed its value most clearly. Until his time nature had been investigated but partially; he was the first to conceive the plan of a methodical and universal investigation. To gather for this purpose the greatest possible amount of material, seemed to him the indispensable task. The ten books of his *History of Animals* bear witness to the zealous enthusiasm which he brought to this work, as also to the variety of inquiries which he directed or inspired. And without doubt they also show us how difficult it was at that time to procure positive information, and to what extent the knowledge of the living world was still imperfect. But the example thus set was none the less excellent. It devolved upon Aristotle to develop these collected materials scientifically; and in his second work the power of his genius shone forth. His remarkable treatises *On the Organs of Animals*, *On the Motion of Animals*, and *On the Generation of Animals*, show us how he proceeded in this work. His penetrating mind excelled in analyzing complex facts, in finding their simple elements, in comparing them according to their similarities, and in classifying them. He was no less skillful, moreover, in discovering the connections of phenomena and their obscure and until then unperceived relations; and intuition, so necessary to the scholar, illumined his observation and made it more fruitful. Finally, the logical vigor of his thought enabled him better than anybody else, by virtue of the power of reasoning, to pass from knowledge already possessed to new knowledge. And there his prudence as an observer placed him on his guard against the danger of hasty conclusions. One of the things to be admired in him is the scrupulous care with which he collected everything that had previously been said on the subjects in question, as also the care which he took to anticipate objections and, when he was unable to meet them, to admit the fact without ceremony. Such, in a general way, is the method which he did not cease to apply to the natural sciences, whether in the works which he himself wrote, or in those which were afterwards written under his inspiration, on physics, on plants, and on celestial phenomena.

The Moral Sciences.—In the moral sciences we find the same spirit, the same method, the same results. Here, too, it is with close observation of facts that his inquiry begins. His morality, condensed in the *Nichomachean Ethics*, leads us to presuppose a preliminary work which consisted in noting the forms of moral life, in distinguishing and defining them. From this inquiry there arose the general ideas which dominate the entire work. Here we recognize the natural moderation of his mind, even in certain particularly contestable points such as the conception of virtue as a mean between two excesses; and here, too, we find his most personal instincts, for example, in the value attributed to the contemplative life, which seemed to him the most complete realization of happiness. Closely related to this morality, his *Politics* proceeds from the same method. Besides the dogmatic work which bears this title, we possess also fragments of a collection on *Constitutions*, in which the institutions of numerous states have been brought together and reviewed. The nature of this collection can be judged by the *Republic of the Athenians* recently discovered in Egypt, which, if it was not a part of that work, serves at least as a sort of sample of it. The *Politics* itself abounds in references to laws, customs, various constitutions, and a thousand historical events carefully presented by the author. It is from experience that he wishes to derive all his teachings, but from an experience interpreted by reason. Thus we find specified and formulated the idea of the family and the city, the distinction between their elements, the theory of the various forms of government, as well as the theory of the dangers which constantly beset them and of the means of guarding against these dangers—in a word, a veritable philosophy of human social communities, the most instructive and most complete that antiquity has handed down to us.

Study of the Human Mind.—No less curious to know the human mind in itself and in its operations than to know the life of the universe and of the beings inhabiting it, Aristotle applied himself with the same zeal and the same perspicacity to observing and describing the former. While his treatise *On the Soul* marks brilliantly the beginning of methodical psychology, the works which, taken together, comprise what the Middle Ages designated by the collective name of *Organon* gave permanent currency to a certain number of fundamental observations on the necessary forms of thought, on its relations to language, on the structure of deductive reasoning, and on the sophisms, as also the means of discovering them (*Categories, On the Expression of Mind, Analytics,* and *Topics*). Few writings have exerted a more profound or more lasting influence than these. To be sure, this influence was excessive during certain ages, but more enlightened modern criticism has been able to restrain it without denying it; for there is no doubt that it is justified by an important body of finely conceived truths. Finally, his *Rhetoric* and his *Poetics* are also solid studies of certain faculties of the mind and their productions; and here again observation plays a no less important part. In the case of the former, it is observation of customs and of passions; in the latter, we have a review of the resources of the poetic art, precepts drawn from the history of literary forms and based upon the psychology of readers or spectators. Altogether it is a doctrine in no sense abstract, but, on the contrary, inspired by a profound knowledge of realities.

The Academy and the Lyceum.—But neither Aristotle nor Plato, great as they were, are to be considered separately if one wishes to appreciate the part attributable to them in the general progress of Hellenic civilization. Both were founders of schools, promoters of intellectual activities which were at first directed by them and then perpetuated after them. The Academy, founded by Plato, was represented after him, in the fourth century, by Speusippus, Xenocrates, and Polemon. It was a school of metaphysicists, mathematicians, and moralists, and we shall see it continuing and undergoing transformations in the following centuries, until the time when many of its doctrines are absorbed in Christianity. The Lyceum, founded by Aristotle and afterwards directed by Theophrastus, was itself to produce, up to the time of the Empire, a long series of philosophers, known by the name of Peripatetics and generally animated by the spirit of positive curiosity which had characterized the master from whom they claimed heritage. Further on we shall see them joining forces with the intellectual movement of another epoch.

(3) ANTISTHENES AND ARISTIPPUS

Other Philosophic Schools.—None of the other philosophies in the fourth century had an importance comparable with those of the Academy and the Lyceum. In a survey of the civilization of that time, however, it is impossible to overlook the names of Antisthenes and Aristippus, since from them were to emerge schools which had the most brilliant fortune in the following period.

Antisthenes.—It is in the moral side of his teachings that Antisthenes especially affirms his originality. Believing, as did his teacher, Socrates, that morality is the science of happiness and that happiness is identical with virtue, he was led by the irreconcilability of his mind to carry this affirmation to the extreme. He wished to be the personal enemy of pleasure; and this he was with an ardent conviction, to the point of paradox, all the more so because he was a subtle and forceful reasoner, a man of brains, and a skillful writer. His dialogs enjoyed great success. It is doubtful whether he convinced many of his readers; but he interested them and amused them by piquant satires, by a mordant criticism of customs, perhaps by allusions which pleased their malignity. The severity of his life, moreover, added prestige to his teachings. He took pride in his poverty. His pupils, as it happens, went still further than he did along the course of renunciation and disdainful abstinence. Diogenes of Sinope inaugurated Cynicism properly so-called, a haughty and somewhat ostentatious protest of stern austerity, not only against luxury and ease, but also against the very habits of mankind, including politeness, discretion, and good behavior. He had continuators. This strange manner of living on the margin of society, and almost in revolt against it, is not one of the least characteristic traits of this time so favorable to individualism. From this tradition, combined with a few different elements, there was to emerge at the end of the century the Stoicism of Zeno, of which we shall have something to say further on.

Aristippus.—In a society in which each individual was more than ever free to live according to his taste, it was

inevitable that a contrary tendency should oppose itself
to this asceticism.   The man who set this opposition up
as a doctrine was another follower of Socrates, Aristippus
of Cyrene.   Since his principle was that happiness is only
an aggregate of pleasures, he professed that the search
for pleasure is the natural law of life, since every living
being instinctively wishes to be happy.   From this point
of view, the pleasures of the senses seemed to him as
justifiable as those of the mind.   This is what he set
forth in writings which had a certain vogue.   Lax as
this morality was, it is nevertheless to be noted that the
sense of moderation so natural to the Greek mind did not
fail to make itself felt even here.   Aristippus by no means
lived in gross debauchery; his was a fine, cultivated mind
which wished that in everything man should take counsel
from reason.   His own practical sense and good taste corrected in him, to a certain extent, the error of his teaching.   Moreover, one may regard him as representing
fairly well the average morality of a large number of his
contemporaries.   But just as the lessons of Antisthenes
were converted by the Cynics into a defiance directed
against humanity, so the doctrines of Aristippus led the
Cyrenaics to the denial of all discipline.   His true thought
was to be taken up once more at the end of the century, with more moderation and a deeper understanding
for philosophy, by Epicurus, who, as we shall see, organized it into a carefully constructed system.

CHAPTER IV

THE ARTS

The Art of the Fourth Century.—As is natural, the changes which took place in the fourth century in customs, sentiments, and ideas, and which are reflected in the contemporary literature, are likewise manifest in architecture, sculpture, and painting. The art of this time is therefore easily distinguished from that of the time of Pericles, from which it is nevertheless a direct outgrowth. The fact is that the art of the fourth century, without renouncing the simple lines, the purity of conceptions, and the intimate harmony from which the Greek genius was unable to abstain as long as it remained true to itself, becomes less severe and, so to speak, less abstract. At this time people admire more than ever before the nobility and serene beauty of the works of Ictinus, Phidias, and Alcamenes, but a more concrete imitation of life is now demanded of the artists; and the latter, on their part, respond to his demand with a more careful study of movement and variety. Thus there appears an art inferior in nobility and in ideal significance, but at the same time charming and distinguished by a fascinating elegance and a graceful freedom which enables each artist better to assert his own personality.

(1) ARCHITECTURE

Evolution of Architecture.—In architecture, the century of Pericles had created models from which it was

thereafter impossible to get away. The Greek temple
had been designed once for all; its form and even its
essential proportions were established as something in-
tangible. It was therefore in ornamentation, in matters of detail, and in the adaptation to given conditions,
that the inventive originality of the artists of the fourth
century was especially able to exercise itself. A few
monuments yet standing, and numerous others the ruins
of which, at least, may be usefully examined, still permit us to form a fairly accurate idea of these qualities.

They reveal the ever-increasing popularity of the Ionic
order and the success of the Corinthian style, the latter
scarcely known in the preceding period. Both tended to
prevail over the more severe Doric order which had previously predominated. More and more it becomes their object to please the eye. The Ionic order grows more or-
nate, more graceful, and acquires a more varied decoration,
as evidenced by the ruins of the Didymæum at Miletus,
those of the Temple of Athena at Priene, the tomb of King
Mausolus at Halicarnassus, and other monuments of the
time. The Corinthian order crowns its pillars or columns
with capitals composed of an ornamental design of acan-
thus leaves, sometimes set off by colors which add force to
its reliefs and carvings. All edifices are adapted to this
new style. The decoration becomes more delicate; it is
animated, as it were, and diversified; it calls for ingenious
inventions. Even small edifices, thus adorned, present to
the eye one of the most pleasing spectacles—as, for instance, the choragic monument of Lysicrates at Athens,
with its graceful form, its slenderness, the fantasy of its
circular frieze picturing a little drama with numerous
characters, the elegance of its crown surmounted by a
tripod of victory which is set off on a support of volutes.

At this time, moreover, architecture is called upon to

satisfy new demands. It is in the fourth century that stone theaters begin to be erected in the Greek cities. Altho the general tendency of these edifices is only to reproduce in their broad lines the wooden theaters of the preceding century, it is none the less evident that, being built to last, they are in reality an entirely new thing. A few general rules are laid down and little by little perfected thru experience. The object is to realize the best possible conditions: to permit the performance to be seen by a large audience, to permit the voices of the actors to be easily heard, to insure the ready entrance and departure of the crowd, and to facilitate the production of the play; and naturally these conditions vary according to the locality. Especially the stage and its appurtenances demand the concurrence of various artists, to whom the architect must furnish his general plan and conception. And altho today it is often difficult to determine positively, under the ruins of later constructions, what is characteristic of this particular time, there is no doubt that the unity of the effect had been preserved without destroying the variety of the details. The architectural type of the theater was undoubtedly one of the most brilliant creations of the art of the fourth century.

(2) SCULPTURE

In sculpture we find the same tendencies, still more clearly characterized. They are represented by artists whose names have remained illustrious—men like Scopas and Praxiteles in the first half of the century, and Lysippus somewhat later. The art of all these men, if one compares it with that of their predecessors, becomes, according to the expression of a competent critic, "more intimate, and frees itself from religious tradition in order to seek in real life an individual and personal character." [1]

This new conception can not be disregarded, according to the ancient witnesses, in the work of Scopas of Paros. Solicited by a large number of Greek cities, which held it an honor to possess some of his works, he filled their temples with statues of gods and goddesses. But what we admire in these statues is not so much their divine majesty as it is the grace of their forms and postures, the suppleness of their limbs, the folds of their draperies. Usually there is something amiable and expressive about these figures, sometimes something pathetic. Thus represented, the gods were offered to the eye as vigorous ephebes, radiant in youth; the goddesses as charming maidens or women in the full glory of their beauty. We know that Scopas assisted in the construction of the Mausoleum at Halicarnassus, erected in 353 B. C. by order of Queen Artemisia of Caria; and there is nothing to prevent us from believing that the frieze of this monument was perhaps executed by his own hand, either entirely or in part, and, in any case, according to a model created by him. It is an evidence that there were associated in this master, together with a most lively instinct for elegance, other qualities of a different order. The frieze, which represents a combat of Greeks and Amazons, is remarkable for its portrayal of the fury of the movements, the boldness of the postures, and the intense passion which animates the combatants; and the dramatic invention of the situations, as well as the gripping representation of the frenzied struggle, make it particularly moving.

The Athenian Praxiteles, a little younger than Scopas, was no less renowned. None of the Greek artists seem to have possessed, to the same extent that he did, an innate gift of grace. All antiquity extoled his numerous

[1] Collignon, *Archeologie grecque,* p. 187.

statues of Aphrodite. Regarded as particularly worthy of admiration was his statue of Aphrodite of Cnidus, which represented the goddess at the moment when she had laid aside her garments for a bath—a masterpiece in which the artist had realized his ideal of feminine beauty, characterized by a youthful delicacy of form. For religious sentiment was substituted a voluptuous seductiveness. Under the chisel of the artist the marble acquired the appearance of life in its full bloom. This refined grace appears again in the figures of young gods which he loved to create. Nobody took so much delight as he in reproducing the god of love, Eros. But this Eros is no longer, of course, the mythological Eros of the aged Hesiod and the theogonies, that is, the contemporary of the origins of the world; nor is he any longer the divine personification of passion, the redoubtable god of whom Sophocles had sung; but rather does he represent sensual and yet splendid love, as conceived by the majority of his contemporaries. It was this love which he had sculptured for Phryne, and which the latter, in turn, wished to consecrate to the city of Thespiæ. Apollo, too, he made an ephebe, quite different from the god of the terrible arrows pictured by Homer. He showed him rather slender in his nudity, giving him a slightly languid posture designed to assert the suppleness of his limbs. And it is still a conception akin to that which we admire in the Hermes of Olympia, an authentic work of his hands happily discovered in our own days. Somewhat mutilated and imperfectly restored, it bears witness to a delightful talent which, without perceptible effort, combines charming sentiment with well-nigh perfect execution.

In the second half of the century the bronze-worker, Lysippus of Sicyon, shows himself more attached to the traditions of the preceding period than do Scopas and

Praxiteles, and particularly to the work of Polyclitus, whose conceptions he followed. Nevertheless he, too, was in certain respects an innovator. Altho, like Polyclitus, he also liked to bring out the strength and play of the muscles, he applied himself, as did his contemporaries, to individual details, notably to the personal expression of the face. This is attested by the great number of effigies which he executed and which reproduced the features of the illustrious men of his day, in particular those of Alexander the Great. He represented the conqueror at various periods of his life, marking with great skill the changing expression of his countenance. Moreover, we know from the testimony of Pliny the Elder that he treated with minute care certain details of his figures, notably the hair, and that he sought to give his subjects an elegant slimness by lengthening the body and diminishing the proportions of the head. This new interpretation of nature had great success. Lysippus has been looked upon, with good reason, as the precursor of Hellenistic naturalism; and when Rome was initiated in the arts of Greece, he was appreciated no less than Scopas and Praxiteles. There came a time when the masterpieces of these artists served to adorn the homes of wealthy Romans; and it was especially under their influence that Latin Italy gained its artistic education.

(3) PAINTING AND CERAMICS

The Highest Development of Greek Painting.—It is necessary to repeat here, concerning painting, what has been said above: owing to the total disappearance of its works we are able to speak of it only on the faith of the ancient writers. From them, however, we know that the great painters of the fourth century, Apelles and Protogenes, were not only worthy successors of Zeuxis, Parrhasius, and Polygnotus, but even surpassed them. What we are told makes it very clear that they did not servilely continue the tradition of the masters from whom they inherited the art. The reputation which Apelles made for himself as a painter of portraits bears witness to a new taste for psychological analysis and a remarkable keenness of penetration, which is quick to comprehend the traits peculiar to a physiognomy and to note the outward indications which reveal the personal character. And it was not only the permanent traits of the individual that he thus discovered; he excelled in giving expression to the agitations of the soul, such as vehement emotions or temporary anxieties. Delicate sentiments, shades of moral life, no longer escaped him; and for the expression of them the precision of his brush was marvelous. Never before, beyond all doubt, had life in its extreme variety been imitated with such perfection. Apelles was very nearly in painting what Philemon and Menander were in poetry. We should not be surprised that he shared with Lysippus the favor of Alexander. His reputation, moreover, seems to have been almost equaled by that of his contemporary, Protogenes. It is impossible, today, to say in what respects they differed from each other.

Among the minor arts, that of the coroplasts and vase-painters deserves especially to be mentioned, in order to complete the picture which we are drawing in broad lines. There is nothing which acquaints us better with the familiar aspects of the Greek civilization of this time. To the fourth century, as a matter of fact, belong the majority of those pretty figurines of baked earth which today are found in all our museums and in all collections of amateurs, and which have popularized in particular the name of the little Bœotian town of Tanagra. Everybody has seen some of these slender statuettes of young girls or young women which have given us so much knowledge of the amusing and gracious details of a refined coquetry. It is a pleasure to the eye to gaze upon their elegance and exquisite grace, to study the naturalness of their postures and the adjustment of their draperies, to get an insight into every-day life in its amusing variety—the walk, the more or less serious meditation, and the games of childhood or of adolescence. As for the series of painted vases referred to above, it was continued without interruption, and we owe to it also some truly living documents—banquet scenes, scenes in the palæstra and in the home, each of them a precise illustration of the customs which have been described above. In the Athenian ceramics, in particular, the decorative art attains at this time a delicacy of execution and a distinction of style in which there is manifested, as clearly as in the works of such writers as Lysias or Menander, everything that is peculiar to Atticism.

PART IV

THE LAST PERIODS OF HELLENIC CIVILIZATION

CHAPTER I

THE HELLENISTIC KINGDOMS

The Decline of Hellenic Civilization.—At the time of the death of Alexander there begins, for Hellenic civilization, the long period of its decline. This period lasted eight centuries, if we fix the end at the time when the last important creation of Greek thought, Neo-platonism, became extinct. It is true that another civilization had already commenced, that of Byzantium, a mixture of Hellenism and Christianity; but in the history of human affairs all distinctions necessarily have something arbitrary about them. This term "decline" has in itself only a quite relative value; for the fact is that these eight centuries were by no means unproductive. It is in works of imagination and sentiment that the diminution of the Greek genius makes itself most keenly felt. We shall see the cause of this and we shall endeavor to understand the type of intellectual petrifaction which was fatal to great poetry. But the environment in which these works were created did not show itself so unfavorable to the search for truth or to meditation on the conduct of life. Learning, science, and philosophy continued to develop; and what they produced at that time can not be overlooked in a general survey of Hellenic civilization. This is especially so because on the whole the work of these periods of relative decadence transmitted this civilization to the following centuries, having deprived it of its extreme individualism and having better adapted it, consequently, to the general needs of humanity.

The Greek World after the Death of Alexander.—When Alexander the Great died at the end of his prodigious conquests, the peoples of the Orient subjugated by him laid themselves open to Hellenic influences. In learning to speak Greek, they made themselves susceptible to the ideas and sentiments of Greece. Everything, in fact, which the Hellenic genius had produced in the way of poetry, science, philosophy, history, and artistic creations thus became the common heritage of civilized humanity. But in the process of diffusion this heritage could not remain unaltered. On the one hand, the peoples who took possession of it ignored what they did not understand and what was not adapted to their own culture; on the other hand, they introduced new elements into it, some borrowed from their past, others related to the political and social institutions which were springing up at that time.

It is well known how the Macedonian generals, after the death of the conqueror, fell into conflict among themselves, and how in the midst of bloody quarrels they divided up his legacy. Here we need recall only that out of the remains of his empire there developed a certain number of kingdoms, among which we should mention in particular that of Egypt under the Lagidæ (Ptolemies), that of Syria under the Seleucidæ, that of Pergamus under the Attalidæ, and that of Macedonia under the Antigonidæ. Alongside of these kingdoms existed a few Greek city-states, more or less independent according to the times and the circumstances, but for the most part survivals of mediocre importance. The characteristic fact of this so-called "Hellenistic Period" was the establishment and organization of these kingdoms.

The Absolute Monarchies; their Character.—All of
them were military monarchies, founded upon the absolute power of one man.   In each of them a sovereign will
dominated.   There were no more elected magistrates, but
only a hereditary ruler served by those whom he himself
chose; and consequently there were no more citizens, but
only subjects. .In Greece itself we now find the old free
city-states subject to local tyrants, clients of the kings.
Hence, there is no more political life, properly speaking;
what here and there remains of it, by way of exception,
scarcely transcends the municipal horizon—petty internal
quarrels involving small interests.   A few groups, like the
Achæan and Ætolian Leagues, soon reduced to the necessity of placing themselves under the protection of the
dominating powers, appear but rarely and then only to
prove by their short duration the permanent extinction of
the autonomous republics.   The great monarchies alone
still have a life truly worthy of attention; and they alone
give the civilization of this time its distinctive physiognomy.

Essentially military in origin and condemned to remain so by reason of being almost constantly at war with
one another, these monarchies depended upon powerful
armies organized in the best possible manner.   It was
in the army, therefore, that the power of the state rested.
And these armies, created and maintained by the royal
treasury, were composed entirely of mercenaries, devoid
of civic spirit and entirely in the hands of the king.   In
order to supply his treasury, it was necessary for all the
resources of the country to be placed at his disposal.
Hence the need of an administration such as free Greece
had never known.   Royal functionaries were assisted by
secretaries, counselors, and agents of all ranks—in short,
by an entire hierarchy, which regulated even the activ-

ity of the people, controled production under the pretext of stimulating and coördinating it, and canalized the public wealth to the profit of the treasury. Thus concentrated, a large part of it was expended in incessant wars, in royal extravagances, and in the pomp of the courts; another large part remained in the hands of those who were charged with collecting it; another, finally, was used for things that were truly useful; and this last was certainly not the principal part. Everything considered, such a régime was calculated to enrich a limited class; and in the long run it was bound to exhaust the people, to paralyze private initiative, and to engender a diminution of truly creative energy.

Those of the monarchies which were properly Oriental, the monarchy of the Seleucidæ, and that of the Lagidæ, inheritors of the traditions of Asia and of Egypt, did not confer upon their representatives merely military and political power; they made gods of them. To the national religions and to those of Greece were added the cult of the king; he became for his subjects an object of worship. A divine majesty surrounded his person. It was not enough for him to impose obedience upon all; it was necessary to impose adoration as well. Until then confined to the Orient, these sentiments now penetrated into the Greek world, and the consecration which they received there was instrumental in causing them to be accepted later on in the Roman world.

The Capitals and the Courts.—These kings of the Hellenistic period were all, in imitation of Alexander, founders of cities. Usually it was about new cities founded by them, or about old cities transformed by them, that the administration and military defense of their kingdoms were organized. To these cities they often gave names suggestive of their own names, or those of members of their families, as if in order to inscribe upon the soil the titles of their dynasties. Each kingdom, in any case, had its capital, which was the seat of its power. Rapidly these privileged cities—Alexandria, Antioch, Pergamus, and Syracuse—residences of the kings, acquired an exceptional importance. It was not long before they surpassed all the others in wealth, in size, in beautiful monuments, in population, in business activity, and in ceremonies and spectacles of which they were the seat. Each of these monarchs had to have a palace in which he could with dignity hold court and receive guests. For the absolute monarchy requires a brilliant entourage which will do honor to it. It is not content with the royal officers and the multitude of servitors. It is anxious to represent all Hellenic civilization; and for that reason it attracts the poets, historians, scholars, and artists. The latter thereafter must glorify the princes, commemorate events of their reigns, and give the greatest possible brilliancy to the ceremonies which they celebrate. These capitals also become renowned centers of culture. A spirit of emulation manifests itself in this regard among the leaders of the states. Almost all of them gratify their vanity by founding libraries for the collection of manuscripts, the latter often purchased at great expense. None of these libraries was more celebrated or important than that of Alexandria, inaugurated by Ptolemy Philadelphus; and his intention of making the city a seat of learning is still more clearly marked by the establishment of the Museum, a sort of Academy where men of learning and of letters gathered together, pensioned by the royal treasury. Altho scarcely equaling Alexandria, other cites, notably Pergamus, also had their schools, their sages, and their libraries. It was thru these foundations, and these new conditions of life, that the writers became clients of the kings. In this way especially the literature of the time acquired its peculiar character; but it also fell under the influence of a social state of which it seems best to point out the principal characteristics.

Society and Classes. Diffusion of Hellenic Civilization.—Most striking is the disappearance of the popular element. The people as such, who were almost everything in the Greek republics, were no longer of any importance in the Hellenistic kingdoms. The peasants, absorbed in a daily labor which hardly sufficed to meet the demands of the public treasury, no longer counted from the political point of view. Moreover, they became less and less numerous; for the city life had a powerful attraction for them. But how was the population of the cities composed? A wealthy aristocracy, a numerous body of officials, held the first rank; around them gravitated a clientele of freedmen, tradespeople, and parasites, who lived in their shadow, so to speak, and in dependence upon them. An army of slaves surrounded and served them. There was no middle class, properly speaking, since the institutions did not insure to persons of moderate fortune any of the guarantees which would make them truly freemen. On the other hand, in the large cities we find an ill-defined crowd, a confused populace, in which men of diverse conditions and professions mingled, often differing even among themselves in respect to religion and nationality, and devoid of any civic spirit. In other words, they formed a multitude now passive, now turbulent, agitated sometimes by sudden and violent movements, but incapable of any concerted and continuous action. Altogether, it is an environment without original character and without a common ideal; and in this environment there is only one truly cultivated class, a small class in which imitation of the princely courts dominates, its members consequently seeking elegance, intellectual refinement, and good breeding, but incapable of producing anything truly original and new.

In this condition of the world Hellenic civilization nowhere encountered any strong resistance. With rare exceptions, the most notable of which was Judaism, the old civilizations were no longer in a position to stand in its way. In these spurious kingdoms, created by rival ambitions, patriotism had lost all its virtue. The ancient traditions were effaced; no group of people possessed the elements of a moral solidarity based upon a deep-rooted attachment to the same traditions. The conquering Greeks alone furnished to these disorganized multitudes a fund of ideas and sentiments sufficiently developed to satisfy the eternal needs of humanity. Moreover, Hellenic civilization alone lent itself to the broadened requirements which the intermingling of the nations had rendered necessary. For it embodied a principle of progress and of liberty which permitted it to modify itself without denying its past, and consequently to adapt itself continually to the new conditions. This adaptation was the essential work of the Hellenistic period. It was accomplished at once by disseminating the wealth of knowledge and thought which Greece had previously amassed and by realizing, or preparing, in morality, in philosophy, and in religion, some syncretisms which were acceptable wherever the Greek language had penetrated.

CHAPTER II

HELLENISTIC LITERATURE

(1) IMAGINATIVE LITERATURE

General Characteristics of this Literature.—All the great sources of inspiration having been exhausted, it was natural that the society of that time sought its pleasure in restricted works, the only ones which were suited to its nature; and these works had to please it especially by the harmony of their details and the ingenuity of their structure. Such is the general character of the imaginative literature of the third century. Moreover, this same literature continues to grow poorer and poorer every day in the two following centuries. Nevertheless, some of its productions are read and enjoyed even to this day; and having served as models for some good Latin poets, such as Tibullus, Propertius, Ovid, and even Virgil, they have inspired imitation even down to modern times. That is why, without tarrying long over them, we cannot well disregard them altogether.

Epic Poetry, Elegy, and Epigram.—Epic poetry had never entirely disappeared in Greece, altho history and tragedy had deprived it, in the fifth century, of its principal reason for existence. In the Hellenistic period it made a curious effort to rejuvenate itself in a less ample but more learned form. The *Argonautica* of Apollonius of Rhodes, which we still possess, furnishes the principal evidence of this; and at the same time it reveals pre-

cisely what made the success of this effort impossible.
A work of erudition and of imitation, it lacks at once
national and religious interest, which is essential to the
epic form, and it also dispenses with the variety of human
passions, which is no less important. A single episode,
that of the love of Medea, is still readable today. Here
the gods no longer play anything more than cold and
artificial rôles. In fact, mythology was dead. Moreover, other writers of epic poems preferred to take subjects from history. Neither the *Messeniaca* of Rhianus
of Crete, nor other poems of the same kind, have come
down to us; and there is probably no occasion to regret
it. Didactic poetry, imitated from that of Hesiod, seems
better suited to this period of scientific curiosity and
erudition. This accounts for the success of the astronomical poem of Aratus of Soli (first half of the third century) and of the medical poems of Nicander of Colophon
(*Theriaca* and *Remedies*, second century), which have
come down to us. The poetic sentiment in them was of
no account.

The elegy, freer from artificialities and less imbued with
traditions transformed into rules, did not present the
same difficulties. No form at that time was practiced
more or enjoyed more. It took the place, to a certain
extent, either of epic poetry, now no longer of any importance, or of the more or less abandoned forms of
lyric poetry, in which vivifying inspiration was lacking. It lent itself either to agreeable narration of love
adventures, which pleased a public very sensitive to the
influence of women, or to the recollection of historical and
mythological antiquities, to explaining old customs and
institutions, or, further, to extoling the kings and to
lending support to the ceremonies of the official religion.
Skillful in assuming many forms, it adroitly mixed a little

sentiment with abundant learning and made the best of old subjects by the introduction of pretty details. This was the merit of Philetas of Cos and especially of the prolific Callimachus of Cyrene, who was placed at the head of the library of Alexandria by Ptolemy Philadelphus. Both of them court poets, they made themselves known as masters of this favorite form, the former by his love elegies which were later to excite the emulation of Propertius, and the latter by the poems which he called *Origins* (or *Causes*), a lengthy and learned composition in which he related to mythological legends, or to simple historical tales, a large number of religious or civil customs. A real talent for story-telling, coupled with a certain grace which is both lively and refined, still lend a certain interest and charm to the few fragments which have come down to us.

From elegy one can not separate the epigram, which is, to tell the truth, but an elegy in miniature. By virtue of its very brevity it was still more apt to seize occasions on the wing and to please by appositeness. It was no less successful in presenting in a few verses a picture, a memory, a moral thought, or an impression. Never before or afterwards did it achieve so much success. At that time we see the appearance of specialists in this form, artists in spirit, whose best creations, similar to finely carved medallions, have been preserved to us in the most ancient part of the *Anthology*. Some of the epigrams of Asclepiades of Samos, Posidippus, and Leonidas of Tarentum, to mention only a few of many names, are miniature masterpieces in this form, the delicacy and ingenuity of which are still enjoyed.

Theocritus and the Bucolic Form.—Alongside of these ancient forms, artificially rejuvenated, appeared an original creation, the bucolic or pastoral form, to which the name of Theocritus remains attached. Altho evidently a very unfaithful picture of the life of the Sicilian shepherds, it was intended to please, and did please, city folk who were somewhat blasé, by the charming depiction of rustic customs and the description of rural countrysides. Moreover, its success was lasting. For the poet had a deep feeling for nature; he painted it in a few free and precise touches; he knew also how to express passion in telling language; finally, he revealed by a discreet and agreeable realism the element of artificiality in his compositions. The same qualities were in his mimes, such as the *Magician* and the *Syracusans*, a transformation of a popular form which, without making it insipid, he adapted to the taste of a polite society. Disdaining with reason the broad epic form, which he considered too heavy for the poets of his time, he nevertheless imitated it in episodical narratives in which his dramatic and descriptive talent shone forth brilliantly. The imitations to which his work gave rise, first among the Latins, then in modern literature, had the effect of bringing out the merits of a model which could not be fully equaled.

The Satiric Form.—Satiric poetry, an outgrowth of the iambic form and of comedy, was no longer lacking at that time when men were seeking to rejuvenate that which had grown old. It acquired some new forms, in the libelous and coarse verses of Sotades, who dared to attack a Ptolemy and paid for his insolence with his life; in the *Sillis* of the philosopher Timon of Phlius, mordant and pitiless adversary of every form of dogmatism; finally, in the diatribes of Menippus of Gadara, mixtures of verse and prose which from the name of their author came to be known as the *Menippian Satires*. These various works, today lost, and probably of mediocre value, nevertheless deserve to be mentioned as attesting

the exceptional survival in the Helenistic world of one
of the characteristic traits of the Greek mind.

The Drama.—As for dramatic poetry, we may say that
it was no longer of any account, altho here and there,
and especially at Alexandria, there were still at this time
writers of tragedies, and altho the obscure names of seven
of them were grouped in a "Pleiad." The only plays enjoyed at that time at the numerous theaters where troupes
of Greek actors exercised their talents, were, with a very
few exceptions, those of the great poets of former times,
which had now become classics.

(2) LEARNED LITERATURE

Principal Forms of the Learned Literature.—But if the
Hellenistic period enriched the poetic patrimony of Greece
but slightly, it at least made a considerable contribution
to learned literature. Philological and literary criticism,
grammar, and even history and geography, owe much to
the laborious activity of its scholars.

Philological and Literary Criticism.—The formation
and constant growth of the royal libraries laid numerous
tasks upon the men charged with satisfying the wishes
of the princes in this respect. First, it was necessary
to procure manuscripts, often scattered, for the purpose
of gathering together the complete works of the principal writers. Then, among the manuscripts thus assembled, it was necessary to determine what was authentic
—a delicate task, in which the critical mind gained its
education. These manuscripts, moreover, were more or
less incorrect. Hence it became imperative to compare
them with one another, in order to correct them, so as to
offer sound texts to the readers, as conformable as possible to the often lost originals. And even this did not

suffice. These old texts had become obscure, either because their language was antiquated, or because they made
reference to forgotten occurrences, or again because the
thought of the author had become unintelligible.   Hence
the need of critical annotations and commentaries, even
of conjectures and special lexicons.   Thus philology and
literary criticism grew out of the requirements of the
time.   It was by works of this worth that certain scholars
made themselves illustrious, among them being such men
as Zenodotus of Ephesus, Eratosthenes of Cyrene, Aristophanes of Byzantium, and Aristarchus of Samos, who
succeeded one another in Alexandria in the course of
the third and second centuries before our era.   At the
end of the same period Crates of Mallus fulfilled the same
office at Pergamus with equal success.   After them, we
must mention Apollodorus of Athens, the Thracian
Dionysius and the Alexandrian Didymus, the most indefatigable of the learned guild.   This is not the place to dis-
cuss each one of them separately or to enter into the details
of their work.   Suffice it to say that we are indebted to
them, not only for the preservation of the ancient texts
the deterioration of which they prevented, but also for a
number of valuable explanations without which many of
these texts would have been in part unintelligible to us.
To them is due, as a matter of fact, the best there is in
the scholia which the commentators of the Roman and
Byzantine periods summarized and too often spoiled.
Literary criticism properly so called, that which judges
the merit of authors, is not lacking in these commentaries;
we still find interesting traces of it in some of the fragments which have come down to us.   But it may be better appreciated in various non-historical writings of
Dionysius of Halicarnassus, who is said to have been
looked upon as the inheritor and continuator of the

Alexandrians, altho he lived at Rome under the Emperor
Augustus.   It would be unjust, however, to impute to
them the personal prejudices which offend us in his works,
when he speaks of Thucydides or Plato.   Engaged above
all in oratorical training, Dionysius claims to offer to
the future orator only the models best adapted to his
art; and this accounts for the fact that he seems to make
it a duty to sacrifice everything to Demosthenes.   This is
a narrow point of view, but one which should not prevent
us from recognizing the precision, and sometimes the acumen, in the critical tradition which he continued.

Grammar.—To this criticism, whether verbal or literary, grammar is naturally related, that is to say, the
classification and methodical definition of the parts of
speech.   Scarcely outlined in the fifth and fourth centuries, it was really put into form by some of the scholars
of this time, notably by Aristarchus, by Crates, imbued
with the stoic logic, and by Dionysius, whose names we
have just mentioned.   They transmitted it in a finished
form to the Greek and Latin grammarians of the following period.

History.—Of all the forms of literature, history is perhaps the one which is the least subject to danger, since
it derives its life from actual events and assumes as its
task that of registering them according as they have
taken place in the past.   Therefore, in the three centuries
of the Hellenistic period, there were many historians.
The best known were Callisthenes of Olynthus, then the
two fellow-countrymen of Alexander, Ptolemy and Aristo-
bulus, also the Sicilian Timæus, Hieronymus of Cardia,
Douris of Samos, Phylarchus, Clitarchus, the authors of
Atthides, and especially Androtion and Philochorus, all
authors whose works have been lost, and Polybius, the
only one whom we are able still to appreciate fully, thanks

to the preservation of a considerable part of his great works. None of them seems to have been equal in talent to the historians of the preceding period; but we should note the innovations they introduced into history.

With Timæus there appears the careful replacing of the local chronologies, notably those which were based upon the lists of archons, ephors, or eponymous priests, by a truly Panhellenic chronology, that of the Olympiads. But when the history of Egypt and of the Orient was better known, when that of Rome was joined with that of the Greek peoples, the need was felt of still further enlarging this chronology, which in its turn had become too narrow. An effort was made, therefore, to constitute a comparative chronology, permitting the establishment of the necessary synchronisms; and this work necessarily led to a general revision of the previous systems of reckoning. This was one of the tasks in which the scholar Eratosthenes made himself illustrious, a man to whom we have already assigned a place among the philologists. He accomplished it by using the data collected by the Hellenized Egyptian, Manetho, who had been a priest of Heliopolis under Ptolemy Philadelphus. After him it was continued by another scholar, likewise mentioned above, Apollodorus of Athens. In spite of errors or inevitable uncertainties, these laborious calculators succeeded, altogether, in laying the foundations of a positive knowledge of the times.

But to Polybius belongs a particular distinction. It is the very horizon of history which broadens out with him. This broadening, which had begun with the conquests of Alexander, could not fail to assert itself more strongly in the second century, when the relations of Greece and Rome were opening to men's mind a perspective over Italy, Carthage, and all the peoples subject to

Roman or Carthaginian influence. The study of the growth of the Roman state in Italy, of its rivalry with the Punic power, of its rapid extension toward the Orient as well as the Occident—what subject could afford greater stimulation to the thought of a man endowed with some degree of interest in things political? Before him there unfolded a long series of historical facts, determined by natural causes which had to be brought to light. Polybius was fully conscious of this. It was in his work that there was defined the idea of continuity in human life, of an intimate logic of things, and of an interdependence among nations, which until then had been able to appear isolated. Thus there was constituted a positive philosophy of history, capable of definitively eliminating the theological explanations which had too long been abused. And this philosophy gave to historical writing a useful political and moral instruction which Polybius succeeded in bringing out emphatically. It also had the effect of making better known the value of the scientific elements of history. Thereafter the latter could no longer consider either geography, or the constitutions of states, their laws and customs and their economic and military organization, as episodical subjects calculated to satisfy the curiosity of readers in a more or less transitory way. All these things became the essential subject-matter of his study. Consequently, he was led to make more methodical and more frequent use of epigraphic documents, of treaties, of decrees, and of public archives. Timæus had already set a good example in this respect. Polybius was not content merely to praise him for it; he followed his example.

Geography, better understood for that very reason, while lending greater aid to history, tended to claim independence from it and to undergo a similar development.

Altho it had not ceased to progress since the remote time of Hecatæus and Anaximander, we may say that in the middle of the fourth century it was still in its infancy. First the conquests of Alexander, then the extension of the Greek world toward the Occident in consequence of its relations with Rome, gave it a vigorous impulse. Thanks to the discoveries of travelers and explorers, such as Pytheas of Marseilles, and Nearchus, an admiral in the service of Alexander, Eratosthenes, whose name is linked with all progress in science, was able in the third century to write his *Geography*, a complete description of the known world at that time, and a work which was epoch-making in summarizing all existing knowledge and in adding to it a remarkable attempt to measure the earth. Polybius, in turn, made corrections and additions to this, founded upon observations which he himself had collected in his travels. And toward the end of the second century this work culminated in the publication of the extensive *Geography* of Artemidorus of Ephesus, utilized in the time of Augustus by Strabo, whose work is still read. It is by means of the latter, consequently, altho it dates from the extreme end of and almost beyond the Hellenistic period, that we are today better able to measure what progress the knowledge of the world had achieved at that time.

With the historiography of the Hellenistic period are connected two works which, altho they also are slightly posterior to the chronological limit, are nevertheless inseparable from it, namely, the *Universal History* or *Library* of Diodorus of Sicily, finished toward the beginning of the reign of Augustus, and the history of *The First Centuries of Rome* of Dionysius of Halicarnassus, composed in the same reign. The former is only an abbreviator of the historians who had preceded him.

All his work consisted in reviewing and summarizing what they had written, in sewing together at the ends, so to speak, the extracts which he culled from them. The chief merit of his work is that of having preserved for us, in this way, some part of so many lost writings. But from our point of view it reveals a need, a very urgent need at that time, namely, that of making a synthesis of a past which people were anxious to comprehend in its entirety. The spirit of the times called for universal history in consequence of the unification of the world by the Roman conquests. As for Dionysius of Halicarnassus, whose works of literary criticism we have mentioned above, his merit as a historian is in itself very slight. On the one hand, his Roman history causes us to feel strongly the influence which rhetoric was then pretending to exert upon historiography, which it regarded as a part of its domain; and, on the other hand, it bears witness to the interest which the Greeks were beginning to take in Roman things and also to the numerous legends which they were introducing into the traditions of ancient Rome in order to relate the latter to their own history. It was for them a sort of revenge for the conquest.

Biography.—Let us not forget, either, that alongside of history, properly so-called, this same period also witnessed the development of biography, a secondary form but by no means negligible. Derived in the fourth century from the oratorical eulogy, biography was first made prominent by the philosophical schools, which were anxious to preserve piously the memory of their leaders. Then, the publication and dissemination of the works of the great writers gave rise to the preparation of notices recounting the principal events of their lives and setting forth the most notable traits of their characters. Once the form had secured standing, biographies of statesmen, generals, kings, and great personages naturally had their turn. The public taste for the details of customs, the more and more lively interest attached to individuals, and also a certain scientific curiosity which was becoming general, insured their success. It is true that none of the biographers of this time, neither Hermippus, nor Antigonus of Carystus, nor Satyrus, seems to have been classed among the writers of renown. Not until the time of the empire, under the Antonines, does the biographic form, thanks to Plutarch, assume its place among the lasting creations of the Greek mind. But the work of Plutarch, of which we shall speak in its place, would undoubtedly not have been possible if the way had not been prepared for it a long time in advance.

(3) RHETORIC AND ORATORY

Oratory. The Schools of Rhetoric.—Need we speak of a Greek oratory in the Hellenistic period? At that time, to be sure, there were deserving orators in all parts of the Greek world; but if nothing of their speeches still exists, this is almost certainly due to the fact that there was nothing in them of lasting interest. Great eloquence had died with the extinction of liberty. Exiled from the public tribune, the oratorical art thereafter had its chosen domicile in the schools.

The principal merit of the teachers of eloquence of this time, therefore, was that of transmitting to the Roman orators the traditions which had been formed in Greece in the fifth and fourth centuries. These traditions proceeded either from examples furnished by the great orators whose principal speeches had been published, or from observations and precepts set down in the fourth century in a few treatises which had become classic, particularly in those of Aristotle, Theophrastus, and Anaximenes. Several of the philosophers of the following centuries, to be sure, wrote in their turn upon the same subject; but it does not seem that any of them or any of the contemporary rhetoricians, brought to the art of persuasion any truly new contribution. Given more to practice than to theory, they cultivated the natural aptitudes of their pupils, especially by repeated exercises. Some of them, who called themselves adherents of the Attic form, remained more or less faithful to the simple manners and methods of the Athenian orators of former times; others, in larger numbers, commended the form which they called Asiatic, the principal initiator of which had been, in the third century, a certain Hegesias of Magnesia—an emphatic and redundant eloquence, full of affectation, which tended to make more or less brilliant improvisation prevail over sane reflection. The great Roman orators did not escape entirely from this unfortunate influence; but the best of them strove to temper it and to revert to the true models which the Hellenistic rhetoric had too much forgotten.

CHAPTER III

PHILOSOPHY AND SCIENCE

Philosophic Needs of the Hellenistic Period.—In an age which lent itself so little to independent and truly useful activity, it is natural that the most vigorous minds turned to philosophy. There, at least, worthy problems were presented to them; and freedom of thought was not trammeled as it was in the domain of politics. Moreover, if philosophy, attached to the essential lessons of Socrates, proposed to regulate the conduct of life, it had much to do to adapt itself to the changes that had taken place in human society. A revision of the teachings which had sufficed in the fifth and fourth centuries was imperative. While the ancient city-state was disappearing, it was a question of assuring to the individual, thereafter isolated and practically reduced to his own resources, the means of preserving everything which makes life valuable. On the other hand, since the legal guarantees were losing their efficacy, it was necessary to realize in some other way the conditions of moral tranquility. It is a credit to the thinkers of the Hellenistic period that they applied themselves to this task and in a general way succeeded, by various methods, in satisfying the numerous generations up to and beyond the advent of Christianity.

Sects.—Several schools were constituted, as we have seen, in the course of the fifth and fourth centuries.

Alongside of that of the Pythagoreans, which tended to eclipse itself, the most famous at that time were that of Plato, or the Academy, and that of Aristotle, or the Lyceum, to which we must add the small group of the followers of Antisthenes, who had become the Cynics, and, on the other hand, the adherents of Aristippus. The Hellenistic period witnessed the growth of two large new sects—Stoicism, or the school of the Portico, and Epicureanism. The development of these rival doctrines and their disputes form a chapter in the history of Hellenic civilization all the more interesting in that they were one of its most active elements.

(1) STOICISM

General Character of Stoicism.—It is undoubtedly in Stoicism that the moral interest common to all the philosophies of this time, is affirmed in the noblest manner. Its dogmas may be criticized, but the moral energy which it exemplifies is deserving of admiration. Its fault lay in its demanding of human nature more than it could give; on account of wishing to elevate its ideals, the Portico lost sight of reality too much. In order to support its uncompromising attitude, it constructed an entire group of paradoxes which exposed it considerably to its adversaries. This defect could not, however, mar the elements of its grandeur.

Its Founders.—Three eminent men built it up, all of them natives of Asiatic Greece—Zeno of Citium, in Cyprus; Cleanthes of Assus, in Troad; Chrysippus of Soli, in Cilicia. Zeno came to Athens at the age of about twenty, shortly after the death of Alexander, and there studied successively under the Cynic Crates, the dialectician Stilpo, and the leaders of the Academy, notably Polemon;

then, at the age of about forty, his doctrine having ripened, he took to lecturing in the Portico called the Pœcile. Everything essential to Stoicism was already in this austere and spiritless teaching, a teaching, however, to which the dignity of his life and the nobility of his character lent a powerful authority. Cleanthes, who was the leader of the school after him, from about 270 to 251 B. C., showed himself his worthy successor. Close application to work and zealous pursuit of truth were his dominant traits. But since his numerous writings, like those of Zeno, have been lost, it has become very difficult to distinguish precisely what is to be ascribed to him in the first development of the doctrine. The third, Chrysippus, certainly played a considerable part. A deserving teacher and a resourceful dialectician, he took his place at the head of the school in the second half of the third century, at the time when it had to meet the most vigorous attacks of its rivals. In order to defend it, Chrysippus was led to define the theories of his predecessors, to supplement them, and even to modify them in certain respects. This is exactly what he did in the writings which he produced in profusion, with a facility which explains but does not excuse the careless form of his works. He has been called the "Pillar of the Portico"; and, as a matter of fact, it was especially upon his arguments that the school subsequently supported its dogmatism.

Fundamental Principles of Stoicism.—The fundamental idea of Stoicism was to consider man as part of an admirably ordered whole. This universal order, or cosmos, appeared to Stoicism as the manifestation of a divine reason, or, better said, as God himself. Here was a pantheism which was at the same time absolute optimism. Such a belief, once accepted in its entirety, procured for the sectary of the Portico an inward peace of mind in the midst of all the hazards of life; for everything, to his eyes, even what is commonly called suffering and evil, tended toward ends conforming to supreme reason, and consequently to good. This is the sentiment which one finds expressed with a touching faith in some extant verses of Cleanthes. It goes back, therefore, to the origins of Stoicism; and it enables us to understand what attraction this austere but profoundly religious determinism was to acquire for those who were troubled and tormented by the spectacle of a world deprived of ideals.

Moreover, this optimism claimed to be based upon a rigorous rationalism, consisting at once of an exact knowledge of nature and of a very carefully studied logic. This was the rather difficult side of the system, the side which always rendered it but slightly intelligible to the masses. In order to understand it, a long and patient effort of the mind was necessary. The Stoic metaphysics, deriving inspiration from the conceptions of Heraclitus and interpreting them in his manner, proposed to explain the formation of the universe and its duration by a series of transformations of fire, considered the original element. But what is important to note here is not the details of these theories, for they were merely arbitrary creations which the progress of science was destined to ruin; it is rather the spirit revealed in them. Above all, Stoicism wished to establish an intelligible relation among the phenomena of which the life of the universe is composed; and since it compared the human soul to a blast of fire penetrating all the organs of the body, it seemed natural to it to explain everything by the transformations of fire. The same need of a rational concatenation made itself felt in that part of their philosophy which the Stoics called "logic." Under this head they classed the study of conscious knowledge, which began with sensation and ended with science, also the study of judgment and reasoning, while passing by that of the categories as renewed by Aristotle. Altogether, their system presented itself as a continuous teaching, which it was necessary to appropriate in its entirety; for the final conclusions, those which constituted morality, derived all their force from the premises established by physics and logic. From this, moreover, it results that logic and physics had scarcely any value for them save by way of introduction to morality. It is the latter, in the last analysis, which has marked the place of Stoicism in Greek civilization, and it is upon its peculiar character that we should place emphasis.

The Stoic Ideal. The Sage.—Most essential was its conception of virtue. While Aristotle had represented virtue as a just mean between two excesses, and Plato as the harmonious development of the human faculties, Stoicism made it the end of a continued progress, toward a goal so far off, so lofty, that only a few men, by way of exception, were scarcely able to attain it. Carried away by the rigidity of their logic, the Stoics, when they wished to define this ideal, were unable to avoid strange paradoxes. They imagined a sage in whom nothing would be lacking, since he would find everything in himself; a man incapable of failure, therefore, and inaccessible to grief, possessing true richness and true power, in short, a mortal resembling a god—a conception manifestly so unreal that it gave the entire doctrine the stamp of utopianism. Nevertheless, it appeared to them necessary for a full realization of this "impassibility," which was for them the supreme form of happiness. And they aggravated this defect still more by denying that there were degrees either of good or of evil, and by affirming, consequently, that all defects were equal, or again that every man who had not arrived at the supreme wisdom was insensate. Herein lay the danger of the excessive dogmatism in which they took delight. In practice, no doubt, these paradoxes corrected themselves, and were toned down by the force of things. Some of the most moderate of their teachers became resigned to concessions; but the doctrine of the leaders of the school persisted, and an endeavor was made to defend it with all the resources of subtile dialectics, which dangerously offset all the good points in their ideas.

Natural Law. Duties. Casuistry.—Perceiving clearly that the law of man can be only an individual application of universal law, and that the latter constrains every being to live in conformity with his peculiar nature, the Stoics had laid it down as a principle that human life is to be regulated according to that which is peculiar to man, that is, according to reason. All their morality was derived from this. This was tantamount to saying that a man was truly a man only if he subjected his instincts, his fears and desires, in a word, all the movements of his soul, to the judgment of this guiding and sovereign faculty. It is an honor to Stoicism that it disengaged and brought to light this simple formula, the foundation of all rational morality. And having thus defined it, the Stoics studied all the practical consequences of it. With them appears in full light the conception of duty, which had remained merely an implied element in the previous systems of philosophy. And they applied themselves to defining it, not only in its general characters, but in the multiplicity of its practical forms. Reluctant to abandon anything to the unreflecting impulses, they set themselves the task of determining the rules of conduct in all doubtful cases which they could foresee. Thus they consti-

tuted what was later called casuistry—a regulation
sometimes excessive, too minute or subtle, but calculated
to arouse the attention of the conscience and to cause
more delicacy to grow in it.   Cicero's treatise on *Duties*,
an imitation of that which the Stoic Panætius had
published in the second century, makes it possible for us
still to judge it; and there is nobody who will deny that
it impresses one as a sane, solid, and precise moral
doctrine.

Stoicism and Personality.—But perhaps the greatest
merit of Stoicism, in any case the most striking, was that
of fortifying marvelously the souls which were impregnated with it.   No doctrine has better emphasized in
each of its adherents the inner power which is the will,
and the use which one can make of it to the end of
rendering oneself truly free.   None has proclaimed•more
loudly that this freedom consists in an adherence to a
superior law, an adherence which depends upon no exterior circumstance and which no authority is able to
prevent.   And if the experience of life does not permit
the admission which the Stoics professed, that this freedom is sufficient to render a man insensible to every blow
of suffering, certainly it is at least one of the best conditions of happiness; and it is also one of those conditions
which contribute most to the development of personality.
The true Stoics were what they wished to be—men, in the
noblest sense of the word.

Cosmopolitanism attributed to the Stoics.—They were
also such by reason of sentiments of human fraternity.
Accustomed to consider in man the common traits of
humanity, they were able to attach only a mediocre
importance to individual distinctions; and consequently
it was much easier for them than for others to rise above
class prejudices, to recognize a brother in the poor man,

even in the slave. That a certain cosmopolitanism necessarily resulted from this attitude, is not to be denied. In the effacement of nationalities, in the fusion of peoples, and at times when political interests tended to become entangled, this sentiment was not unnatural, and it is not to be imputed to any particular doctrine. That of the Stoics is assuredly very appropriate in this case, as are all philosophies and religions of a universal character. Still, cosmopolitanism is not a necessary consequence of Stoicism. Among the Romans, such as Cato of Utica, far from weakening patriotism, it seems, on the contrary, to have given it greater energy.

Influence of Stoicism.—Stoicism owed much to the philosophers of the preceding age, notably to Socrates, Antisthenes, Plato, and Aristotle. In turn, it exerted a considerable influence upon the thinkers of the following centuries. It helped to lead the Academy away from the course of semi-scepticism which it had followed since the third century; and later on it became an element in the formation of Neo-platonism and Christian asceticism. Since then, moreover, something of its teachings or of its examples have always survived in all moral doctrines characterized by a generous ideal.

(2) EPICUREANISM

General Character of Epicureanism.—Alongside of, or rather in the presence of, Stoicism, there rose at the same time another new philosophy, Epicureanism, likewise inspired by the desire to regulate human life with a view to happiness, but claiming to succeed in this by an opposed method. Whereas Stoicism demanded a prolonged effort, Epicureanism, on the other hand, wished to suppress all effort. As it held forth a great promise, while demanding almost nothing, it naturally found numerous adepts. What, essentially, did it teach? It taught the art of living quietly, of throwing off cares, and of including some pleasures without excess or fatigue. Nothing is better suited to easy-going natures, devoid of ambition, but sufficiently reflective to perceive the dangers of action and too listless to face them. Moreover, Epicureanism won adherents by its moderation; from the Greek tradition it had preserved the sense of moderation—which lent to its doctrine, mediocre as it was, the appearance of wisdom.

Epicurus and His School.—The Athenian Epicurus, who gave his name to this doctrine, does not seem to have been a teacher, properly speaking, save for the physical part of his philosophy, which he borrowed from Leucippus and Democritus. But it was he who formulated its essential principles, deriving his inspiration from the writings of Aristippus. The school which he opened in Athens in 306 B. C. was a sort of gathering-place for friends, whom he invited to attend his lessons in his garden. His influence upon them was great. All of them loved him, and all were persuaded that he was bringing to them the secret of a happy life. His confidence in himself, the clearness of his affirmations, and the simplicity of his reasoning and of his precepts, attracted minds which were scarcely anxious to examine anything very profoundly. He excelled in freeing them from the principal causes of trouble, and in furnishing them with practical counsel adapted to all circumstances of life. A prolific writer, he composed numerous treatises, in which he repeated to satiety ideas which varied but little but were always listened to with respect by his admirers. Of this literature, there have come down to us only two letters containing a summary of his doctrine, and a collection of *Maxims*, which was the manual or the vademecum of the Epicurean. A school which, basically, disdained science and abstained as much as possible from discussion could scarcely undergo any notable changes. Furthermore, it had no development. It lived several centuries, but remained, until its disappearance, the same as its founder had made it.

Incredulity in Religious Matters.—One of its characteristic traits was the negation which it opposed to the common belief relative to the activity of the gods. Epicurus regarded the idea of a divine providence, and everything that depended upon it, as the principal cause of many of the anxieties which at that time were tormenting the majority of minds. He wished to free them once for all from such anxieties. He demanded of them the inclination toward a conception of the universe founded entirely upon chance. The atomistic doctrine of Leucippus and of Democritus furnished him with all the elements of this. The exposition of it is to be found in the didactic poem of the Latin poet Lucretius. This atomistic doctrine, as we have seen, explained the formation of the universe and all the phenomena of nature by the fortuitous coming together and mechanical combining of particles eternally falling in space. Thus everything was reduced to matter and to motion. The soul, being itself material, could not have any destination other than the body. Therefore, we hear no more of survival; all apprehension relative to another life had to disappear. Epicurus, it is true, did not deny the existence of the gods; but he conceived them as being relegated to absolute idleness, indifferent to human affairs and finding their happiness in this very indifference. For man, such gods were as if they did not exist. In fact, the supernatural element, in all its forms, was eliminated; humanity had nothing to demand of these happy beings who ignored mankind, and it had nothing to fear of them. Thus it was in vain that the Epicurean defended himself against the charge of atheism; common opinion held him an atheist; and, everything considered, there is no doubt that Epicureanism contributed its share to the ruin of the ancient religion.

Morality of the Epicureans.—The morality of the Epicurean harmonized with his conception of the universe. Since everything in the world depended upon chance, man, according to him, had only to obey the instinct which led him to seek pleasure. But anxious to do away with every cause of inward uneasiness, he had to eliminate from pleasure itself everything which might cause it to degenerate into pain; and pleasure was thus reduced to a sort of quietude. For the Epicurean, therefore, the art of living happily consisted of guarding as much as possible against desires, which are almost always followed by deceptions, or against fears, which are vain anticipations of an unknown future. The wise man, in his eyes, was one who knew how to shut himself up in the present, to live from day to day, without ambition, without projects, concerned only to enjoy the passing moment, forgetful of troublesome memories, his mind closed to worry over things of the future. A tranquillity consisting of an indefinite series of pleasant sensations—such was his ideal. Physical atomism, in which he believed, was reflected in this sort of moral atomism. In practice, however, this did not work out without some difficulty. Nature does not easily allow itself to be subjected to an artificial discontinuity which is so contrary to its laws. The Epicurean also had to supply himself with an abundance of precepts and to have them incessantly present in his mind. He could remain on the right path only by carrying in himself a collection of rules, brief and imperative formulas, destined to place him on guard against his unreflecting impulses, often even against his sensations. One succeeded in being happy, according to the idea of the master, only by firmly persuading oneself that one could always be happy, thanks to these traditional recipes. All in all, one purchased the illusion of an easy life at the price of a discipline subject to many errors.

Influence of Epicureanism.—Those who adopted this form of life liked to associate closely with one another, in the first place, no doubt, because they felt that they were unfavorably judged on the outside, and because they felt the need of escaping, by the pleasure of companionship, from the inner void which such a doctrine could not fail to produce in them. A few testimonies bearing upon these circles of Epicureans depict them as gatherings of friends, passing the time agreeably without definite purpose or determined action. But, undoubtedly, it is not solely by these adherents, faithful to the thought of the master, that it is fitting to judge Epicureanism. Let us not fail to recognize that the doctrine contained in itself elements of moral dissolution, which its easy discipline was not capable of checking. In persuading a man that he had a right to live without really doing a man's work, it encouraged moral dispositions which tended to bring about the ruin of the old Hellenic civilization. To free the individual from every obligation, to allow him to live his life at the pleasure of circumstances without making any effort to direct them, was equivalent to breaking the power of the will, which alone assures the progress of human society.

(3) OTHER SCHOOLS

Old Schools and New Spirit.—If we set apart Stoicism and Epicureanism, the other schools of philosophy, the activity of which is manifested in the Greek world between the death of Alexander and the establishment of the Roman Empire, did not profess to be new. The Academy pretended to perpetuate the teachings of Plato, the Lyceum those of Aristotle, and the Pythagorean sect those of Pythagoras. But without declaring it, perhaps without wishing it, they accommodated themselves more or less to the spirit of their times; and consequently they, too, brought with them certain innovations. Three tendencies deserve especially to be mentioned here, namely, Scepticism, Eclecticism, and Mysticism.

Scepticism.—Scepticism, as it appeared at the end of the fourth century with Pyrrho of Elis, was in a sense a condensation of the doubts which had previously been raised, either concerning the evidence of the senses, or apropos of judgments themselves. A certain lassitude of general intelligence, in the face of excessively abstract speculations and of incessant controversies, also had something to do with this. Neither Pyrrho, nor his pupil Timon, is sufficiently well known to us today to enable us to reconstruct all their doctrine exactly. It consisted, essentially, of a refusal to declare themselves upon anything whatever, of a systematic abandonment to custom, of a sort of passivity, which was to result, according to them, in peace of mind; for this was, for the Sceptics as well as for the Epicureans, the final object of philosophy.

But it was in the Academy, in the third century, that this tendency of thought took a scholarly form. The initiator of this change was the Æolian Arcesilaus of Pitane, a pupil of Crantor. He became the leader of the school about 280 B. C. and directed it for a period of forty years. Endowed with a brilliant, cultivated, and resourceful mind, he was an indefatigable disputant, charming by virtue of his amiable and disinterested character. His ideas, transmitted to his successors, in the following century found a no less remarkable representative in Carneades of Cyrene, an eloquent orator, always ready to attack or to parry and thrust, who directed the school from about 160 to 120 B. C. Academic scepticism was their common work.

The truth is, it was only an attenuated scepticism, rather well defined by the term "probabilism," which commonly serves to designate it. Setting itself especially the task of refuting the trenchant assertions of Stoic dogmatism and the negations of Epicureanism, its representatives professed that neither the senses nor reason could procure certainty. They pretended to revive for their purpose the expectant attitude which Plato had attributed to Socrates in many of his dialogs. Affirming nothing, they contradicted everything which the rival schools supported. The only concession which they consented to make was that certain opinions, everything taken into account, are more probable than others, and they admitted that it was wise to acquiesce in them provisionally, without, however, renouncing the freedom of scepticism. In the long disputes which they had with their opponents they brought up almost all the arguments of which the sceptics have since then made use; and for that reason they exerted an influence which has never entirely ceased. They have been reproached, with reason, for the inconsistency which lies in saying that the mind, incapable of discerning the truth, is nevertheless able to recognize probability.   But what is not to be denied them is the recognition that they made vividly clear the difficulties of absolutely certain knowledge.   Would it be fair to be severe with thinkers who, in refusing to acquiesce in premature and over-confident dogmatism, considered scepticism a necessary factor in progress of the human mind?

Eclecticism.—The Academy, however, did not persist indefinitely in this semi-scepticism.   In the first century before Christ, Antiochus of Ascalon, its leader, repudiated it formally.   The new dogmatism which he adopted was, however, an eclecticism, in which Platonic, Peripatetic, and Stoic ideas were fused.   In this he followed a tendency which was general at that time.   Philosophic speculation had multiplied hypotheses.   None of them had been able to impose itself in the long run, but almost all of them had brought to light some interesting aspect of things.   After so many efforts, men were little disposed to attempt entirely new explanations; it seemed best to revise what had previously been said, to appropriate the good from everything, and to reconcile as much as possible all things that were not irreconcilable.   The Academy tried this, but went at it too timidly; it did not dare to construct; it was content to repair.   But its eclecticism at least marks the beginning of a movement which was destined to continue and from which Neoplatonism was later to emerge.

To the same tendency is related the renewal of Peripateticism, which had attracted scarcely any attention since the time of Theophrastus.   Toward the beginning of the first century before Christ, we find it coming to life again at Athens in the person of Aristonicus of Rhodes, and Boethius.   Zealous commentators of Aristotle, whose manuscripts they revise and whose ideas they interpret, they themselves attest by their turn of mind this mutual penetration of doctrines; but what must warrant them a place in the general history of Greek civilization is especially the fact that they illuminated the totality of the Aristotelian philosophy, the influence of which was destined to be so great in time to come.

Mysticism.—In a general way, all these philosophies pretended to deal with reason; but we should certainly have an incomplete idea of them if we overlooked the part played by Mysticism, which became more and more bound up with them. Disseminated everywhere, it nevertheless manifests itself most completely in the Neopythagoreanism of the first century. It was probably at Alexandria, a decidedly cosmopolitan city, that the Neopythagorean doctrine was created and first developed; and there is reason to believe that it resulted from a fusion of traditional Greek Orphism, the Jewish and oriental religions, and certain elements of the ancient Pythagorean wisdom, which formed its core. Various borrowings from the philosophic doctrines enumerated above were later added to it. But the truth is that this Neo-pythagoreanism was only a particular manifestation of a general state of mind. The Hellenic world, morally weakened, sought in the supernatural a strengthening and a source of hope. Never had it been so strongly attached to mysteries, to revelations which opened prospects of future life to believers. It eagerly accepted belief in the new gods, or in beings intermediate between men and gods. Purifications and expiations found favor with uneasy and troubled souls tormented by vague superstitions. Nothing seemed to them more desirable than to enter into communion with divinity by initiations and theurgic practices, sources of privileged grace. Ideas were now confused, now coördinated in doctrines, more compact and precise with some, and more indistinct with many others; but already their great importance was about to become preponderant in the last stage of Greek civilization.

(4) THE SCIENCES

Inequality of Progress in the Various Sciences.—As regards the sciences properly so-called—mathematics, physics, mechanics, astronomy, and biology—the three centuries of the Hellenistic period offer us a spectacle of striking inequalities. While the mathematical sciences made remarkable progress at that time, the sciences of life remained almost stationary. The reason for this, undoubtedly, was that the former are made by a logical sequence of ideas which rises only from the work of the mind; from every established truth there immediately follows another truth which is a consequence of it. In the sciences of life, on the contrary, the first collected observations convey to the mind only a confused mass of materials, enormously complex, full of enigmas and apparent contradictions; and when a few superior minds have once classified them, long and patient study is required to verify the interpretations, to note the errors, and to draw from the observations everything usable that they contain. Moreover, antiquity lacked many of the indispensable resources; it had at its disposal neither the microscope nor chemical analysis. Under these conditions it could not easily do better than Aristotle and Theophrastus.

Natural Sciences.—Here, accordingly, we may review this category of sciences very rapidly. In the field of zoölogy, of botany, and even of medicine, the Hellenistic period did not produce anything which deserves to be mentioned in a survey as brief as this. Medicine, however, by reason of its practical utility, showed itself always active, but without realizing any appreciable scientific gains. Besides a dogmatism which pretended to perpetuate the tradition of Hippocrates, but which, very unfaithful to his spirit, fixed itself in rigid formulas, there developed at that time an empiricism, which, denying itself all coördination of facts, led to the very negation of science. The greatest merit of the physicians of this time was that they kept alive an art which was to be renewed in the following period by Galen and transmitted by him to the Middle Ages.

Mathematical and Physical Sciences.—On the other hand, in the mathematical and physical sciences, the first progress which had previously been realized by Pythagoras and his successors, Plato and his school, Theodorus of Cyrene, and Eudoxus of Cnidus, continued with glory. At the beginning of the third century, Euclid published his celebrated *Elements,* which have entitled him to be called "the great geometer," and which we still read. He laid down in it the foundations of geometry, such as they have continued to exist to our day. Some of the most notable qualities of the Greek mind are nowhere more vividly manifested than in this work. Shortly afterwards, Archimedes, at Syracuse, gave proof of a marvelously inventive genius, both in the theories relative to the measurement of the circle and of the cylinder, in the properties of the parabole, in the study of curves, and in physics and mechanics, discovering at once new principles and their unknown applications. Toward the end of the same century, the Pamphylian Apollonius, of Perga, composed the first treatise on conic sections; and finally Heron of Alexandria, at the beginning of the first century, likewise made progress in physics, mechanics, and pure mathematics.

Almost as remarkable were the works of the astronomers. To the scholar Aristarchus of Samos, who taught about 250 B. C., falls the honor of having discovered and dared to assert, for the first time, in spite of many vehement contradictions, that the earth revolved on its axis and made an annual revolution around the sun. To the same age belong the astronomical works of Eratosthenes, mentioned above as a critic and as a geographer, namely, his didactic and scientific poems, *Hermes* and *Erigone*, and his *Catasterismi*, in which he rivaled with the *Phenomena* of Arotus, who had preceded him a little. Both of them, it is true, did little more than popularize knowledge already acquired, and they mixed legend with science. Nevertheless, we may conclude from the success of their books as to the interest taken by their contemporaries in knowledge of the universe. But the great astronomer of this time was the Bithnyian Hipparchus, of Nicæa, who lived in the second century, inventor of the astrolage, creator of trigonometry, the actual originator of astronomical computations and measurements, and first author of tables indicating the movements of the sun and the moon. By the totality of these works it may be said that astronomy was at that time emerging from its infancy and inaugurating truly scientific methods.

Let us not go further. It suffices from an enumeration of these names and from a rapid review of the principal discoveries which made them famous for the reader to form a general idea of the contribution made by Hellenistic science to the fund of knowledge which Greece handed down to subsequent civilizations.

CHAPTER IV

GREEK CIVILIZATION UNDER THE EMPIRE

Survival of Hellenic Civilization under Roman Domination.—The establishment of the Roman Empire caused the last Greek states to disappear. In the Orient as in the Occident they were no longer anything but Roman provinces. Whatever autonomy had been able to persist until then was utterly annihilated. Under the authority of governors of various kinds sent out by Rome, everything emanated from the imperial power, which held the entire world under its domination. But Greek civilization did not perish with the destruction of the Hellenistic kingdoms. Far from it. On the contrary, it imposed itself upon the conquerors. Already, in the last centuries of the Republic, Rome had profoundly fallen under its influence. In the first centuries of the Empire it succumbed to it still more, and in the time of the Antonines we find a Roman emperor writing the journal of his intimate life in Greek. The Latin culture scarcely succeeded in grazing it, and never penetrated it. Thus the history of Greek civilization continues under the Empire, with no sudden or very apparent change, until the time when, with the creation of an Eastern empire, the Byzantine civilization commences. Neither the general aspect nor the intimate constitution of society are very perceptibly modified during these four centuries. Nevertheless, society undoubtedly underwent a crisis

242

which had its causes in the decline of polytheism.   In the second century, Christianity, which was growing and expanding, began to shake the foundations of the old religion.   In the third century, it placed itself in rivalry with paganism; it had its apologists, its teachers, and its schools; it fortified itself even in persecutions.   In the fourth century, it triumphed with Constantine and his successors.   And no doubt the new religion, according as it attracted the intellectual aristocracy, became impregnated with Greek culture; indeed, it even developed into a new form of the ancient civilization, at least in the East.   But it is too distinct a form, inspired by a very different spirit, for us to study it here.   Greek paganism is the limit beyond which we should not pass.

While declining, therefore, this ancient civilization gave proof, during these last centuries, of a vitality which can not be ignored.   If even seems that, thanks to the Roman peace, it experienced at that time something in the nature of a second flowering, assuredly somewhat pale, as is natural in Indian summer, but not devoid of charm in spite of everything.   Some of the works which issued from it belong among those whose influence has persisted down to our day.   They acquaint us with a society which, to be sure, compared with a glorious past, did not conceal its inferiorities, and which, on the other hand, no longer felt itself turned toward the future with firm hopes; but, at least, it attached itself with zeal and love to its traditions, and applied itself to the best of its ability to perpetuate them.   It found pleasure in this and succeeded thereby in doing honor to itself.

The Life of the Cultivated Greeks under the Roman Empire.—It is in the first and second centuries of our era that the life of the cultivated Greeks of this time presents itself to us in its most interesting aspect.

Everything considered, the life of the cultivated classes was an intelligent one. Plutarch, whose works we shall mention further on, has left us testimonies in regard to this point, which give us a truly favorable idea of that age; and what he says of himself, or of his family, having nothing exceptional about it, may be broadly generalized without risk of error.

In a small city of Bœotia, at Chæronea, three or four generations pass before our eyes between the time of Augustus and that of Hadrian. It is at first the great-grandfather of Plutarch, Nicarchus, witness of the civil wars the effects of which made themselves cruelly felt about him, then his son, Lamprias, and his grandson, the father of Plutarch, who, one after another, seem to have quietly enjoyed the reëstablishment of order in the world. They occupied themselves in turning their lands to account, in replacing in good condition their family fortunes—honest people, devoid of ambition, content with the public esteem which they enjoyed and little troubled with regrets for the national independence a long time lost. In these surroundings, in which the spirit of the family passed from father to son, intellectual and moral culture was highly appreciated. All the fine traditions of Greece, all its memories, were held in honor there. Thus Plutarch and his brothers were sent as young men to Athens, which still remained the seat of polite studies. Celebrated schools attracted thither from all points of the Greek world the best teachers and studious young men. Nowhere were the relations between the professors and the pupils better regulated; under the guarantee of a sane discipline, they were familiar and cordial. There were friendly gatherings and talks around a hospitable table; random debates about this and that; contests in intelligence, in erudition, and in ingenious and subtile reflec-

tions. A very active taste for literature, for philosophy,
for the sciences, and for religious questions prevailed in
all the circles. On the other hand, there was little or
no discussion of politics. It seems that the exchange
of ideas had become the principal object of life. Moreover, it did not cease outside of the schools. People
traveled much at this time, assuredly for business reasons,
but also for curiosity. The means of communication
being surer and easier than formerly, men went from the
Orient to the Occident, from Greece to Italy, and from
Italy to Greece. Plutarch, his education completed,
visited Egypt, the great city of Alexandria, then Rome
and Italy, where he sojourned on several occasions.
Here he gave lectures, for conferences were in vogue;
he visited the philosophers, for they were everywhere, and
he himself taught philosophy; but he also visited the celebrated places, he made the acquaintance of great personages, he familiarized himself with Roman history by
questioning the descendants of those who had participated in the making of it. The mutual penetration of
the two civilizations appears to us there actively.
Then he returned to his own country; and, having decided not to abandon it, he occupied himself with
municipal affairs, without neglecting his own affairs.
He held local magistracies, frequented the near-by sanctuary of Delphi, so rich in monuments and in traditions, and even allowed himself to be connected with
priestly functions. Gradually he became celebrated.
Distinguished strangers came to see him and were received by him. On his part, he wandered about in
Greece, betook himself from time to time to Athens, his
intellectual domicile, whither the education of his sons
soon drew him. The best part of his time he spent in
reading and in writing. What did he write?—treatises

on ethics, letters, but especially biographies, of which
we shall soon have to speak. For the present, what
interests us in him is his mode of life; for it represents
that of a large portion of his contemporaries and his
compatriots. A laborious idleness, a peaceful existence,
an activity which ends in dissertations, a varied culture,
a taste for knowledge—such are the characteristics
which give the best Greek society of the century of the
Antonines its proper physiognomy. We shall find them
again in its literature, and the latter will reveal to us at
the same time some other aspects of this same society,
some of the changes which it underwent under the influence of circumstances.

*General Character of the Intellectual Production under
the Empire.*—In the time of the Hellenistic kingdoms, intellectual production had already lost much of its
spontaneity; already imitation was tending to stifle
originality. Under the Empire, notwithstanding the
number and variety of its works, and notwithstanding the
merit of some of them, this character becomes still more
discernible. In all things men now succeeded only by
imitation. There is hardly anything new in literature,
and still less in the arts. Science and philosophy alone
give evidence of a certain creative power. It is chiefly
with them, accordingly, that we have reason to occupy
ourselves here. Nevertheless, it is necessary to cast
at least a glance at the literary movement as a whole,
from which philosophy is inseparable.

Oratory and Rhetoric. The Atticists.—It is a curious
circumstance that the art of speaking was never more
strongly cultivated or more greatly admired than it was
in this period, in which it had lost its real bases for existence. The Greco-Roman world, in the second century,
abounds in orators; Asia, Greece, and even Italy, acclaim

these masters of the spoken word, these marvelous improvisers, these artists of oratory, who have taken the title of sophists, which had fallen into disuse, and who bear it proudly. The schools in which they teach the secrets of rhetoric are frequented more than ever before; but it is especially in orations of great ostentation that they triumph—eulogies of cities, compliments to official personages, harangues delivered at public ceremonies. More serious occasions are offered to them, when they come to convey to the Roman magistrates, sometimes to the senate or even to the Emperor himself, the grievances or the congratulations of their fellow-citizens. And besides that, they always attract a large audience to oratorical exhibitions. Some names were then illustrious which have long since fallen into a just oblivion, such as those of Scopelian, Favorinus of Arles, Ælius Aristides, and Philostratus. Their eloquence lacked every substantial element, and posterity has had the right to look upon it as sonorous verbiage. Nevertheless, we must recognize that these artists performed no useless task in reawakening the sense of literary beauty which their immediate predecessors had too much neglected. Those who at that time were called "Atticists," grammarians and rhetoricians, while exaggerating their scruples as purists, restored to honor correctness and good form in language. They purified it by imposing upon the orators and writers the authority of the best Attic prose-writers of former times, and in this way they prevented it from degenerating too rapidly. Evidently it was not in their power to do more, or to give it the freshness and spontaneity which constitutes the eternal charm of masterpieces.

History.—The historical form was better protected, by its very nature, against the danger of frivolity. In the second and third centuries there were Greek historians whose works have survived and are justly esteemed. Imitators of Thucydides, Xenophon, and Ephorus, their common merit is that of having clearly and honestly set forth, in correct and pure language, the events which they undertook to chronicle. They made use of information which without them we would not have today. It is to them that we must have recourse for the knowledge of important periods. We owe to Arrian of Nicomedia, a contemporary of the Emperor Hadrian, the best account that we have of *The Expedition of Alexander*, remarkable for its simplicity and its veracity. Appian of Alexandria wrote in the reign of Antoninus his *Roman History*, of which we still possess important parts —a rather dull composition, without originality or personal criticisms, but well ordered and composed, in general, of good materials. Neither of these writers was equal to Dio Cassius, the most remarkable historian of this time. Of his great *Roman History* only some twenty books, a little more than a fourth of the work, remain. Here we find set forth, in firm language, the tragic events of the end of the republic, the civil wars, and the history of the empire under the first Cæsars; but it is to be regretted that Dio, having used Thucydides as a model, did not succeed in appropriating his freedom of thought or his independence of judgment. After him, the Syrian Herodianus, whose history of the *Successors of Marcus Aurelius* is still read, merely deserves mention.

The work that does the most honor to the historiography of this time is undoubtedly the collection of the *Parallel Lives* of Plutarch. Thanks to these *Lives*, biography, which until then had remained a subaltern form of history, truly acquired a new value. No doubt, one can not consider Plutarch either a great writer or a vigorous and daring thinker. Even as a historian, indeed, he lays himself open to serious reproach. In him we find neither a careful criticism of the sources, nor a sufficient regard for chronology, nor a complete understanding of great political plans. Plutarch's work is moralistic and curious above all, and by his portrayal of customs and his description of varied details, he succeeds in making the majority of the remarkable men of antiquity, Greeks and Romans, live once more before our eyes. A rich fund of information, drawn from reading as abundant as it was varied, enabled him to gather not only a quantity of secondary but suggestive facts, but also numerous traits and customs which reveal the character of his personages. Careful to seek out the motives of their action, to inform himself as much as possible regarding their private life, and to catch them unawares, as it were, in their moments of abandon, to the end of ascertaining their secret sentiments, their moral habits and their underlying natures, he often succeeds in acquainting us with them better than the historians properly so called have done. We may add that he could tell agreeable stories, that he possessed dramatic sense to a high degree, and that the often long-winded reflections with which he interspersed his accounts, lacked neither astuteness nor power. Hence the work as a whole reveals almost all the aspects of ancient civilization. The popularity which he has enjoyed since the Renaissance is thus explained. It has provided more subjects for tragedies than any other work; it has been enjoyed by some of our best moralists; and nothing, perhaps, has contributed more to the influence which Greece has exerted upon certain moments of our own French history, especially upon the period of the Revolution. Thus even today, altho the progress of historical criticism has weakened its authority, it is one of the works of which we can not be ignorant if we wish to know the moral life of ancient Greece.

Satirical and Fantastical Literature. Lucian.—In a very different form, another writer of the second century, Lucian of Samosata, likewise earned a lasting reputation. Like Plutarch, he owed much to the classical writers of the past; but, also like him, altho he borrowed a great deal, he was, in rather large measure, a creator; and as such he had his influence. He was, by profession, one of those sophists of whom we have spoken above; but his turn of mind revealed itself very quickly as quite different from theirs. Deriving his inspiration both from the ancient comedy and from the biting satires which the Cynic sect had placed in fashion, he gave scope to his sparkling and scoffing verve in light and varied works, dialogs of the dead, pleasant conversations of the gods and of mythological persons, treatises or dissertations, pamphlets, and fantastical compositions; in these he poked fun, now at the superstitions and fables of polytheism, now at the teachings or the follies of the contemporary philosophers, criticizing all dogmatisms, tearing off all masks, piercing with his darts all charlatanry. He was fundamentally a sceptic, who perhaps sought above all an opportunity to show off his talent. But his scepticism, associated with a sharp good sense, could not fail to awaken many reflections and to fortify many doubts. He lets us see the emptiness which at that time was conspicuous in many minds under the ancient beliefs. Moreover, a vivacious imagination, grace, ironic enjoyment, and a brisk and piquant style, seasoned with Attic salt, made him a master of satirical prose. His work has remained the model of a form which has attracted many an imitator.

The Novel.—Let us mention, finally, among the literary

creations of the time of the Empire, the novel; for it is
in the novel that the free imagination, being diverted
from poetry, found especially a means of exercising itself at that time. The Greek novel is not a fiction of
any kind; it is essentially a love story inserted in a narrative of adventure. It proceeds at once from the earlier
erotic literature, and from the accounts of voyages, true
or fabulous. Thru its characters as a whole, it represents
well the state of mind and the customs in the Greek world
for which it was made. A society detached from all
great things, and one in which the influence of women was
considerable, could not fail to make love one of its preferred subjects. Moreover, it was too frivolous to demand profound psychological studies of its novelists.
What they represent is not a passion in conflict with other
passions, or with a sense of duty. If love, in a Greek
novel, is opposed, it is opposed only by exterior obstacles
and by imaginary events more or less improbable. Complicated adventures, abductions, tales of brigands and
pirates, fortuitous meetings, incidents upon incidents—
such are its ordinary elements. The lovers, separated by
some accident, are marched across the world, tossed about
by the caprices of fortune, until the time when they
finally come together again, always faithful to each other,
and having escaped by miracle the most terrible dangers.
In these rather incredible fictions, the marvelous abounds.
In reading them one quickly senses that they were composed for minds to which real life seemed unattractive,
and which even found pleasure in detaching themselves
from it. A rather childish curiosity is associated in them
with a total lack of critical spirit. Their credulity accepted without the least resistance all theatrical happen-
ings, all unforeseen interventions of the gods, and all
fortuitous combinations, even the strangest. Thus these

novels, in spite of the diversity of the fictions and of the characters, all resemble one another astonishingly. It is always the same general traits which one finds in the narrations of an Antonius Diogenes, an Iamblichus, a Xenophon of Ephesus, of the Syrian Heliodorus, of the Alexandrine Achilles Tatius, and of Chariton, composed and published between the first and fifth centuries of our era. Among these authors there is scarcely any difference of talent. Possibly Xenophon of Ephesus with his *Ephesiacs*, and Heliodorus of Emesa with his *Æthiopica* or *Adventures of Theagenes and Chariclea*, are the least bad. It is difficult for us today to become interested in such works. Nevertheless, they were not without influence upon the growth of the modern novel. And this is still more true of the pastoral of Longus, *Daphnis and Chloe*, the precise date of which is unknown, but which certainly belongs to the same period. The love of two children is here described with an ingenuity more apparent than real, but not without some charm. In spite of a note of affectation and overdone nicety, this little book is one of those which have not ceased to be read.

Erudite and Technical Literature.—We must not neglect entirely in this review, summary as it is, the erudite literature; for it also shows us to what extent Greece was living at that time in its past. What, in fact, are the treatises of rhetoric due to the masters of the second and third centuries, such as those of Hermogenes of Tarsus, Apsines of Gadara, and Menander of Laodicea, unless they are collections of oratorical recipes drawn from the classical works or extracted more or less skillfully from the special writings of Aristotle and of Theophrastus? The small book of Longinus, *On the Sublime*, mixes with precepts inspired with the same spirit a commentary, sometimes eloquent, composed of beautiful

passages taken from the poets or the orators of former
times.   The grammarians, on their part, labor to study
in its minutest details the language of the ancient authors,
which is coming to differ more and more from the
current speech, and seek to establish rules governing it;
this is the work of such writers as Apollonius Dyscolus,
and Herodianus.   They select as their collaborators zealous lexicographers, giving them the task of collecting
from the ancient writers words that have fallen out of use,
rare terms, and those which allude to forgotten usages.
The lexicons of Harpocration and of Julius Pollux, composed toward the end of the second century and transmitted to us, bear witness to their labors.   And *The Banquet of the Sophists*, of Athenæus of Naucratis, published
a few years later, places before our eyes, as it were, the
work of a passionate collector of old curiosities, who, not
wishing to let anything of this precious antiquity be lost,
applies himself to introduce, in an interminable dialog,
all the notes which he has been able to collect in his
laborious reading.

CHAPTER V

SCIENCE AND PHILOSOPHY

General Survey.—The lessening of creative activity in literature which has just been discussed could not fail to make itself felt in science and philosophy as well. This is true, not because there were fewer savants or philosophers at that time, but because both applied themselves more to the task of coördinating or discussing the ideas of their predecessors than to that of conducting new researches. Greek thought retired within itself, so to speak, instead of continuing to expand freely. Nevertheless, the work thus accomplished was by no means lacking in interest or results. For, in spite of everything, this revision of the previous ideas, knowledge, and systems inevitably gave them new life, to a certain extent. Thus with materials in large part old, edifices of an appreciably different aspect were constructed. And altho this renovation, in the sciences properly so called, was not very considerable *in toto*, it led in philosophy, as we shall see, to the formation of a doctrine the influence of which was destined to be deep and lasting.

(1) THE SCIENCES

Mathematical and Natural Sciences.—Alexandria, which in the Hellenistic period had been a seat of such intense studies, produced again in the following centuries some of the most remarkable representatives of the mathematical and physical sciences. First among them ranks Claudius Ptolemy, who distinguished himself as an astronomer, as a geographer, as a musical theorist, and as a physician, in the second half of the second century of our era. His great *Treatise on Astronomy*, known in the Middle Ages, after the Arabic translations, by the title *Almagest*, remained the foundation of the science of astronomy until the time of Copernicus. It preserves for us all of the observations made both by the author himself and by his predecessors. In his *Geography* we find gathered all the information which the science of that time had at its disposal for determining the latitude and longitude of the places mentioned on the maps; it was the greatest work of this kind that had ever been executed. His *Harmonics* give him the reputation of being the continuator of Aristoxenus and the Pythagoreans in musical theory. Finally, besides his treatise on *Optics*, of which we possess a Latin translation, he wrote various lost works on mechanics and on a few phases of physics.

In the field of mathematics, another great name worth mentioning is that of the Alexandrian, Diophantus, who seems to have lived in the third century of our era. His *Arithmetic*, the text of which unfortunately has come to us mutilated and altered, today represents the sum total of the researches undertaken by the Greek mathematicians on numbers. Precisely what part of this work is to be attributed to Diophantus himself? That is a point on which the specialists are not entirely agreed. In general, however, it is admitted that the Alexandrine scholar did more than merely set in operation, in a series of problems, methods already employed before. At the very least he chose the best methods and brought out their value. He may be looked upon as one of the creators of the theory of arithmetic, and also as the one who furnished the Arabs with the component elements of algebra.

Biological Sciences.—The rôle of Galen in medicine, using this word in its broadest sense, was very nearly the same as that of Ptolemy in astronomy and geography, and of Diophantus in arithmetic. Like them, he summarized in his writings all the knowledge acquired by his predecessors; but like them, also, he developed this knowledge by his personal observations. Well informed in philosophy and in letters, he bore everywhere, whatever may have been the subject to which he applied himself, the habit of methodical reflection; he knew how to coördinate and to generalize, and he reasoned well and clearly. A long medical practice at Pergamus, his birth-place, and at Smyrna, Alexandria, and Rome, under the reigns of Antoninus, of Marcus Aurelius, and of Commodus, had given him a rich experience. A prolific writer, he turned this experience to account in his very numerous works, the most important of which have come down to us. In them one finds evidence of the progress which is due to him in anatomy, in physiology, and in pathology. An admirer of Hippocrates, on whose principal works he wrote commentaries, he deserves to be compared with him in the history of Greek medicine. The former was the initiator of medical science; the latter gave it the form under which it was to be transmitted to modern times pending the appearance of new methods and increased knowledge.

(2) PHILOSOPHY PRIOR TO NEO-PLATONISM

Rôle of Greek Philosophy under the Empire.—But at that time the rôle of philosophy was much more important than that of the sciences in the survival of Hellenic civilization. Already, during the Hellenistic period, it had come out of the schools and had penetrated widely into Greek and Roman society.   At the time of the Empire it exerts a still more varied and extended influence. In truth, one finds philosophers everywhere.   In their capacity as professors, they continue to gather all the cultivated youth around them; state chairs are instituted in their favor, besides those maintained by the cities and those of a private character.   As intimate counselors, as guides of the conscience, they become more and more the familiar associates of great men and at the same time they give moral advice to a host of restless souls, either orally or in writing.   But even this does not suffice for them.   They transform themselves into veritable preachers, and many of them go thru the world carrying the good word from city to city.   Some of them address themselves especially to chosen hearers, who are not indifferent to beautiful language, and who wish to be instructed or taken to task in delicate terms, with a certain elegance and literary polish.   Others, less refined or more daring, go straight to the people; they face crowds and criticize vices in public places, wherever they find the opportunity, in the stadia or theaters.   Naturally, this philosophy imparted in speeches or lectures can scarcely live only on commonplaces.   It is in small circles, in the intimacy of genuine thinkers or of superior natures, that we must seek, on the one hand, the best examples and unusual virtues, and on the other hand, personal ideas, which become organized into doctrines.

As for general spirit, what characterizes this Greek philosophy of the Empire is the development of the moral tendency previously mentioned, to which is added a religious and even mystical interest, which becomes more and more pronounced.   In this way it is related to the Platonic tradition, and ultimately it leads to a renewal of Platonism.   But in its progress it gathers and absorbs in a broad eclecticism many elements proceeding from other schools, notably from Stoicism and from Pythagoreanism. It also endeavors to save everything in the national religion which does not seem irreconcilable with moral law and with the idea of God. Thus it becomes the superior form of paganism, and is the form which best represents the latter in the face of growing Christianity. From this results the inevitable conflict which leads to its ruin.

Previously, however, and even toward the middle of the third century, the sects of the Hellenistic period are still in existence—some of them at least—and their activity and true value are brought to light in works which can not be slighted.

Stoicism under the Empire.—Among them, the first place undoubtedly belongs to Stoicism. We have seen how the doctrine of the Portico was definitely constituted in the preceding period, and what prestige it had acquired even in Roman society. It had nothing more to gain from the dogmatic point of view; and, on the other hand, if it supported in certain respects the influence of general eclecticism, this was so only to a small extent, to such a degree did its original rigidity preserve it from outside encroachments. True to the lessons of its founders, it discovered in their teachings everything that seemed necessary to assure the wise man internal peace in the midst of the difficulties of life and political revolutions. Thus refusing to rejuvenate its dogmas, it endeavored to make all their efficacy felt; and this sort of daily verification of their value became the occasion of a practical teaching which has survived in a few particularly precious works.

First and foremost is the *Handbook* of Epictetus, with the collection of his *Discourses*, both written in a sense under his dictation by the historian Arrian, who has already been mentioned in another connection. The *Handbook* particularly, for the reason that it contains in a condensed form the entire substance of this lofty morality, has survived as one of the most refreshing books handed down to us by Greek antiquity. Nowhere has the power of the human soul been affirmed more energetically, resolved to free itself from all servility by its own strength. We read here the proud and somewhat rude words of an ancient Syrian slave, a freedman, whom the edict of Diocletian against the philosophers, in 89 A. D., had driven from Rome. Retiring to Nicopolis, in Epirus, he lived there in poverty and solitude, without a family, without intimate affections; and yet a profoundly religious optimism breathes in everything which has been collected of his utterances. Persuaded that the universe is good as it is, that all events take place according to the law of a superior wisdom which leads everything to ends determined by it, he finds complete satisfaction in the adhesion which he gives without reserve to all the wishes of that benevolent Providence in which he has faith. And from that time on, certain that this adhesion depends only upon himself, that nothing in the world can prevent him from giving it, he feels both free and happy; free in spite of everything which seems to oppress him, happy in spite of exile, in spite of misery, in spite of the suffering and of everything which troubles the majority of men. He feels it and he wants others to feel it as he does; for he is a master of moral force and of happiness, but an exacting master, imperious in his benevolence.

Such is the book of the slave; we may compare it with that of an emperor, Marcus Aurelius, thoroly similar in virtue of its doctrine, thoroly inspired by the same faith and the same ideal. But whereas the slave gives a lesson to his disciples, the emperor addresses only himself and can correct only his own weaknesses.   Fully conscious of his immense responsibility, of the extent of his duties, he examines his conscience and notes his thoughts day by day in order to judge himself and to better himself.   He is a judge without indulgence, whom nothing escapes, since he is at once the accused and the accuser.   Moving by virtue of his sincerity, attracting by virtue of the nobility and delicacy of his sentiments, he lets people see his scruples, his intimate conflict with inevitable discouragements, his resistance to dangerous influences, his secret worries, and, above all that, his constant will to do good, his admirable force of soul.   No book has ever better revealed the man in the author; and this man to whom it introduces us is one of the best types of manhood, one of the most worthy of admiration and love.   He is not, however, an exceptional being.   He resembles each of us in some respect; and thus this book of personal confidences, this discourse which he holds with himself, offers us in its psychological analyses an always true image of the human heart.   It has never ceased to be read, having never ceased to be profitable.

The Platonic Tradition.—While Stoicism thus maintained itself almost intact up to the end of the second century, the Platonic tradition, on the contrary, appeared in a blended form from the beginning of the Empire.

We find it, much impregnated with Judaism, in the work of the Alexandrian Jew, Philo, in the first half of the first century of our era.   Nothing is more curious than to see Greek philosophy thus penetrating a milieu which seems necessarily to be the most refractory to its influence.   In Philo it is mixed with Judaic theology to the point of modifying it profoundly.   Borrowing from the Stoics their allegorical method of interpretation, this teacher of Israel claims to rediscover in the Old Testament the majority of the ideas of Plato, and he does not even hesitate to believe that Plato borrowed them from the sacred books. As for his morality, it is in large part Stoic. But in this philosophy, which owes almost everything to the past, there appear elements indicative of new tendencies. The most important is the effort whereby Philo, while remaining faithful to the monotheism of Israel, nevertheless seeks to enlarge it. The god which he conceives manifests himself by "forces," which in his eyes seem to acquire, at times, a sort of individual personality. The principle is the "logos" or divine word, to which he attributes the rôle of an intermediary between God himself and men. Here we have already something in the nature of a first outline of the Neo-platonic doctrine.

The tradition of the Academy is also found again, but more influenced by Stoicism, in the work of the Bithynian, Dio of Prusa, surnamed Dio Chrysostom. A rather strange individual, at first a sophist according to the custom of the time in the early part of his life, then proscribed by Domitian and turning a philosopher in exile, he becomes a sort of preacher of morality under the reigns of Nerva and of Trajan. Those of his discourses which have been preserved bear witness to a rich and varied culture of mind, to a flowing eloquence, and to a distinguished talent for writing. We find, naturally, many commonplaces, the banality of which the author does not always succeed in dissimulating by pleasing details or by ingenious inventions. But it is interesting to hear him reproach the people of Alexandria for their frivolity, their turbulence, and their delight in the games of the circus and the horse-races. On the other hand, philosophy with him plays a rather beautiful rôle, when it traces to the Emperor himself the ideal image of the king, or when it denies that slavery is founded on right, affirming that moral quality alone establishes a real distinction among men. We may add that in certain of his discourses we find a lofty conception of God, conceived principally as the supreme realization of everything which reason adjudges excellent. That is why, altho there is nothing truly original in Dio other than his personality, we must recognize that his work is at least the interesting expression of a whole group of ideas and sentiments which show us Greek wisdom in the process of perfecting itself.

But the most renowned of the Platonists of this time, the one, in any case, who is read the most even today, was Plutarch, to whom we have to revert rapidly in order to complete what we have said about him above. For this biographer was also an open disciple of the Academy; and in this quality he combated Stoicism and Epicureanism, but took pleasure in invoking the authority of Plato. His treatises on morality, in which he discourses agreeably on questions of conduct by mingling anecdote with counsel, reveal him under the aspect of a guide of the conscience, who combines observation and the lessons of experience with a sane doctrine, without exaggerated rigor and without excess of indulgence. Nevertheless, what is perhaps the most interesting in the philosophic part of his work is the section on religion. On the one hand, he makes himself the zealous defender of the traditional beliefs of Greece; he remains devotedly attached to the ancient cults, he tries to demonstrate the veracity of the oracles, and he either refuses to admit their failure or explains it in a manner designed to preserve the divine character. On the other hand, the foreign religions, particularly those of Egypt, interest him greatly, not as simple objects of curiosity or study, but because he believes he finds in them, under different names, the same gods of Greece. It is this which he undertakes to prove by ingenious relationships, founded on allegorical interpretations. The result is that he groups the principal varieties of polytheism in a syncretism which preserves the Hellenic character. In reality, the foreign influences make themselves felt strongly. Dualism, against which Plato had not been able to defend himself entirely, acquires with Plutarch an entirely different importance. In contradistinction to the supreme God, the principle of good, he recognizes as necessary a bad principle, from which all evil in the universe proceeds. And this principle is not matter; for he represents it as purely passive, and therefore equally capable of good and of evil. It is an active power, essentially evil-doing, which opposes itself with all its forces to the divine power, the source of all good. He relates it to the Ahriman of Zoroaster, and to the Typhon of the Egyptians, thus bearing witness to the penetration of Oriental beliefs into Hellenism. Between these two contrary powers, intermediaries are indispensable. These are the beings which Plutarch calls demons, as did Plato previously. His philosophy attributes a varied rôle to them. Very unequal and dissimilar, some of them for him are the very gods of Greek polytheism, while others appear to him as impure spirits; and it is in this way that he believes he can explain a large part of the mythological traditions as well as the violent or gross cults which are sanguinary or immoral. A singularly complex theology, apparently, which attests the dilemma of the best minds, their desire to abandon nothing of that which they looked upon as a sacred heritage, and at the same time their need of not remaining obstinately unreceptive to foreign influxes. In this confusion the Greek genius persisted in seeking coördination and harmony.

Neo-pythagoreanism.—Analogous provisions are found
in Neo-pythagoreanism, the formation of which was mentioned above at the end of the Hellenistic period.   Reconstituted at that time as a school, we see it undergoing a
notable development under the Empire.   It is represented
principally by Apollonius of Tyana and Moderatus in the
first century, by Nicomachus and Numenius in the second,
and by Philostratus at the beginning of the third.   But
its doctrines in themselves, in which Platonic, Aristotelian,
and Stoic elements are mixed with old Pythagorean ideas,
offer nothing very original.   Only by virtue of its morality and its idea of life, is it of interest in the history
of civilization.   The biography of Apollonius of Tyana,
written by Philostratus, shows us clearly what element of
credulity and superstition was associated in its adherents
with a spiritualism which was sometimes confined to
asceticism.   Philosophy, as they conceived it, was less a
science than a form of life entirely permeated by religion.
Purity of customs and practice of abstinences constitute
its essential discipline; and this discipline was especially
for the Pythagoreans a means of placing themselves in
close contact with God.   Their demonology represented
this contact as facilitated by supernatural intermediaries.
And thus, monotheists by profession, they not only worshipped the Greek gods and certain foreign gods, but they
made Pythagoras himself and, later on, Apollonius of
Tyana, if not gods, at least divine men, prophets,
magicians, thaumaturgists, as well as sages endowed with
infallible reason.   It was the school in which was most
strongly manifested that mysticism which was later to become one of the principal elements in the Neo-platonic
doctrine.

Scepticism.—In opposition to these various dogmatisms, it was natural that scepticism likewise demanded

its rights.   After Ænesidemus, of whom we know scarcely more than his name, the physician and philosopher Sextus, an empiric, who seems to have written at the end of the second century, made himself the convinced defender of them.   His *Pyrrhonian Hypotyposes* and his treatises *Against the Mathematici* summarize all the arguments which Greek scepticsm of the preceding centuries had successively opposed to the doctrines of the various schools.   He even pretends to overturn all science, all positive teaching; it is the most systematic defiance which has ever been cast into the face of human reason.   But if the tendency which it represents is to be noted here, it can be noted only in passing.   There is no doubt that it remained confined to a narrow circle.   The general intellectual movement tended at that time in an entirely different direction; it was destined to end in Neo-platonism.

(3) NEO-PLATONISM

Origins and General Character of Neo-platonism—. Outlined at Alexandria, in the first half of the third century, by Ammonius Saccas, the Neo-platonic philosophy was definitively constituted at Rome, a few years later, by one of his pupils, the Alexandrian Plotinus, between the years 245 and 270 A. D.   This was truly the last great creation of the Greek genius; and the effort to which it bears witness shows what vitality there was still left in it. Refusing to deny its own self or to consent to dissolve itself miserably, it sought to coördinate in a broad eclecticism everything superior which had formerly been produced, and it succeeded in adapting the doctrine thus formed to new needs, of which it was fully conscious. This doctrine presented itself as a renewal or rather as an interpretation of that of Plato.   In any case, it was a very free interpretation, which associated with the teachings of the Academy many ideas borrowed from the Pythagoreans, from the Peripatetic tradition, and from the Portico, without counting those which it added on its own account. Naturally strange contrasts had to result from this fusion of a far-off past with a present so different. No school carried abstraction further; none, moreover, attributed more importance to sentiment; on the one hand, an extreme subtlety, an abuse of analysis ending in a maze of innumerable distinctions; on the other hand, a fervor carried to the point of exaltation. This double character, so ill designed to please the modern mind, was nevertheless the very reason for the success of Neo-platonism. By its abstraction and subtlety, it succeeded in reconciling, at least in appearance, beliefs, traditions, and diverse doctrines; and by its appeal to the senses, it gave satisfaction to the mystical tendencies which were then prevalent. The result was a construction which was no doubt fragile in its totality, since it could succeed in lasting scarcely more than two centuries, but which nevertheless contained elements that have continued to exist in other forms and in other combinations.

The Monotheistic Element in Neo-platonism.—For centuries, as we have seen, the Greek mind, without freeing itself entirely from polytheism, tended to modify it by subordinating it to the conception of a supreme god, in whom was condensed, so to speak, the essential idea of divinity. This tendency was carried by Plotinus, whose thought is characterized by a boldness of abstraction which stops at nothing, to the point where it resembles a defiance to human intelligence. The god of Neo-platonism, as a matter of fact, is beyond all sensible forms, beyond all imaginable attributes, beyond all precise determination; he can not be defined or, consequently, named. It is only by a logical operation that the mind, incapable of attaining him directly, can form an idea of what he is. Plurality reveals to the mind the unity from which it proceeds; the visible effects permit it to go back to a first cause; and the varied forms of good, the existence of which it verifies, constrain it to conceive an absolute Good, which is its source. Thus it is the natural movement of the mind which lifts it up to the absolute Unity, from which all existence proceeds. Such a unity being admitted, how it is to be related to the plurality which our senses make known to us? Plotinus was persuaded that he could render this communication intelligible without destroying, by the very act, the idea of absolute unity. Everything that exists derives its existence from God; but God, according to him, in producing life in its variety, does not undergo either change or diminution. The living forms are only reflections which he projects without exteriorizing himself. Such formulas are apt to conceal the intimate contradictions of a system; they do not suppress them; but they deceive their very authors. Thus we see Plotinus treating these reflections as so many distinct beings. He multiplies them at pleasure, no doubt in order better to manage the transition between two irreconcilable extremes. He thus comes to conceive an immense chain of existences, which grow weaker and more obscure according as they draw further away from the first cause. Around the central seat, a first zone is outlined in his metaphysician's imagination; he sees it entirely illumined by this seat, and for him it is that of the reason; beyond is a second zone, already less brilliant, more related to the darkness of the sensible world, which begins to invade it: it is that of the soul; and finally, contiguous to the second zone, but entirely darkened, entirely enveloped in material night, is the last zone, that of the body. In running over them, the thought follows a descending movement. Nevertheless Plotinus thinks, as did Aristotle and others after him, that all these beings aspire to God, from whom they seem to draw away indefinitely. This is so ordered that an equally progressive ascension corresponds to the progressive degradation which has just been described. Such is the general course in which his thought moves.

Of course, it would be scarcely possible to follow this thought here step by step. The details of the combinations which he imagines are strangely complex and often obscure. But we should note the effort of a philosophy which, manifestly, wishes to detach itself more than it is able to do from transitory and contingent things. The supra-sensible world is the only one which seems to it truly intelligible; it makes of it its own object. Far from seeking life in movement and in change, it states as a principle that life is to be found only outside of time, in eternal identity and in absolute immutability. What, then, is matter, which seems to the common run of men most real? Plotinus is disposed to see only nothing in it; and if it is absolutely necessary to consider it under a positive aspect, he would gladly say that it is evil. It is true that sometimes, from another point of view, he admires the visible universe; he does not admit that one can fail to recognize its beauty or that one can criticize its organization. But let us understand the good. The true object of his admiration is not that which pleases the senses—such things as movement, variety, fugitive charm of forms and of colors, the marvelous play of light, the enchantment of artists and poets; it is harmony and the arrangement of parts, the intimate order which reflection discovers; in short, it is the element of reason behind the things which one sees and touches. This reason, which is God himself, he feels and proclaims to be present everywhere. Hence his profound optimism, analogous to that of the Stoics. In a world ordered by the Supreme Good, he is unable to find anything which is not good in its relation to the totality of things.

Neo-platonism and Hellenic Polytheism.—Here we have, certainly, a theology which, more than any other, was turned by a sort of inner impulse toward the idea of divine unity. And yet, who does not see at the first glance how large a place it takes in polytheistic beliefs? Polytheism did not, to be sure, take much account of the theory of the hypostases, which seemed to distinguish several persons in God. The Neo-platonic hypostases resembled abstractions more than the mythological gods. But the pantheism of Plotinus permitted him to reconcile his belief in the divine unity with the conception of an entire world of gods, simple emanations of the Being of beings. To this world belonged the stars, regarded as divine, and nothing prevented the entrance also of the ancient Greek gods, or those of foreign nations, on the sole condition of interpreting by the allegorical method the myths relative to each of them. No doubt, this Olympus differed greatly, in the thought of the philosopher, from that which the poets had imagined and which the masses, following their descriptions, represented vaguely to themselves. What was this intimate difference, if it did not manifest itself externally either by word or by deed? But Neo-platonism showed itself respectful of the cult and of the common practices of religion. The worship of images, the belief in oracles, prayer, and the sacrifices, were explained, justified, and even recommended by ingenious reasons. The philosopher could therefore reject in spirit the coarse absurdities and puerile superstitions; and thereby he did not detach himself from the traditional Hellenism, nor did he cease to take part in the religious ceremonies, in the consecrated acts. In this respect, moreover, demonology came to the aid of theology properly so called. We have already seen what use Plato had made of it in the preceding century. We find it again developed or, better said, organized, in the doctrine of Plotinus. Entirely distinct from the gods, the demons for him are intermediary beings between the divine world and the terrestrial world. He holds them immortal, much superior to men in intelligence and power, but, like them, subject to a life of the senses, susceptible of passions, and, consequently, inconstant, differing among themselves, and beneficent or maleficent according to their underlying natures and according to circumstances. In accordance with such endowments, a sort of inferior religion became necessary to regulate the relations which it was expedient to maintain with them. And one immediately sees what a large opening was thus left by philosophy to a number of superstitions, to theurgical operations, and to magic. This was one of the weaknesses of Neo-platonism, one of the traits which make it appear, in spite of everything, as the work of a decadent epoch.

The Destiny of Man and Morality.—The spirit which dominated this philosophy could not fail to manifest itself also in its views regarding the destiny of man and his morality. Like Plato, Plotinus affirmed the preëxistence of the soul. He thought that, having emanated from the supra-sensible sphere, it was destined, by birth, to unite itself with a body, and that from this union there resulted for it a duality in a sense congenital. A part of the soul, according to him, tended instinctively toward the superior region, the place of its origin, whereas the other part inclined toward the world of the senses, in which it

found itself captive, without its will ceasing to remain
free, however. He thought that it should make use of this
freedom in order to prepare its future destiny; for immortality was no less certain for him than it was for
Plato, whose arguments he took for his own account. To
attach oneself too narrowly to the body, was to condemn
oneself to undergoing in a series of successive lives a
union with other bodies; and this captivity, incessantly
renewed, ran the risk of being all the more oppressive,
all the more humiliating, for this soul come from heaven,
inasmuch as it would be more chained to matter. It then
saw itself threatened with passing over into the bodies of
animals, or even temporarily reduced to the purely
vegetative condition of the plant. On the other hand,
the soul which would succeed better in maintaining its
integrity, could have the hope of assuming superior human forms, or even of freeing itself more and more from
the degrading contact with matter. To these liberated
souls was promised a life of happiness and of light in the
stars, and to the purest of them all, the definitive return
to the source of being, the union with God in absolute
felicity.

A profoundly spiritualistic asceticism was the necessary consequence of these conceptions. Every effort of
morality found itself turned toward renunciation, toward
absolute detachment. Matter being evil, everything had
to be given to the mind. Action could only be sacrificed
systematically to meditation; and the latter was to have
as its rule the elevation toward the invisible. It was
necessary for the mind to form the habit of always look-
ing upward, of searching for God in everything. It is
here that Neo-platonic mysticism manifested itself in all
its force. For this philosophy which craved God, the
ordinary operations of the spirit were not sufficient; they

were too timid and too short for its desires. What was necessary for it was the immediate vision of the supreme unity, the direct contact with it. How was this to be done, unless by abolishing thought itself? This is precisely what it pretended to realize by ecstasy, a state of the soul truly indescribable, in which, forgetting its own self, it identified itself in a sort of transport with the God which it was seeking.

Nothing shows us better than this mystical dream the extent to which the Hellenic soul was tired, at that time, of reasoning. It made use of reason in order to show the impotence of the power of reasoning. What it realized in this large intellectual construction, in which it seemed to revive its entire past, was, on the whole, the renunciation of this very past, which had been characterized essentially by practical wisdom and reasoned activity. And this was not an individual fact. Neo-platonism was destined to prove, by its success, that it was indeed the adequate form of that older Hellenism which had outlived itself.

CHAPTER VI

THE END OF HELLENISM

Last Resistance of Hellenism.—The last part of the
third century and almost the entire fourth century witness the end of Hellenic civilization, at least in the sense
that at the close of this period, ceasing to live on its own
resources and in its integrity, it continued to exist thereafter only partially in Greek Christianity, which derived
its principal force from other sources. But before thus
effacing itself, it sought to erect a dam against the rising
tide which was about to submerge it. It is necessary to
describe briefly the nature of this opposition, in order to
form a judgment of the resources of life which still remained to it.

(1) THE CONFLICT OF THE RELIGIONS

Invasion of Foreign Religions.—For a long time, as we
have seen, the relations of Greece with the peoples whom
it called barbarians had had the effect of introducing
foreign elements into its national religion. But this sort
of invasion, slow and insidious, had never given rise to a
conflict. As a rule, indeed, Greek polytheism had admitted the foreign gods and had finally conferred a sort
of naturalization upon them. During the Hellenistic
period, especially, many Oriental cults, of Phrygia, of
Syria, and of Egypt, had become Hellenic cults. Their
gods were recognized and celebrated in the kingdoms of

Greek origin which had succeeded the ancient local monarchies, and the official theology was charged with assigning to these newcomers a place of honor on Olympus. On the other hand, the philosophy was never short of allegorical interpretations, which were applied as well to the beliefs of hellenized nations as to the ancient religion of Greece proper. Never, therefore, had the latter been profoundly troubled by that which it received from without.

Judaism alone had refused, even in accepting Greek culture, to allow itself to be absorbed in this way. Its strict monotheism did not lend itself to any compromise with polytheism. But the propagation of Judaism was neither sufficiently rapid nor sufficiently intense to disquiet Hellenism. It was the same with Christianity during the two following centuries. So long as it appeared to the representatives of Greek polytheism only as an obscure sect, it inspired in them scarcely more than a sentiment of misapprehension; and none of them took the trouble to combat it. The disbelievers themselves, such as Lucian, who make satire of the public cults, contented themselves with aiming a few stinging darts at it in passing; and probably Celsus, who seems to have attacked it more directly, did not take it for a very redoubtable adversary either. Nevertheless, about this time, toward the end of the second century, it happened that things began to change. The apologists were succeeded by teachers. The teaching of Clement of Alexandria marks a new epoch; and this teaching was enlarged and strengthened and rendered more precise in the course of the third century, according as the Christian Church organized itself and opened schools. In the face of the philosophies of paganism, one sees rising at that time a Christian philosophy which opposes its doctrine to the doc-

trines of the celebrated sects; and naturally it is Neo-
platonism on which devolves the duty of resisting it.   At
the beginning, however, it seems that no very well defined
position was taken on either side.   The Christian teachers
were themselves Platonists.   Origen had perhaps the
same teacher as Plotinus; and in any case their writings
attest a certain community of ideas on many points.   On
the other hand, Plotinus does not seem to have taken issue
with Christianity either in his teachings or in his writings.
It is after him that the rivalry is openly declared.

Porphyrus.—It manifested itself in two forms in the
works of Porphyrus, his most celebrated pupil and his
continuator: by direct attacks against the Christians,
and by a very frank wish to rejuvenate polytheism and
to fortify it by placing it under the protection of philosophy.   There is preserved for us almost nothing of
the work of fifteen volumes which he composed against
the Christians; only the writings of the Fathers, notably
St. Augustine, indicate the fame which he had in his
time.   Insofar as we are able to judge of it, it was not
an injurious diatribe.   Porphyrus looked upon Jesus as
a man of remarkable virtues.   It was not His person
that he attacked, therefore; it was the idea of a God
made man and the fundamental dogma of redemption as
well as its practical consequence.   He was to see in this
theology, as a matter of fact, a new principle contrary
to the essential idea that Neo-platonism had made of
God and of His relations to humanity.   But this criticism
of Christianity had for Porphyrus himself, probably, only
a secondary importance.   What concerned him especially
was to affirm the doctrine of Plotinus.   The latter had
charged him to publish his writings; he placed in order
the *Ænneades* and made of it the work which we read.
His erudition and activity as a writer were great.   A

grammarian, a commentator, a literary critic, he had a variety of knowledge which his teacher did not possess, altho otherwise he was very inferior to him as regards originality of thought. All his resources were placed at the service of philosophy, which was very dear to him. Several things in his works deserve to be emphasized.

Porphyrus had a very strong notion that the entire Hellenic tradition was at stake in the conflict of ideas in which he was engaged, and that consequently it was this tradition which Neo-platonism was to defend. For him it was a question of bringing to light both examples and ideas. This was the object of his *History of Philosophy*, of which we still possess the first book, devoted to the *Life of Pythagoras*. The latter was represented in it, not only as a thinker, but as an inspired sage, almost superior to humanity, endowed with a truly miraculous power and authority over souls. Legend is mixed with history. The devotees of Hellenism found in such a book an apology of their beliefs and a subject of edification. The same intention existed, no doubt, in the work entitled *Philosophy according to the Oracles*. Hellenic polytheism lacked a sacred book to which it might have recourse. Porphyrus thought that the collections of oracles which were current at that time might constitute this fundamental book if some one could comment upon them in such a way as to establish that they contained a doctrine. This was the object which he proposed to himself. He wished to show that his religion, that which he opposed to Christianity, was not a work of human invention, but that it proceeded from a divine revelation, and that this revelation, well interpreted, was in accord with the modernized Platonic teachings. In this enterprise his syncretism did not hesitate to mix with the Greek oracles those of

the Chaldæan astrologers, faithful in that to the spirit
of the time, which no longer conceived the religions as
national.

As regards morality, Porphyrus seems to have had
analogous intentions. His four volume treatise on *Abstinence from Meat*, otherwise multilated, is anything but
an occasional work such as its title might suggest. It
is in fact a sort of body of precepts, designed to regulate, if not the common life, at least that of souls
touched by a high ideal of perfection. The question of
aliment is here considered only in its relation to spiritual-
ity, which for the author is everything. What he teaches,
what he demands with a stern conviction, is absolute
renunciation of the satisfaction of the senses ; it is detachment, from which for him all virtues result and without
which he adjudges the latter impossible. In this we see
Neo-platonism veering decidedly toward asceticism, as if
it felt the need of exalting its forces, of redoubling its in-
most energy, in order better to defend itself. At the
time when he seems to concentrate all Hellenic civilization in himself, it is curious to observe that, by the force
of circumstances, he loses precisely that sense of moderation which had been one of its most original characteristics in the heyday of its glory.

Iamblichus and Julian.—Porphyrus was succeeded, as
head of the school, by another Syrian, Iamblichus, in
whom the tendencies which have just been set forth were
still further exaggerated. The Orient penetrates more
and more into Hellenism, while exaltation and mysticism
develop at the expense of sane reason. Iamblichus is for
his pupils more than a man; there is something divine
in him. The pious admiration which attaches to his person is not justified by the force of his thoughts; it is
due to the mysterious power attributed to him. His

rôle is that of an interpreter of God.   One listens to him
with devotion; and in listening to him, one feels clarified,
consoled, and exalted.   From the little that remains of
his numerous writings, and from references added to them,
we are able to picture him less as a philosopher, properly
speaking, than as a sort of preacher.   He discusses
hardly at all; he comments piously and with abandon;
he teaches people to believe and to pray.   His subtle
mind finds in the writings of Plato, of Aristotle, of the
Pythagoreans, and of Plotinus, and also in those of the
Orphics and the Chaldæans, everything necessary to his
theology.   With him, moreover, practical religion is inseparable from doctrine and apparently more important.
He attaches the greatest value to sacrifices, to prayer,
to the worship of images, and to divination; he lives
and he maintains his pupils in the belief in miracles.
Magic itself found acceptance in this milieu, in which
the critical sense was obliterated more and more, and in
which the strangest credulity developed.

This was the time at which Constantine was converted
to Christianity, which was becoming the official religion
of the Empire.   If the Council of Nicæa did not succeed
in destroying the disagreement which compromised it, it
nevertheless gave to its fundamental dogmas an authority
which was to insure its success in the long run.   Moreover, the Arianism of Constance was no more favorable
to polytheism than was the orthodoxy of Constantine.
Against this spiritual power which triumphed, this degenerated philosophy, so disloyal to the principles which
it pretended to represent, was a very weak defense.   The
reign of Julian (361–363 B. C.) could, it is true, delude
for a moment those who remained attached to it.   The
young prince had nothing more at heart than to regen-
erate polytheism and to make it once more the religion

of the State; and in order to accomplish this reform he became inspired with Neo-platonism, the doctrines of which he had embraced with ardor. Iamblichus in particular, altho he had been dead thirty years, was the object of his most active admiration. He therefore did everything in his power, both as an emperor and as a writer, to give new life to the ancient cults and to insure them of the support of an appropriate theology. His premature death put an end to an attempt which was destined, in every way, to prove useless.

Hellenism at the End of the Fourth Century.—From that time on Hellenism was doomed to proceed rapidly to its end. In the last half of the fourth century, those who still perpetuated its traditions were only men of the second order, philosophers or rhetoricians. Alongside of the Neo-platonists of the Athenian school, the only ones that we have to mention here are the philosopher Themistius and the rhetoricians Libanius and Himerius. Themistius, who taught philosophy at Antioch, at Nicomedia, and at Constantinople, and who became a political personage under the reign of Theodosius, had a logical but superficial mind, and was an agreeable writer and a deserving orator, but who, all in all, did not rise above an elegant mediocrity in his paraphrases of various writings of Aristotle, or in his speeches either. His contemporary, Himerius, gained a wide reputation with short works, school compositions, in which his brilliant imagination created a sort of reflection of classical works by which he was inspired. Libanius of Antioch is more entitled than either to mention in a historical survey of Greek civilization. It can not be denied that he represented it with a certain glory at the moment when it was about to become extinct. His renown, the friendship of several emperors, the honors conferred upon him, pro-

cured for him a high consideration in the Greek world
of that time. In his numerous writings that have come
down to us, speeches, letters, scholarly compositions, bio-
graphical and historical notices relative to Demosthenes,
we recognize a remarkably cultivated mind, an extensive
knowledge of classical literature, and a generally sane
judgment. The man himself does not fail to inspire one
with esteem and sympathy. In the midst of the religious
conflicts which divided the Greco-Roman world at that
time, he succeeded in maintaining the attitude of an honest
man, a stranger to violences of language, attached without irreconcilability to a tradition which many others
detested from interest. For that reason he holds honorably his place at the end of that long gallery of figures
which, one after another and in widely varying degrees,
expressed the changing aspects of Hellenism.

The Last Neo-platonists.—Altho decisively driven back
by Christianity from the time of the death of Julian,
Neo-platonism continued as an independent sect thruout
the entire fifth century and the first third of the following
century. It would be of no interest to enumerate here
the names, long since forgotten, of those who professed
his doctrines at that time, either at Alexandria or at
Athens. Let us merely do them the justice of recognizing that they gave proof, in their attachment to the past,
of a firmness which was not lacking in nobility. Men of
tradition, of timid mentality and devoid of originality,
but of sincere conviction, they could not make up their
minds to deny so many admirable teachings, of which they
felt themselves to be the inheritors. On the other hand,
they were not capable of developing them by new researches. Free scientific investigation, which alone would
have been able to furnish their thought with a truly productive element, was foreign to them. Men no longer

studied directly either nature, or the human race, or society.   It seemed that concerning these subjects, however
inexhaustible, everything had been said.   Science appeared
to them achieved, and they thought they possessed it in
perfect form in the works on which they did not cease to
meditate.   Was it reasonable to wish to outdo Plato and
Aristotle?   All their intellectual activity was employed
in commenting upon them.   The most illustrious of these
commentators was the Syrian, Proclus, of whose works
there is still extant a considerable number relative to various treatises of Plato, two epitomes of the Neo-platonic
doctrine, and a few secondary opuscules.   Others have
left us an entire collection of commentaries on Aristotle.
Their common fault is a prolixity, which is all the more
regrettable for the reason that it tends less to clarify
the true thought of the author under consideration than
to alter it ingeniously to the end of bringing it closer
to the Neo-platonic doctrines.

As little dangerous as were these last representatives of
Greek polytheism, their refusal to adhere to the victorious
religion was imputed to them as a crime by the Emperor
Justinian.   An edict which he issued in 532 A. D. ordered
the closing of the School of Athens and interdicted the
teaching of a philosophy which the Christian Church
disapproved.   Its last representatives had to take the
road of exile.   They took refuge with the king of the
Parthians, Chosroes.   The truth is, however, that the
civilization properly called Hellenic had ceased to exist
long before the Greek empire had pronounced the death
sentence over it.   It gradually became extinct in the
course of the fourth century.   A part of its vigor had
then passed over into Christianity and had animated the
eloquence of such men as Basil, Gregory of Nazianzus,
and Chrysostom.   Another part had for a long time been

incorporated with Latin civilizations. Hence we may now evaluate Hellenic civilization in its entirety, but first let us cast a retrospective glance at the evolution of Greek art during the Hellenistic period and in the time of the Empire.

(2) HELLENISTIC AND GRECO-ROMAN ART

General Survey.—After the admirable productions of the fifth and sixth centuries B. C., Greek art found itself in possession of school traditions and of models of all kinds. This was at once an advantage and a danger for it. It was relatively easy for the artists of the following centuries to imitate their predecessors, and by imitating them they could produce beautiful results. On the other hand, it was difficult to achieve something different and to show oneself truly original. Imitation imposed itself, in a sense, upon talent. It is not surprising that, on the whole, it dominated the works of this time. What is remarkable, is the fact that it did not more completely paralyze inventiveness and that the latter actually manifested itself—at least during the Hellenistic period —in so large a number of works of art which bear witness to the brilliant vitality of the Greek genius.

Architecture.—The building up of the kingdoms which were established after the death of Alexander gave occasion for important architectural works. The orders of the cities were succeeded by commands of the kings. The latter had to create the greatest possible impression of their power, and, in order to satisfy their political ambitions or their vanity, they scarcely took the question of expense into account. A certain pomp was for them a means of government, and the absolute power at their disposal gave them the assurance of abundant resources.

Desirous of glory, they demanded that everything about them should acquire an air of magnificence. What had formerly appeared large in their eyes was now too small. Art had to become commensurate with their pride. Moreover, were they not obliged, since they resided in the Orient, to rival the imposing or even colossal works which the ancient civilizations of Assyria and of Egypt had produced and which struck so many visitors with astonishment? The problem which the Greek architects had to solve was that of adapting these new demands to their traditions of harmony and of moderation. Several of them extricated themselves from this difficulty to their honor, thereby giving evidence that the inventive faculty was not stifled in them by respect for the great models.

Nothing is better calculated to give us an idea of the building passion which reigned at that time than the description of Alexandria which we read in Strabo. It lays before our eyes an immense city, sprung from the ground in 331, and growing almost visibly during the successive reigns of the first Ptolomies. Each of them wished to have an entirely new residence, and so a series of contiguous palaces were added, one after another, to that of the founder of the dynasty. The royal quarter finally occupied a quarter or even a third of the city. There the Museum was erected, a vast edifice containing a library, porticoes, exedrae, halls of conversation, and planted courts. Not far from it was the necropolis of the kings, with the tomb of Alexander and the princely sepulchers. A part of these magnificent structures overlooked the sea. All around and behind them lay the city, built upon a rectlinear plan, with its two long streets, broad and straight, perpendicular to each other, into which the secondary streets led. Along the shore were the port, the quays, and the docks, appropriate to the

needs of a great commercial center such as the city was
at that time, protected by an immense mole and covered
on the broad side by the island of Pharos, on which rose
the celebrated tower, considered one of the wonders of
the world, which had been erected by the architect Sos-
tratus of Cnidus.   In the city itself, there were numerous
admirable temples, the great gymnasium with its porticoes more than a stadium in length, the spiral belvedere
called the Paneion, from which the view embraced a vast
perspective, the hippodrome, and numerous special structures.   Beside the extraordinary grandeur of the plan,
this description reveals a truly characteristic harmony
of conception.   One finds here the geometric spirit which
Greek architecture never abandoned; but one also senses
a free originality which can adapt itself to a new
state of things.   What is thus attested as regards one
of the largest capitals of that time applies also, save for
variations of detail, to the majority of the others, to
Antioch, to Seleucia, to Pergamus; and, in a certain degree, to some of the cities of the Greek mainland, notably
to Athens, which owed to the Lagidæ and to the kings
of Pergamus embellishments and new buildings.

The ruins of some edifices, carefully studied in our day,
bear witness to the taste which was then general.   We
may cite particularly those of the temples of Artemis Leu-
cophryne at Magnesia on the Meander, of Dionysus at
Teos, of Apollo at Didymus, of Ascelpias at Tralles, constructed in the third century, those of the porticoes of
Eumenes and Attalus at Athens and of the temple of Zeus
Stratius at Alabanda, constructed in the second century.
In almost all of these architectural creations there is
manifested the desire to strike the imagination at once
by the magnificence of the plan and the richness of the
decoration.   The use of marbles, of colored stuccoes and

of incrustations, and the ornamentation of the capitals
and friezes, add to the peculiar beauty of the lines and
proportions the charm of a rich and varied ornamentation.   The architects seem to take pleasure in softening the rigidity of the profiles by graceful undulations;
they multiply and ingeniously diversify the color effects
obtained by the polychrome.   They seek the contrast of
light and dark places.

One of the most remarkable specimens of this architectural decoration has been furnished to us by the ex-
cavations at Pergamus.   In the second century, the Attalidæ, proud of the extension given by them to their
kingdom in consequence of their victories over the Gala-
tians, wished to commemorate them by a monumental
building.   They built in their capital a sort of gigantic
altar, which resembled an artificial acropolis.   In the
middle of an immense esplanade there rose a square foundation, reposing upon a powerful stone surbase, which
was itself elevated upon some degrees and surmounted by
a cornice.   The superior surface was surrounded by a
full wall, save on the south side, where the foundation of
the surbase was notched by a broad stairway of twenty-
four steps giving access to the platform.   By these steps
one reached the interior court, which was surrounded by
a portico of Ionian columns.   In the middle there rose
the altar of Zeus and Athena.   Two sculptured friezes
formed the exterior ornamentation of the monument; one
of them, the larger, decorated the surbase and the sides
of the stairway, extending for a length of more than 120
meters; the other, smaller, ornamented the height of the
wall.   No doubt an Athenian of the time of Phidias and
Ictinus would have felt strongly that in this entire conception there was a degree of pompousness resulting
from the too perceptible disproportion between the gran-

deur of the plan and the purpose of the edifice; but in a very different society there were lacking new means of producing an effect, and one can not deny to the architects of Pergamus the merit of a bold invention which was not without beauty.

The necessary result of these numerous and diverse works was to develop and perfect, in certain respects, the architectural technique. Led to solve multiple problems, the builders of this time had to conceive appropriate means and, little by little, to make rules which were laid down in formulas. For the fitting up of the theaters particularly, for the drainage of the cities and for the instalation of baths, gymnasia and stadia, experience and observation suggested views from which theories were soon derived. In this way was constituted a doctrine which the Greek architects of the Hellenistic period transmitted, on the one hand, to the Latin architects and, on the other hand, to their successors of the first centuries of the Empire. We find it condensed in the treatise of Vitruvius, composed in the reign of Augustus, and we know what influence it exerted upon the architects of the Renaissance. In the legacy of Hellenic civilization, therefore, this is an element which is not to be overlooked.

Sculpture.—The circumstances which favored architecture were not less propitious to the arts which contribute to the ornamentation of buildings, especially to sculpture and painting. The Hellenistic period saw both of them flourishing thruout the entire Greek world. But never were the workshops of sculpture more active or more numerous than during these three centuries. The kings vie with one another in ordering new statues, groups, and bas-reliefs; and as might be expected, private men of wealth followed the example of the kings according to their means. Thus encouraged and stimulated, remarkable artists were not wanting. Naturally they could not carry into their work the religious and national inspiration which had animated the masters of the preceding centuries. There was no longer any fatherland for them, properly speaking; and the gods were not looked upon with the same sentiments of profound piety and respectful fear. On the other hand, the Hellenistic sculptors were no less subject than the architects of the same time to the influence of the models which claimed their admiration. However that may have been, the inventive genius of Greece continued to live in them. Their prolific activity succeeded in creating, even in imitation, an art which had its own originality and the influence of which was great. Some of their works, saved from destruction, are still justly admired.

Modern science has been able to classify these artists in schools, or at least in local groups. It has distinguished the workshops of Pergamus, of Rhodes, of Tralles and of Alexandria, each of these cities being represented either by famous works or else by families of sculptors whose names it has collected and whose relationship it has reconstituted. Here it will suffice to define some of the traits which characterized the art of this time.

One of the most striking is that desire to work on a large scale which we have already discovered in the works of the contemporary architecture. The sculptural decoration of the gigantic altar of Pergamus mentioned above offers the most conclusive evidence of it. The lower frieze referred to, the one which surrounded the surbase and the sides of the monumental stairway, represented the victory of Zeus and Athena over the giants, a symbol of the victory which the Attalidæ had won over the barbarians. Never had Greek art made a similar effort to give expression to the deployment of muscular force, exalted by the fury of combat. Convulsed bodies, violent gestures, monstrous but skillfully combined forms, made an ensemble of powerful effect. The majesty of the victorious gods was opposed, moreover, to the desperate rage of the conquered giants. The nobility or the grace of several figures attenuated happily what there was of necessary brutality in certain other parts. Thus from the spectacle of this tumult, from this superhuman contest, the spectator clearly gained an impression of the superiority of a force which is at once intelligent and master of itself. In this, as also in the technical merit of the work, the perpetuity of the Greek tradition manifested itself. Yet it was no less evident that new means were also being used.

Another interesting trait of the same art was the search for the pathetic. It seems that the increasing success of the classical tragedy was an important factor here. Sculpture, deriving inspiration from the most popular tragic scenes, was itself led to an attempt to represent, by its own means, touching situations. To the Hellenistic period belong some celebrated groups which bear witness to this tendency. We need but mention the Laocoön, the entreaty of Dirce (known as the Farnese Bull), the death of the Niobe—all subjects borrowed from the legends which the theater had popularized. In all these works there is exhibited the same care to translate into the immobility of the marble, by expressive attitudes, what poetry had described or laid before the eyes of the spectators. Certain it is that one might well make reservations on the opportuneness of this alliance between statuary and literature; but in any case the renown of the works just mentioned bears witness to the influence which Hellenistic art has continued to exert even in our day.

Technical perfection also was instrumental in engaging the sculptors in difficult undertakings. Possessing all the secrets of the trade, it is only natural that they were tempted to make a show of them. Too much of science runs the risk of lapsing into virtuosity. Hellenistic sculpture did not always escape from this. In the analysis of the details of the human body, in the observation of movements and gestures, the masters of this time had nothing more to learn. They delighted in proving it by the finish of their productions. The well-known statue known as The Dying Gladiator, which probably represents a Galatian defending himself against a horseman, is in its technical perfection almost a study of the anatomy of a living body. Moreover, if the Aphrodite of Melos and some of her sisters are also, as there is reason to believe, works of the same epoch, one can not deny that this virtuosity sometimes produced exquisite beauty. In any case, it permitted those who possessed it to reproduce, at their pleasure, and with the greatest precision, all the variations, all the caprices even, of nature. So it is that they exceled both in the marble or bronze portrait and in the sculpture of genre. No epoch has produced more sculptured effigies, each one attesting, by means of expressive traits, an individual resemblance which was bound to be striking. None, moreover, imagined more gracious or amusing subjects, laughing or angry cupids, children playing with one another or with domestic animals, and grotesque figures. Still better than marble, bronze and sometimes gold or silver lent themselves to these caprices of artistic invention. All our museums have statuettes, groups, chiseled reliefs on cups or vases, mirror frames, which permit us to admire the variety of imagination and the ingenious skill of their authors; and the Greek Anthology has preserved for us a goodly number of epigrams which contain descriptions of these pretty things.

Painting.—There is no doubt that for the decoration of the buildings spoken of above, the art of the painters was drawn upon as much as the art of the sculptors. And the taste for the portrait, which the latter had to satisfy so frequently, called no less for the talent of the former. Unfortunately, the productions of the brush are essentially perishable. Nothing is left which enables us to appreciate for ourselves the works which at that time made famous artists, such as Aëtion, Theon of Samos, and others whose names are mentioned by various authors. But we should state that the Hellenistic taste, as it has just been characterized in sculpture, likewise manifested itself in painting. There, too, the artists delighted in pathetic scenes, inspired by the tragedies; and on the other hand, they showed themselves no less interested in the study of details. They sought to translate, by the means which were peculiar to them, such phases of sentiments which the renowned actors had realized, the moral tortures of Medea, her supreme fears and her ragings, the somber resolution of Ajax, the horrors of the entreaty of Iphigenia, the distraction of Agamemnon. Fascinated by naturalism, they put into fashion familiar scenes, subjects of genre, views of interiors, in which the reproduction of the real objects did not exclude a bit of fantasy. It seemed probable also that, under the influence of the pastoral form, they gave a new importance to the countryside; many legends lent themselves to this, notably those which placed on the scene centaurs, inhabitants of the mountains, Polyphemus and Galatea, the gods of the sea and their adventures.

Even caricature appears to have been in honor at that time. In the absence of the originals, many painted vases still bear witness to this diversity of efforts, which were often successful. And from this we draw, on the whole, the idea of an art which no doubt lived much from imitation, which probably produced nothing great, in the true sense of the word, but which gave proof of a remarkable technical skill, associated with grace, sometimes with emotion, and almost always with an ingenious or amusing inventiveness.

Greek Art under the Empire.—Between this Hellenistic art and the Greek art of the imperial epoch there was no interruption of continuity. The second is only the prolongation of the first. Only thru the effect of the political unification which the imperial régime imposed upon the world did the exchange of ideas, the mutual penetration of examples and of influences, become increasingly free at that time. The Roman taste made itself accepted everywhere, but it was itself entirely penetrated by the teachings of Greece. Thus from the first century A. D. it is very nearly impossible to distinguish what is properly Greek and what is Roman or Oriental. There is scarcely an artistic production of this time which does not contain elements of diverse origin. What one may say, however, is that in all the arts, up to the time when Christianity predominates, the Greek tradition, in the Orient, is much the strongest. Architecture particularly, in the first and second centuries, remains in this part of the Empire a Greek architecture in all its essential traits. The emperors, from the Cæsars to the Antonys, embellish the Greek cities, especially those of Asia, as much as or more so than the kings of the Hellenistic period. But whatever may be the number and importance of the works of art which they bestow upon them, neither the

art of the builder nor that of the sculptor or painter
appear to be marked at that time by original creations.
And as for the combinations which they realized more
or less happily, they can not be studied here. All in all,
it is the Hellenistic taste, diversely modified in details,
which continues to prevail; and whereas the knowledge
and the practice of the profession maintain themselves,
the art perpetuates itself honorably. The decadence does
not make itself definitely felt until after the third century,
first in consequence of civil wars, later as the result
of barbarian invasions. But it is also at that time that
there commences, under the influence of Christianity, a
new Greek art, which will be the Byzantine art. We have
not to speak of it here. The arrival of Byzantine civilization marks the time when Hellenic civilization, properly so called, ceases to exist.

CHAPTER VII

CONCLUSION

Lasting Value of Greek Civilization.—Thus this summary survey of Greek civilization comes to an end. And now that we have passed over the entire scene in review, how does it behoove us to judge it as a whole? A purely individual appreciation would have little value here. It is to history that we must refer. Let us ask ourselves, therefore, what influence this civilization has exerted upon the evolution of humanity. The facts consulted will speak for themselves, and we shall have only to collect their testimony. At first sight, however, it appears that something of Hellenic civilization is visible in almost all the civilizations that have succeeded it. We find it present and active in Imperial Rome and at Byzantium, then, across the Middle Ages, in the epoch of the Renaissance, and in modern times. What thus endures necessarily has in itself a virtue which can not be contested; and the best means of determining it, no doubt, is to note its effect where it makes itself felt most strongly.

(1) GREEK CIVILIZATION AT ROME

It is a commonplace but an incontestable truth that Rome, in order to achieve its intellectual and moral education, had to go to school in Greece. The Romans themselves were the first to recognize this, and they were proud of it. There is no doubt that this acceptance of a foreign

293

influence was not with them a renunciation of their own character. While hellenizing themselves, they still remained Romans. But their culture was mainly a Greek culture. It was to Greece that they owed their literature, their philosophy, their scientific knowledge, and their arts. It was Greece which made them completely human. That, at the same time, it brought to them defects and even vices, is not to be denied. Does there not exist in every well developed civilization the inevitable counterpart of good? Greece, grown old, could not react vigorously enough against this interior evil, nor yet could Imperial Rome. It is none the less true that, in her very decadence, the highest virtues which subsisted in Rome were inspired by Greek idealism.

In the political order Rome was least subject to the influence of Greece; it even seems that, if one holds to institutions, it escaped this influence altogether. The republic developed with the Roman people three causes which were peculiar to them, outside of every external influence; and the Empire followed the Republic because circumstances had made ready for its arrival. But the history of institutions is not to be confounded with that of ideas and sentiments. If we consider on the one hand the political theories, and on the other hand the laws and the sentiments of the Romans, we are bound to recognize that the part played by Greece was large. The Republic of Cicero would not have been conceived if Thucydides, Plato, Aristotle, Polybius, and other historians or philosophers had not written beforehand; and if the Republic is the work of a student, we should not forget that this student was also a man of state in constant relations with others interested in the same subjects. As for the Roman laws, is it not also under the influence of Greek philosophy that we see them softening down and humanizing themselves, according as it injects the Hellenic spirit into Latin society? Finally, if the sentiment of liberty still existed under the Empire, if sometimes it manifested itself even in the form of opposition, how can we fail to recognize that alongside of traditional hatred of aristocratic tendencies the Stoic doctrines were also a factor? All this is so evident that there is no reason even for dwelling upon it.

(2) GREEK CIVILIZATION AND CHRISTIANITY

If we pass from Roman paganism to Christianity, the part played by Hellenic civilization is not less manifest. Let us not speak here of the evangelic period of the new religion, altho even there the Greek influence can be felt and pointed out; in any case, it is only secondary. It is a little later that it acquires all its force, when Christianity penetrates into the cultivated classes. What does it encounter here, as a matter of fact? Minds prepared by Hellenic civilization for spiritual things. Its first apologists, notably Justinian, the most remarkable of them, are disciples of Platonism, who in the Greek schools have acquired the habit of reasoning and of the study of ideas, and who seek to formulate their sentiments in the language of Greek philosophy. Then come the teachers properly so-called, such as Clement, Origen, and the members of the Alexandrian School, who organize the theology of Christianity—which amounts to saying that they insert new beliefs into the intellectual frames prepared by Hellenistic thought. And when the Christian religion finally prevails, in the fourth century, the literary flight which accompanies its victory is in a sense a taking possession of Hellenism by its conquerors. In the eloquence and dialectics of its orators, in the erudition

of its historians, in the patient labor of its chrono-
graphers, it is the very spirit of Greece, the knowledge
constituted by it, and in part its methods, which return.
The charming facility of St. Basil, the ingenious abundance of St. John Chrysostom, the learned elegance of
St. Gregory of Nazianzus—did they not proceed from
Greek literature, poetry as well as prose, as their natural
source? We may add that Hellenism penetrated Christianity in still another way. It was Greek philosophy
which nourished all the heresies; and it was Greek
philosophy, too, which furnished orthodoxy with many
of the weapons which served to combat them. It was
present, so to speak, in all the discussions from which the
dogmatic formulas grew; and it inspired almost equally
the parties in conflict. On the other hand, outside of the
conflicts, in the more peaceful domain of morality, did it
not provide Christian teaching with the richest variety of
precepts, of counsels, of observations and examples?—a
treasure which the latter could appropriate without
scruples, since it found here the exquisite expression of
the practical reason and of the best sentiments on which
humanity lives. Thus Christianity, from the time when
it felt assured of victory, itself recognized its obligation to Greek civilization. The homily of St. Basil
to the young people *On the Manner of Drawing Profit
from the Profane Authors* is like the manifestation of a
reconciliation, which, no doubt, did not take place without
serious reservations, but which was none the less the
avowal of a broad community of sentiments.

(3) GREEK CIVILIZATION IN THE MIDDLE AGES

The alliance thus contracted in the fourth century was
destined to undergo more than one vicissitude, but it clung

to causes too natural ever to be entirely broken. As one might expect, it was in the Greek orient that it maintained itself most solidly. Altho Christian, Byzantine civilization showed itself the heir and in many respects the continuator of Hellenic civilization, from which it proceeded in direct line. It could not have been otherwise. In the Occident, things presented themselves under a different aspect. There it was Latin civilization which was everywhere extended. It was Latin civilization again which, after having undergone the assault of the barbarian invasions, restored little by little the tradition of learning and raised the human mind from its temporary downfall. It is all the more curious to see Greece exercising her influence in this domain, altho it seems foreign to her. It is well known by what roundabout ways Greece penetrated there. It was Latin translations, or rather the poor Latin manuals, which kept alive some remnants of Hellenic science and philosophy, and which rendered possible, in the time of Charlemagne and his first successors, the restoration of the schools. Already under this form, something of the thoughts of Plato, of Aristotle, and of Plotinus insinuated itself into this semi-barbarism. Thanks to Johannes Scotus Erigena, to Gerbert, to Berenger, to Lanfranc, to Peter Damianus, and to St. Anselm, this first knowledge was enlarged between the ninth and the eleventh centuries. Toward the end of this period, and at the beginning of the twelfth century, at the time of Roscellinus, of William of Champeaux, and of Abelard, the quarrel of the realists and the nominalists opposes the partizans of Plato to those of Aristotle, whose *Organon* had been known in the Orient since the reign of Charlemagne, but the reputation of which was increasing in the midst of these conflicts. It increased rapidly when new writings of his were rediscovered in the course of the twelfth century, in the guise of translations which the Arabian philosophers had made. These translations the Jewish philosophers retranslated into Hebrew, and thru the Hebrew rendered them accessible to the scholars of this time. So it was that in the thirteenth century Alexander of Hales and Albertus Magnus made themselves the propagators of Aristotelianism, interpreted to their spirit. St. Thomas Aquinas, by adding elements borrowed from Plato and from Neo-platonism, drew from it a large doctrine, more wisely coördinated, to which Duns Scotus raised opposition which was continued more actively by his pupil, Occam. Altogether, it was Greek philosophy which, with the teachings of the Fathers and the dogmas defined by the Councils, furnished the subject-matter of these long and memorable disputes. Under the subtleties with which scholasticism enveloped it, it was the ferment which aroused men's minds, and already, while placing itself ordinarily at the service of theology, it made ready for the arrival of an independent philosophy.

(4) HELLENIC CIVILIZATION IN THE MODERN WORLD

With the Renaissance there opens, from the end of the fifteenth century on, a new period for the influence of Greek civilization. Confined in the Middle Ages to the domain of philosophy and theology, it thereafter makes itself felt not only in philosophy and the sciences, but also in literature, in the arts, in politics, and even—for a while, at least—in manners and customs. In other words, more or less powerful according to the period and locality in question, it becomes one of the integral elements of modern civilization. But since the principle of liberty involved in it inevitably emancipated the minds upon which it exercised itself, the result was that it tended to eliminate itself by its very action, at least as regards its external forms, reducing itself more and more to the rôle of a factor of intellectual and moral enfranchisement. To give a survey of an action so extended, so varied, would evidently be an endless task, the subject of a large volume. Here we must content ourselves with a few rapid indications.

In philosophy, this force for emancipative stimulation is particularly noticeable. In the fifteenth and sixteenth centuries it is around Plato and Aristotle, thereafter studied directly thru the medium of all their works, that scholarly discussions revolve. In order to interpret them, to develop their thoughts, recourse is had to Neo-platonism, to Plotinus, to Porphyrus, and to all their commentators, according as they reappear to light. At that time, however, it was the custom to inform oneself in this same way of the other philosophic systems of Greece as well. New interest is taken in Pythagoras and his school, in the Ionians, in the atomism of Democritus and Epicurus, as also in Stoicism and Scepticism. It is an entire world of thoughts, an entire totality of problems and of solutions of various kinds which are thus revealed. What stimulation for vigorous minds! Suddenly, the sterility of scholasticism appears; and here it is that one feels the need of reëntering upon all these researches and of creating new methods. The seventeenth century inaugurates them with glory. Neither Bacon nor Descartes wishes to be a disciple of Greece; they are innovators who are themselves breaking new paths. But in the face of Descartes, Gassendi still remains attached to Greek thought, which he essays to defend with the newly acquired knowledge. And do not the innovators themselves proceed from the movement of ideas which

Greek philosophy had started in the two preceding centuries? Leibnitz associates himself with the conceptions of Aristotle and Plato, altho modifying them. This emancipation, it is true, continues to accentuate itself; Greece seems more and more forgotten by the philosophy of the eighteenth century. On the other hand, the rapid development of the sciences carries to reflection so large a quantity of new materials that each day it becomes more and more absorbed in their study. It is to their organization that philosophy applies itself especially in the nineteenth century; and it does so in an entirely independent spirit. However, no great effort of attention is required to perceive that at bottom the great agitated questions are always the same, and that the apparently new solutions are very often nothing more than those of Greek antiquity rejuvenated and brought up to date. Relative to mind and to matter, to the nature of knowledge, to the eternal enigmas of the world, to the relations of the infinite and the finite, and to the destiny of man, is it not remarked every day that the doubts, the hypotheses, of the Greeks are still the same, or very nearly the same, as ours? Furthermore, has not the history of Greek philosophy been profoundly studied and almost rejuvenated, according as it has become the habit to revert to the origin of questions in order closely to study their entire development? What matters it, on very many points, that we feel the Greeks very far from us? We can not fail to recognize that they presented the data of the most difficult problems with a simplicity and a conciseness from which we can always learn much.

In literature, something analogous has happened. In the sixteenth century, when the masterpieces of Greek poetry and prose were brought to light again, the best minds seemed dazzled by it. In the face of these models, it seemed to them that there was nothing better to do than imitate them. In France this is true of Ronsard and of La Pléiade. Thus practiced, imitation manifestly harmed originality. But in this assiduous and somewhat superstitious reading of the works of antiquity, judgment was formed and strengthened. Montaigne has told in excellent words how much he owes to Plutarch, and his testimony, such as he offers, applies to many of his contemporaries. Moreover, the Latin influences, which at that time were associated with those of Greece, were themselves, in large part, indirect Greek influences; and it is the same with a certain number of Italian influences. In the seventeenth century, we note a change. Our French classical art, altho it continued to draw its inspiration from antiquity, formed at that time a quite different idea of imitation, and everybody practiced it according to his taste. Honoré de Balzac and Corneille are more Roman than Greek, altho the latter borrows numerous subjects from Greek history; but with Racine and Fénelon the sentiment of Hellenic beauty is extremely active. There is something like an immediate contact of souls between Euripides and the poet of *Phèdre* and *Iphigénie*, between Homer and the author of *Télémaque*. And what thus draws them together, is less their direct borrowings than a certain form of sensibility or a certain turn of imagination. Something of the Greek mind truly passed over into them and penetrated, by virtue of the adaptations which they made of the ancient subjects, the taste of a public far removed from the ancient simplicity. The evident fact is that writers had ceased to copy; they admire quite as much as in the preceding century, but they endeavor to rival more freely. La Bruyère began by translating Theophrastus; then, having learned from him the value of precise observation, he observed on his own part and made an original work. It even comes about that the new masterpieces inspire in some the idea of a revolt against antiquity. The celebrated quarrel of the ancients and the moderns bears witness to a desire for independence, which is born of the progress of knowledge and the demands of a more advanced civilization. This sentiment becomes stronger and still more general in the eighteenth century. Voltaire, who represents its spirit better than anybody else, places strong reservations upon his admiration for the Greeks. And the very scholars who translate them and comment upon them, understand them but poorly. Nevertheless, in the second half of the century, under the influence of Rousseau, a reaction takes place against the abuse of the mind and worldly frivolity; men go back to nature, they are charmed by simplicity, by ingenuousness, even by civic virtue. Plutarch, expressly praised by the author of *Émile*, regains a popularity which he shares with his great men. The Abbé Barthélemy leads his numerous hearers into ancient Greece, following his young Scythian, Anacharsis. André Chénier, in his delicate and charming poems, which were not to be published, it is true, until the beginning of the following century, draws his inspiration at once from Homer, from Theocritus, and from the poets of the Anthology. Finally, the image of idealized Sparta dominates the first period of the Revolution. Then, thruout the nineteenth century, it seems that this Hellenic influence, now exalted, now suppressed and momentarily diminished, tended to acquire its just value. It has become evident that it can not impose itself upon the modern men of letters as a sole type of perfection. Too many new thoughts have come up, too many sentiments which Greece scarcely knew have developed, too many forms of art created by other peoples have seduced the modern soul, for the latter to confine itself henceforth to the limits of the ancient conceptions. But precisely because taste has broadened, because sensibilities have become more supple, has it become easier to understand them and to appreciate their simplicity, often associated with so much profound truth.

And what is true of literature, is also true of the fine arts. Certain it is that since the Renaissance the study of Greek architecture and sculpture has not ceased to be productive. It has become even more so than ever, since in the place of a too confused admiration it has substituted an attentive criticism which is able to discern and distinguish periods, to note individual characters, and, in a word, to classify and judge by comparison both artists and works. But if this criticism has taught us better in what respect Greece is a magnificent school of beauty, and what services it will always render in this capacity to man's innate craving for an ideal, it has also taught us to find again in other creations of the human genius, under very different forms, the same aspirations and realizations which give value to those of Greece. The architecture of some of our cathedrals today does not seem inferior to that of the Parthenon, nor does the artistic merit of certain statues of the Middle Ages seem unequal to that of certain works of Scopas or of Praxiteles. More and more there is revealed to us, moreover, the art of other peoples, previously too little known. The Orient, better studied, astonishes and attracts us. From this enlarged experience results the very clear sentiment that art can not enclose itself in traditional and immutable formulas, that it should not even attach itself servilely to the same models, howsoever beautiful they are, and that, on the contrary, variety and incessant renovation are the very law of its life. On the other hand, if it can not become a simple abandonment of the imagination to all its caprices, if it must after all always resort to certain essential precepts of nature and of reason, why can it not find tomorrow, as yesterday and today, in the example of Greece, some excellent lessons, which it devolves upon each one to appropriate to his time, to his milieu, to his personal talent and to his conceptions?

In politics the influence of Greek civilization has been, until the present time, very limited. The great modern states, constituted as monarchies, could demand nothing, in the way of example or lessons, from the small Greek republics, whose conditions of existence were so different from theirs. And the democracies themselves, such as those of the two Americas, dominated by conditions peculiar to themselves, did not imagine that they had anything in common with the miniature states of olden times, of which they knew, moreover, so little. However, the political theorists did not share this indifference. Bossuet, in his *Universal History*, devoted a chapter to the governments of ancient Greece, and so called to them the attention of reflective minds; mingling numerous errors with a few strong observations, he showed what these republics owed to the love of liberty and to the civic virtues. Montesquieu, in his *Spirit of the Laws*, without presenting a complete view of their public life, nevertheless insisted in his turn upon a certain number of their characteristic traits. Thanks to these great writers, the study of ancient Greece holds a place in political science. It suggested, as we have seen, some ideas and certain arguments to many of the men of the Revolution. But the reëstablishment and succession of monarchic governments relegated it anew to the domain of theories. In our day, however, let it be noted that the extension of the republican and democratic form of government to a large number of nations gives it an interest of actuality. It is again becoming for us a historic experience of high value, and this change coincides with an increase of knowledge which is perceptibly augmenting its importance. Today we know the institutions of Athenian democracy much more accurately than they were known during the last century, and our own country (France) is itself a democracy in relation with other democracies. Why should we not profit by investigating a history which is so manifestly related to our own?

But this history is instructive; it is doubly so by reason of the defects and good qualities which it discloses. Democracy, like every other form of government, has need of a solid but flexible organization; it has all the more need of it because its natural tendency toward individualism exposes it, more than any other, to the danger of having its elements disintegrate. Did Athens succeed in realizing this organization? No. What it lacked especially, as we have seen, was an executive power capable of giving the people a course that they might follow. It did not succeed in establishing a government which sufficiently insured the continuity of its policy by preserving it from improvisations and unreflected errors. To this first defect is added a second—the poor constitution of the judiciary power. In entrusting to tribunals the care of rendering justice, tribunals which were veritable assemblies, it placed justice at the discretion of ignorance and the passions. In so doing it removed almost all value from the conception of personal responsibility, so just in itself, which it attached to every public function. Finally, it did not subject the exercise of popular sovereignty to restrictive conditions, all the more necessary in that this sovereignty resided in the most fickle of crowds, particularly accessible to those unforeseen movements to which a mass of men is always exposed. Here, in a few words, we have the part which it is well to assign first of all to criticism, to the end of determining more readily that which deserves to be praised. The glory of Athens consists in its having been first to show, in antiquity, what a people which governs itself is capable of doing in order to assure itself a place of honor in history. Athens made itself worthy of this honor by its civic spirit, its humanity, and its superior culture.

Nobody can deny that the Athenians, in the best days of their democracy, did not have a truly high idea of the rights and duties of the citizen. At that time they showed themselves genuinely solicitous of the public good, ready for all services which the interest of the State imposed upon them, courageous and enduring under arms, respectful of discipline, accepting with good heart the necessary sacrifices and fatigue, and, beyond all this, facing without complaint the duties assigned to them, proud of the reputation of their city, and happy to contribute to the increase of a noble sentiment of solidarity. A patriotic ambition animated the entire city, conscious of the glorious destiny which seemed to open up before it, since it contributed more than any other city to the defense of the national independence.

This energy, moreover, was reconciled with a natural amiability which won for it a deserved reputation for humanity. No doubt when we reflect that slavery was looked upon, at Athens as well as everywhere else in the ancient world, as a natural fact, and when, on the other hand, we see reported by the historians certain acts of cruelty of which the Athenian people were guilty, we are led to make reservations regarding this point. But nothing would be less fair than to judge the things of the past from the modern point of view. What we must consider is that the condition of slavery was nowhere of shorter duration than among the Athenians; the law itself assured it a certain protection, and the customs were often still more indulgent than the law. As for the acts of cruelty which are attested, if it would be excessive to excuse them, it should nevertheless be recognized that some of them are to be explained by transitory impulses of anger, others by the condition of international law, which was still in its infancy. These, moreover, are isolated facts. In general, the Athenian democracy was hospitable to foreigners. It held it a matter of honor to attract, not only Greeks from other cities, but also the barbarians. It was at Athens that the sentiment of human fraternity found the moral dispositions most favorable to its development. And this instinctive humanity manifested itself even in national politics. In its capacity as a democracy, the Athenian republic felt itself obliged to support democratic principles everywhere. It was therefore the natural enemy of oppressive powers, the protector of the weak; it had for its watchword the defense of liberty. And if we can not deny that this rôle was not always as disinterested in reality as it seemed to be in the speeches of its orators, it is none the less true that there is moral profit and honor for a people in being able to direct its activity in this way toward a generous ideal. There results for it a habit of thought which ennobles it by raising it above the constant obsession of purely material interests.

But among all the titles which recommend the name of Athens, none is equal in value to that which it acquired by its brilliant intellectual, moral and artistic culture. And what is particularly interesting to note is the close relationship of this culture to its democratic institutions. We know with what accent of pride the poet Æschylus,

in his tragedy of the Persians, exalts thru the mouths
of the old men of Susa, before the queen astounded by
what she hears, the redoubtable force of this people which
has no monarch. This vivifying influence of liberty was
likewise emphasized by a foreigner, Herodotus; and one
must recognize with him that it was one of the principal
sources of the sentiments which animated the Athenians in
the fifth century, beginning with the greatest of them,
Pericles. It was in an atmosphere of democratic liberty
that all the great works of that time were produced. No
milieu was more favorable to the brilliant development
of the tragedy, which was able to represent the human
passions in a spectacle, before a public prepared by public
discussions to understand the play of opposing interests.
No other public would be equally prepared for the bold
traits of the comedy and for its insolent and incisive criticisms, which made people think. And what is to be said
of the orators and historians, matured in this fertile agita-
tion of the spirits, in this conflict of ideas, in which one
learned to study events, to scrutinize motives, and to note
consequences, that is to say, to judge and to evaluate?
Was it not Athenian liberty which made a Thucydides,
as it had made a Pericles? Philosophy itself, at least
moral and social philosophy, which showed itself severe
toward democracy—from what was it born if not from
this democracy which it condemned?   Is Socrates imaginable elsewhere than in Athens? This observer needed
the human spectacle which was found only there, and this
ironic moralist and mocker required the freedom of speech
which at the time existed nowhere else to the same extent.
Finally, as regards art, it was not entirely by chance,
certainly, that it enjoyed at Athens, at that same time,
so marvelous a development. Without any possible
doubt, it was due not only to the desire, common in all

Athenians of that time, to give their city a distinction worthy of its grandeur and to honor the gods to whom they attributed it, but also to a general refinement of taste resulting from the activity of all, from their mutual relations, from the incessant exchange of ideas, from the reception accorded to men of talent from all countries. All in all, it was because freedom was responsible for the education of Athens that this city, in its turn, was able to contribute so largely to the education of humanity.

Thus, we see clearly that Hellenic civilization, far from losing any of its value for us, according as it buries itself in the past, seems on the contrary to acquire greater value in our day, in proportion to the efforts put forth to know it better. Considered in the succession of epochs which we have rapidly traversed, it assuredly presents, as does everything human, great inequalities and, alongside of brilliant traits, many weaknesses. But if in place of considering it so, century by century, according to the historical method, we take in at a single glance everything good which there was in it, everything which has been and still remains profitable to humanity, it appears as a marvelous source of wisdom, and of light, and of beauty. That is why the last word of this study can not be anything but an expression of a sentiment of admiration and of recognition for this little nation of antiquity to which we owe so much.

THE END

INDEX

311